Praise for *Broke: A*...

Rick Parsons is well-positioned to describe the financial crisis and its effects on basic retail and commercial banking. Bankers, directors, lawmakers, and regulators will benefit from this informative and passionate book.

—WILLIAM F. GITHENS,
President and CEO, The Risk Management Association

Broke: America's Banking System is a lively and incisive evaluation of the major problems plaguing the U.S. banking system. Rick Parsons has blended experiences from a long and distinguished banking career with historic perspectives of the industry and statistical analysis of recent performance to identify the causes of recurring failures in the system. *Broke: America's Banking System* not only diagnoses problems, but also offers thoughtful and sometimes provocative prescriptions for curing the most important chronic problems in U.S. banks.

—RANDAL GORMAN,
Retired Senior National Bank Examiner, OCC

This book is a welcome reminder to policymakers, regulators, and bankers that rebuilding banks' human capital is as important as rebuilding their financial capital. It should be read by all involved in renewing our broken banking system.

— SIMON THOMPSON,
CEO, Chartered Banker Institute, Edinburgh, Scotland

Richard Parsons's perceptive analysis of bank-crisis causes over the last 50 years is based both on his decades of deep but varied experience in the industry and on his independent research. He presents his reasoning and conclusions in nontechnical terms that make them accessible to the general public as well as to the banking profession and its supervisors. Parsons makes substantive recommendations for dealing with the problems he sees coming in the future as well as for past problems that remain uncorrected. Even if one doesn't agree with his suggestions, they should stimulate thoughtful discussion. A very valuable book for the industry.

— WILLIAM W. SIHLER,
Ronald Edward Trzcinski Professor of Business Administration,
University of Virginia Darden School of Business

A great analysis of the history and causes of bank failures. It should become a required primer for new directors and a provocative call to action for existing boards. Highly recommend!

— DANIEL C. REGIS,
Independent Director and designated "Financial Expert,"
Columbia Banking System, State of Washington

While Mr. Parsons is very analytical in his approach, this is not a dry theoretical treatise. He mixes real and timely stories with intriguing research to make the case for radical change in the banking industry. Mr. Parsons makes a compelling case that the banking industry does not have the talent to run tomorrow's banks. He calls on bankers and their directors to embrace risk management, certification, and continuing education to change the paradigm from *banking industry* to *banking profession*. We would do well to listen.

— DOUG CRUICKSHANKS,
Vice Chairman, FirstBank, Nashville

Drawing on his 30+ years in retail banking and his painstaking review of recent bank failures, Rick Parsons effectively paints a compelling picture of a major challenge to America's banking system—the ability to identify and manage operational risk. *Broke: America's Banking System* is a must-read for bank directors and executives.

— SCOTT A. CAMMARN,
Partner, Cadwalader, Wickersham & Taft

Current and prospective bank directors could not wish for a better review of the complicated range of responsibilities they must discharge if they are to take their roles seriously. And take their roles seriously they must. No longer is it sufficient for directors to show up at periodic board meetings, listen to PowerPoint presentations and then leave for convivial dinners. Managing and directing a bank is an important position involving considerable shareholder and public trust. Rick Parsons has written an elegant work of great insight and understanding. Reflecting his deep knowledge of how banks work, Mr. Parsons writes with deep credibility and in a way that makes the most complex issues easily understandable. He also adds a great range of valuable insights and recommendations that are rich with wisdom, experience, and careful research and reflection. Having been on the inside, I cannot recommend this book strongly enough to bank directors and, for that matter, regulators and executives in banks both large and small.

— LAWRENCE G. BAXTER, PH.D.,
Professor of the Practice of Law, Duke Law School,
and former Executive Vice President, Wachovia

BROKE

America's
Banking System

BROKE

America's Banking System

Common Sense Ideas to Fix Banking in America

Richard J. Parsons

rma℠
THE RISK MANAGEMENT ASSOCIATION
Serving the Financial Services Industry

RMA is a member-driven professional association whose sole purpose is to advance sound risk principles in the financial services industry.

RMA helps our members use sound risk principles to improve institutional performance and financial stability, and enhance the risk competency of individuals through information, education, peer sharing, and networking.

Edited by Kevin McLaughlin
Cover design by Arielle Morris
Text design and composition by Stephen Druding
Illustrations by Michelle Tomm
Front cover photo by Thinkstock.com
Back cover photo by Yellow Cape Communications

RMA Product Number: 640291

ISBN: 978-0-9886379-0-0

Library of Congress Control Number: 2012955450

Printed in the United States of America.

Contents

London, 1873

He [Danny] shook his head. "I've got a new idea. You see, it's happened to me twice, that my life has been wrecked by a financial crash. The men who own banks are the stupidest people in the world. They never learn, so they make the same mistakes again and again. And it's the working people who suffer...."

1879: a conversation between Danny's sister Maisie and Hugh, her husband, a junior banker:

"The men who ran the City of Glasgow Bank should go to jail," Maisie said shortly before dinner.

"That's a bit hard," Hugh responded.

The remark struck her as smug. "Hard?" she said irritably. "Not as hard as what happened to the workingmen whose money was lost."

"Still, no one is perfect, not even those workingmen," Hugh persisted. "If a carpenter makes a mistake, and a house falls down, should he go to jail?"

"It's not the same!"

"And why not?"

"Because the carpenter is paid thirty shillings a week and obliged to follow a foreman's orders, whereas a banker gets thousands and justifies it by saying he carries the weight of responsibility."

"All true. But the banker is human, and has a wife and children to support."

"You might say the same of murderers, yet we hang them regardless of the fate of their orphaned children."

"But if a man kills another accidentally, for example, by shooting at a rabbit and hitting a man behind a bush, we don't even send him to jail. So why should we jail bankers who lose other people's money?"

"To make other bankers more careful!"

"And by the same logic we might hang the man who shot at the rabbit, to make other shooters more careful."

"Hugh, you're just being perverse."

"No, I'm not. Why treat careless bankers more harshly than careless rabbit-shooters?"

"The difference is that careless shots do not throw thousands of working people into destitution every few years, whereas careless bankers do."

—FROM *A DANGEROUS FORTUNE*, BY KEN FOLLETT (1993)

Introduction:
Why I Wrote This Book

B anking is not quite the oldest profession. But like the oldest, it has few advocates.

When times are good, people cautiously knock on the banker's door in search of capital to start businesses, pay off debt, buy homes, and pay for college educations. When times are bad, society is reminded a banker's capital comes with strings attached. Bad times reveal the banker's purpose: to make money.

Money is a touchy subject. In the Bible, Jesus talks about money in 11 of the 39 parables. Timothy writes that the love of money is the root of all evil. Hebrew sacred literature includes an entire chapter in Nehemiah describing the bankers' hard hearts. The Koran expressly forbids lending money when repayment requires the added burden of interest.

Author Ken Follett's *A Dangerous Fortune* tells of the rise and fall of the House of Pilaster, a fictional London banking family. Banking in 19th-century England paralleled the tumultuous century of banking in the United States. England had its panics of 1825, 1847, 1866, and 1890. One-upping the English, the U.S. experienced no less than six panics during that time.

The Great Depression of the 1930s triggered the failure and closure of 9,000 financial institutions in the United States. Despite draconian measures passed by Congress in 1932 and 1933, less than 60 years later another 3,000 U.S. financial institutions failed during the banking crisis of the late 1980s and early 1990s.

In contrast to the Great Depression and the banking crisis of the 1980s and 1990s, the current financial crisis has witnessed a far less devastating number of bank failures. At 457 failures since early 2008, this most recent banking crisis seems rather tame.

In their masterpiece overviewing eight centuries of financial crises, *This Time Is Different,* economic historians Carmen Reinhart and Kenneth Rogoff argue that every financial crisis shares certain features. They describe the "fickle nature of confidence" trap that leads people throughout history into believing this time is different.

Historians enjoy distance and time to sanitize and filter their analysis of events. By contrast, those of us living in this current crisis feel the heat and passion of the moment. Our financial crisis sure feels different. Consider the following:

- During the Depression, bankers were either Potters or Baileys. Frank Capra's classic movie, *It's a Wonderful Life,* paints a celluloid canvas of good versus evil. By 2009, evil Mr. Potter is evil Mr. Wall Street incarnate. When the President of the United States lashes out at greedy, "fat cat" bankers, it feels like this time really is different. Powerful Washington lawmakers seem to take special delight in parading a rogues' gallery of bank CEOs before congressional committees. The hearings come as close as modern America can to slamming miscreants into pillories.

- Eager to display scalps (and perhaps to divert attention from their own mistakes), federal regulators report nearly weekly a running tab of lawsuits directed against mostly community bank presidents and bank directors. The so-called authorized

D&O defendants climbed from 11 in 2009 to 98 in 2010 to 264 in 2011 and are on pace to hit nearly 400 in 2012. The George Baileys of Main Street are a dying breed. Many banks across the nation cannot find candidates to be presidents or directors.

- Depression-era legislation prompted straightforward changes to banking. In fewer than 50 pages, Senator Glass and Representative Steagall in 1932 introduced new banking laws that prevented bank failures for the next 50 years. By contrast, the more than 2,300-page Dodd-Frank Act of 2010 is so complex that three years later regulators (and many high-paid lawyers) are still sorting out the details.

- Traditional protectors of the free market are now calling for even greater government control over banks. In early 2009, at least one panic-stricken Republican senator said he "would not take the idea of nationalizing the banks" off the table. By the election of 2012, one Republican candidate for president proposed breaking up the big banks.

Whether this time is truly different, time will tell. What we do know is the financial crisis revealed substantial design flaws in the U.S. and global banking systems. Although public policy makers like the Federal Reserve have done an admirable job of preventing the crisis from becoming the Second Great Depression, the system remains flawed. As a result, the U.S. is vulnerable to future banking shocks that could lead to greater government intervention and more financial hardship for Americans.

What I share with you in this book are insights I learned during my 31 years in the banking industry. My story is fairly similar to that of other people who chose to make banking their career. In 1980, when I entered the business as a trainee in the credit department of a medium-sized southern bank, I was told the industry was on the verge of massive change. I had no idea then just how wild the ride would prove to be.

After about a year of training in the credit department, where I was taught how to evaluate and underwrite loans to big and small companies as well as consumers, I was promoted to the job of bank branch manager. I loved being a branch manager. Every day was different. For the next 15 years, my career grew as my bank grew. Throughout those years—even as I moved from North Carolina to Florida, back to North Carolina, across the country to Texas, and back to North Carolina—all my jobs connected me to my passion for community banking.

Over the first half of my career, I lived and worked in my many hometowns, gathering deposits and making consumer, small business, and commercial loans. During those years, I oversaw increasingly larger organizations of employees and branches. By the time I left Texas in 1995, I was an executive vice president responsible for my bank's consumer and small business banking in Texas. My work shifted during the second half of my career to our bank's headquarters, where I assumed corporate roles. Over the next 16 years, I was assigned jobs in corporate functions like Online Banking, Strategy, Operations, Marketing, Human Resources, and Risk Management.

From my career as a banker, I combine practical community banking knowledge with hands-on experience in global banking, macroeconomics, risk and control, and bank strategy. So why did I write this book? More importantly, why is it worth reading?

My purpose is to use my experience and insight to recommend systemic improvements to basic banking in America. I want to share lessons I learned in the Banking School of Hard Knocks. I want to offer common sense ideas to transform the industry and help the banking industry regain its stature. Banks can be a source of stable, reliable fuel to grow the economy while also demonstrating the highest ethical standards.

The title of the book is *Broke: America's Banking System*. It is not about the megabanks; it is about the other 7,240 banks in America that look a lot more like the kind of bank I joined in 1980. Sometimes it is difficult to comprehend just how different the megabanks are from the typical bank in the country, but let's try.

The Apple Creek Banking Company in Ohio with $100 million in assets is such a bank. In contrast, JPMorgan Chase has $2 trillion in assets. Imagine Apple Creek Bank is a one-story building 15 feet high. By comparison, JPMorgan Chase would be a building 57 miles high poking into the earth's thermosphere. How is that for apples and JPMoranges?

Broke is different from other books about the financial crisis in three other important ways. First, to my knowledge, it is the only one written by a roll-up-your-sleeves, lifelong banker whose work for 31 years cut across virtually every aspect of modern banking. I fought on the front line of the 2008-2011 financial crisis and in the trenches of Texas and Florida during the horrific banking crisis of the late 1980s and early 1990s. I have made $5,000 car loans as a branch manager and also have spent time in the offices of billionaires talking about banking. I have worked in Indian Rocks, Florida, and Mesquite, Texas, and have spent time in London, Singapore, Hong Kong, and Tokyo evaluating bank risk.

The second difference is that *Broke* provides a much-needed historical backdrop to develop a fact-based, common sense view of why more than 3,400 financial institutions have failed in the U.S. since the mid-1980s. I offer insights about macro patterns to understand not only the "what" of bank history but the "why." Most analysts of the current banking crisis fail to appreciate the nation's historical banking challenges. Very few of the more popular books written by journalists acknowledge the industry's 200 years of repeated banking failures.

The third difference is that *Broke* is about basic retail and commercial banking in America. It is about the kind of banking practiced by 99.7% of America's banks and about the banking services used by 99.9% of America. It is not about investment banking, proprietary trading, investment management, and esoteric banking activities the nation's community and regional banks do not practice. Maybe someday I will address those issues, but not now. Someone needs to talk about basic banking in America.

Unlike many entertaining books about the financial crisis, this book is not a kiss-and-tell or whodunit. As you will discover, I am a student of history. More than 2,500 years ago, Herodotus, known as the "father of history," is reported to have said, "Circumstances rule men, men do not rule circumstances." This truth must not be lost at times of great emotion.

Finding fault with individuals is not my priority, but understanding the circumstances leading to the crisis is critically important. My ultimate purpose in writing this book is to shape circumstances by influencing bank managers, directors, regulators, and lawmakers to learn something new and stop making the same mistakes over and over again.

Two bank crises in one lifetime are enough.

Preface:
An Overview

Now I know why authors write both an introduction and a preface. There are two kinds of people in this world: people who read every page of a book and people who pick and choose pages based on interest and perceived usefulness.

I know a number of bankers in the latter group. They are thoughtful people, but also by nature somewhat impatient. They like short meetings, short PowerPoint presentations, and short books. Feel free to jump to the parts of the book you think will be most helpful. For readers who appreciate context, you will find reading the book sequentially makes the most sense.

Part 1 establishes the foundation. The first chapter chronicles bank failures in America since the mid-1980s. The next two chapters are a case study of America's greatest community banker, "Old Man" Mueller of Winesburg, Georgia. We meet him as a young man in the 1930s and follow his remarkable career. Mueller represents the best in community bankers. He is a man of honor who believes bankers have a duty to society to build banks that last. If you understand Winesburg banking, you will understand U.S. community banking.

Part 2 is a call to action for bankers and bank directors. Banks always face risk. 10X risk is the risk, or combination of risks, that kills banks. Lawmakers and regulators alone cannot solve all the industry's ills. Directors and bankers need to step up and fix the industry. Bank failures are almost always tied to weak directors and management who lack capable processes to identify and mitigate risks. Certain conditions, including external events, heighten the risk of failure. Operational risk—risk associated with people, processes, systems, and external events—is the true root cause of 10X risk.

Bankers must collaborate to protect banking in America. The first priority is to define the banker's duty to society. The next priority is to build skills in the industry, starting with operational risk management skills needed to run and govern banks. Directors and bankers have their work cut out for them. A paradigm shift is required if commercial banking is to get on track. The industry suffers from a severe shortage of skilled bankers and directors, and the problem will only get worse before it gets better. Board composition requires enormous work. Bankers need to establish standards and processes to protect the industry from incompetent, so-called bankers.

Part 3 chronicles the rocky history of banking in America. Bank failure is as American as apple pie and Chevrolet. Periodic epidemics of bank failure were common in the 19th century. Accounting for financial institution failures and closures improved in the 20th century when more than 12,000 financial institutions failed. During the dark days of banking—of which there are many—lawmakers pass new laws. Sometimes the laws worked well, although more often they led to unintended consequences.

Part 4 addresses critical questions lawmakers, regulators, bankers, and directors need to debate. Lawmakers need to evaluate whether the current system for regulatory oversight of community and regional banks makes sense in the 21st century. Regulators need to determine if there are better tools and processes to supervise banks. Bankers and directors need to look over the horizon to identify risks before those risks trigger the next epidemic of bank failure.

Part 5 is the conclusion of the book. Chapter 16 offers 24 possible scenarios for bankers, directors, regulators, and lawmakers to consider as they develop strategies and tactics to address industry needs during the next eight years. Chapter 17 highlights four common sense ideas to fix basic banking in the United States.

The appendices provide an introduction to specific operational risk management tools and processes. Bankers and directors will find the appendices to be a source of practical applications to jump-start or accelerate their operational risk management programs. Appendix 3 posits bank formation rates as a leading indicator of U.S. bank failures.

I have tried to avoid banking jargon. Whenever I find the use of jargon unavoidable, I define the term in plain English. A few such terms are used throughout the book. Some of the most critical are:

Megabanks, regional banks, and community banks: Banks fall into one of three categories. The megabanks are coast-to-coast and global banks that operate many different types of businesses and generally have total assets greater than $1 trillion. Regional banks, as a rule of thumb, have between $25 billion and $300 billion in assets and operate in many states. Unlike the megabanks, they do not engage in a wide variety of businesses, most notably activities associated with securities and broker-dealers. Community banks make up more than 99% of U.S. banks and, in the vast majority of cases, they are much smaller than $25 billion. Most operate in one or a few towns, although some have several hundred branches and operate across two or more states.

CAMELS: Bank regulators examine banks periodically. When the exam is completed, the regulator issues CAMELS ratings. CAMELS ratings are similar to a report card and use a 1 to 5 scale, with 1 being outstanding and 5 meaning the bank has one foot in the grave. Each letter stands for something. *C* is for capital adequacy. *A* is for asset quality. *M* is for management quality. *E* is for earnings. *L* is for liquidity. *S* is for sensitivity to market risk. It is important to note that CAMELS ratings are a backward view of the bank's health.

Basel: Basel is a city in Switzerland where bank regulators from across the globe have been meeting for the past 25 years to determine the most effective ways to oversee banks. The Basel Committee's primary focus is capital adequacy of banks and the banking systems.

Operational risk management (ORM): Although not new in many industries, ORM is a relatively new risk management discipline for banks. ORM covers risks associated with people (the bank's employees), processes (how the bank gets its work done), systems (technology and reporting), and external events (risk factors that exist outside the bank).

Scenario analysis: Operational risk management includes a number of tools, one of which is scenario analysis. Scenario analysis is called "war games" or "what-if exercises" by other industries. It requires bankers and directors to evaluate the probability and potential financial impact of adverse events occurring in the future.

Risk and control assessment (RCA): The RCA (also known as the risk and control self-assessment, or RCSA) is a risk management tool used periodically by banks to identify inherent and residual risks associated with business processes, systems, and people/organization capabilities.

IMMR: Effective risk management requires risk identification, monitoring, mitigation, and reporting (IMMR).

10X risk: A risk or combination of risks that causes a bank to fail.

Material loss reviews (MLRs): Congress requires the FDIC, OCC, and Federal Reserve to examine the root causes of bank failures. MLRs are conducted when the Bank Insurance Fund experiences a loss over $25 million due to bank failure. Because so many banks failed between January 1, 2010, and December 31, 2011, however, the Dodd-Frank Wall Street Reform and Consumer Protection Act raised the reporting threshold to $200 million for banks that failed in 2010 and 2011.

Acknowledgments

Many friends and colleagues helped to write this book. To all of them I say thank you.

It would be impossible to overstate the significance of the collaboration and support I received from The Risk Management Association. RMA's enduring contribution to the banking industry is best evidenced by its celebration in 2013-2014 of 100 years of service. Some 2,500 institutions are members of RMA today. When I was a trainee in 1980, my bank used RMA training material to develop my commercial lending skills.

A special note of appreciation must go to Ed DeMarco, who embraced the idea for this book and made it possible for RMA to publish it. Kevin McLaughlin edited *Broke* and worked tirelessly to coach me through the writing process. Kathie Beans, the editor of *The RMA Journal,* was of great help in my effort to write several articles related to the book for *American Banker.*

Through my volunteer work with RMA, I am able to work with some of the industry's top bankers as well as a few directors. Their insights and ideas about banking shaped this book. In RMA's classroom sessions, I meet real bankers who are dedicated to developing their skills and raising the bar for the banking industry.

Writing this book would be impossible without smart friends and smart friends of friends who selflessly gave of their own time to review, challenge, and sharpen my early drafts. Professor Bill Sihler and retired banker Henry Mueller were among the first readers of the draft and paved the way for me to work with RMA.

I am indebted to former colleagues and other friends in the industry who read the first couple of drafts and offered page-by-page edits as well as constructive challenges to my thinking.

Also to be thanked are the countless number of bankers who over the years taught me what it means to be a real banker. Most notable are those who urged me to pursue a career as a community banker and made sure I had the training and mentoring to do the job.

I need to recognize the executives of NCNB, who envisioned coast-to-coast banking and provided the experiences I needed to have a wide-ranging career in banking. If one experience shaped my view of bank risk more than any other, it was my five years in Texas when the state was healing from more than 800 bank failures. So many Texas bankers offered me the benefit of their counsel during that time.

My wife, Yvette, knew before anyone of my desire to help fix banking in America. Throughout my journey, she has fueled my passion with words of encouragement and boundless support. I am blessed to have her in my life.

Case Study: The Community Banking Crisis in America

The Other Banking
Crisis in America

I t is time for an experiment. If you are on a plane, try to act cool and not attract attention.

Extend your left arm in front of you. With your left hand in a clenched fist, point your left index finger (not the middle one!) skyward. For a few seconds, with both eyes open, stare at your left index finger. Don't move your finger. Now, close your left eye and stare at the finger again. Did your finger "move" or did it "stay still"?

Keep your finger pointed to the sky and now close your right eye and open your left and stare at your finger. Same question: Did your finger "move" or "stay still"?

If your finger did not move when you stared at it with only your left eye, you are left-eye dominant. If the finger did not move when you stared at it with only your right eye, you are right-eye dominant.

This experiment actually comes in handy in real life. For example, a marksman must know which eye is dominant. It helps for batters in baseball to know which eye is dominant. Did you know it is better for a right-handed batter to be left-eye dominant and for a left-handed batter to be right-eye dominant?

You are probably thinking that sticking your finger in the air is a strange way to start a book about banking. So why did we just do the experiment? You can say it is an analogy for how Washington politicians think about banking today. They are so "megabank-eye dominant" that they have lost focus on the other 99.7% of banks in America that still matter to this country.

To hear some experts speak, it seems the only banking issue in America is that a few banks are "too big to fail," but this is not true. There are towns across the country suffering because of community bank failures. As Figure 1.1 shows, since 2008 a total of 457 community banks in the U.S. have failed through October 12, 2012, and 3,400 financial institutions have failed since 1980. Bank failure is epidemic in America. It is nothing short of a national disgrace, and no one seems intent on fixing it.

Investors in bank stocks have been seriously disappointed by the industry's problems. While the stock prices of the big banks get all the headlines, the fall in the average community bank's five-year stock prices from January 1, 2007, to January 31, 2012, also has been painful. Keep in mind the numbers shown in Figures 1.2 and 1.3 are for a period when the stock price of the Vanguard Total Stock Market ETF (symbol VTI) decreased 5.4% (split adjusted, from $71.42 a share at the end of January 2007 to

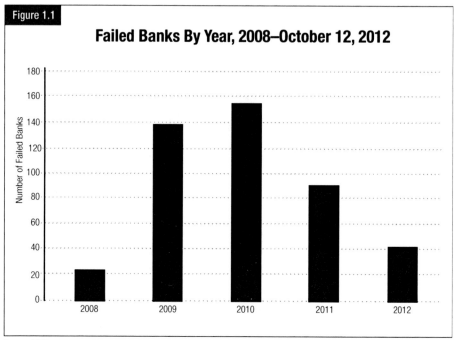

Source: FDIC

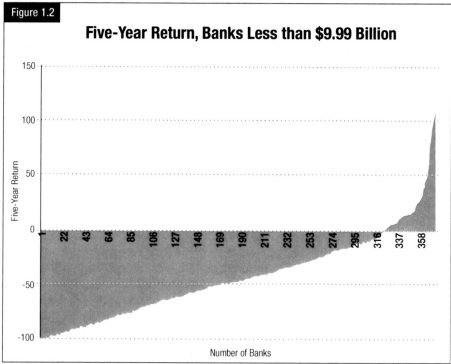

Source: Morningstar

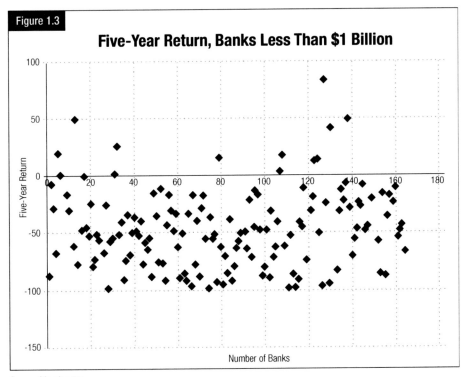

Figure 1.3

Five-Year Return, Banks Less Than $1 Billion

Source: Morningstar

$67.56 five years later). Although no one would ever be satisfied with a 5% loss, compared to banks, the Vanguard Total Stock Market ETF five-year return actually looks quite good.

Of the nation's 7,246 commercial banks and savings institutions, fewer than 10% are actively traded on stock market exchanges. Figure 1.2 shows the five-year return, as of January 31, 2012, for 382 publicly held U.S. community banks with less than $9.99 billion in assets. Each bank's return is plotted out in the chart. More than 320 of the 382 banks had a negative return. The average drop in stock price for the 382 banks is 43%. This list excludes publicly held banks that failed before January 31, 2012. If those had been included, the overall return obviously would be even worse.

Some pundits suggest running banks with less than $1 billion in assets is easier than running bigger banks, for example, banks with $1 billion to $9.99 billion in assets. Figure 1.3 highlights that smaller community banks have not performed better than bigger community banks for the same five-year period ending January 31, 2012. Again, excluding failed banks, the average stock price of the roughly 160 publicly held community banks with assets of less than $1 billion fell 45% during those five years. Even more disturbing, more than 90% of these smaller community banks' shareholders experienced a negative return in their stock price.

There are many implications for a country when its banks fail, but there are also implications when its community banks are unable to create anything close to reasonable returns for shareholders. Chief among the concerns is the investing community's reluctance to invest new capital into banks. During tough times, banks need access to fresh capital to ensure adequate capitalization. Just as serious, when the industry suffers, even profitable banks can lose access to capital needed for long-term growth.

A deeper dive into bank failure is warranted. Of particular concern is that a significant majority of the 457 bank failures since early 2008 have been concentrated in a handful of states. Stunningly, 10 states account for 327 or 72% of all bank failures in the U.S. from January 2008 until October 12, 2012 (Figure 1.4).

Five states stand out as the ignominious leaders in bank failures. Georgia, Florida, Illinois, California, and Minnesota account for 57% of the nation's recent 457 bank failures (Figures 1.5, 1.6). This percentage is well over twice what would be expected based on the states' share of U.S. financial institutions. Why? Georgia's 83 bank failures have had devastating implications for job creation, home values, and tax revenues.

One problem in comparing state bank failures is that banking varies so much across the nation. As Table 1.1 shows, North Dakota has 92 banks as of 2011, or one bank for every 7,283 people in the state.

In contrast, highly populated Arizona has only 33 banks headquartered in the state, or one bank for almost every 200,000 people in the state. A few states—Washington, Arizona, and Nevada—have alarming bank-failure rates as bad as Georgia's. However, because these states have far fewer banks, they do not make the top-five list.

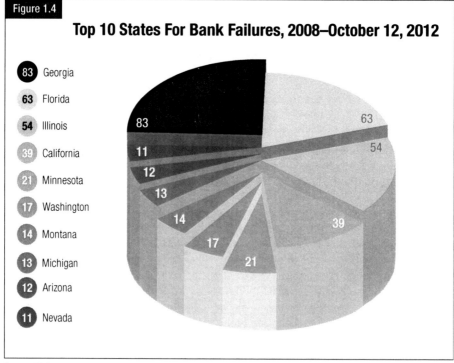

Figure 1.4

Top 10 States For Bank Failures, 2008–October 12, 2012

- 83 Georgia
- 63 Florida
- 54 Illinois
- 39 California
- 21 Minnesota
- 17 Washington
- 14 Montana
- 13 Michigan
- 12 Arizona
- 11 Nevada

Source: FDIC

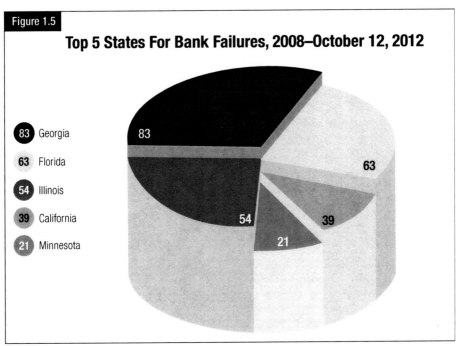

Figure 1.5

Top 5 States For Bank Failures, 2008–October 12, 2012

83 Georgia

63 Florida

54 Illinois

39 California

21 Minnesota

Source: FDIC

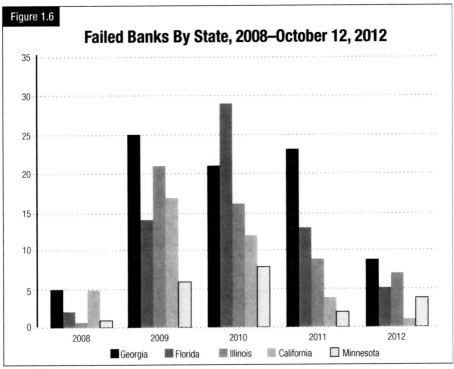

Figure 1.6

Failed Banks By State, 2008–October 12, 2012

■ Georgia   ■ Florida   ■ Illinois   California   □ Minnesota

Source: FDIC

Table 1.1

Banks and Population per Bank for 50 States

State	State Total Banks	2010 Population (millions)	Population Per Bank	State	State Total Banks	2010 Population (millions)	Population Per Bank
North Dakota	92	0.67	7,283	Maine	29	1.32	45,517
Nebraska	221	1.82	8,235	Colorado	109	5.00	45,872
Iowa	348	3.00	8,621	Utah	57	2.76	48,421
Kansas	320	2.85	8,906	Ohio	237	11.50	48,523
South Dakota	83	0.80	9,639	New Hampshire	23	1.32	57,391
Minnesota	395	5.30	13,418	South Carolina	80	4.60	57,500
Montana	73	0.99	13,562	Pennsylvania	209	12.70	60,766
Oklahoma	242	3.75	15,496	Maryland	85	5.77	67,882
Wyoming	36	0.56	15,556	Connecticut	52	3.60	69,231
Missouri	333	6.00	18,018	Virginia	112	8.00	71,429
Wisconsin	271	5.70	21,033	Michigan	133	9.90	74,436
Illinois	585	12.80	21,880	Rhode Island	14	1.05	75,000
Kentucky	195	4.30	22,051	New Jersey	116	8.80	75,862
Arkansas	127	2.90	22,835	Florida	233	18.80	80,687
West Virginia	63	1.85	29,365	Idaho	18	1.56	86,667
Louisiana	150	4.50	30,000	Vermont	9	0.80	88,889
Delaware	27	0.90	33,333	Washington	73	6.70	91,781
Mississippi	89	2.97	33,371	North Carolina	98	9.50	96,939
Tennessee	188	6.35	33,777	New York	187	19.40	103,743
Alabama	142	4.80	33,803	Nevada	25	2.70	108,000
Georgia	246	9.70	39,431	Oregon	34	3.80	111,765
Massachusetts	160	6.55	40,938	Alaska	6	0.71	118,333
New Mexico	50	2.06	41,200	California	261	37.20	142,529
Texas	600	25.10	41,833	Hawaii	9	1.36	151,111
Indiana	143	6.50	45,455	Arizona	33	6.40	193,939

Source: FDIC, U.S. Census Bureau

Let's go back 25 years and examine the bank failures of the late 1980s and early 1990s. Figure 1.7 shows the enormous spike in financial institution failures and assisted transactions during this time. Consider this fact: There were nearly 3,000 financial institution failures in the most advanced economy in the world.

To some people, including politicians and even bankers, bank and S&L failures 25 years ago are ancient history. They see little value looking back for lessons learned. They are wrong.

Figure 1.8 provides several interesting insights. The first, as repeated during the recent financial crisis, is that a handful of states in the 1980s and first half of the 1990s

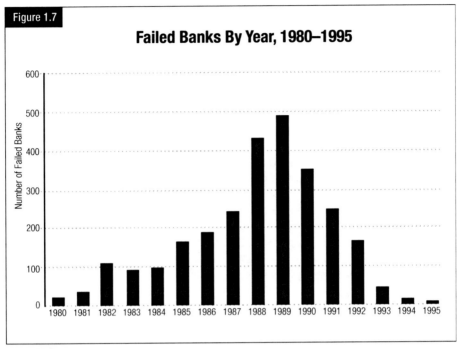

Figure 1.7

Failed Banks By Year, 1980–1995

Source: FDIC

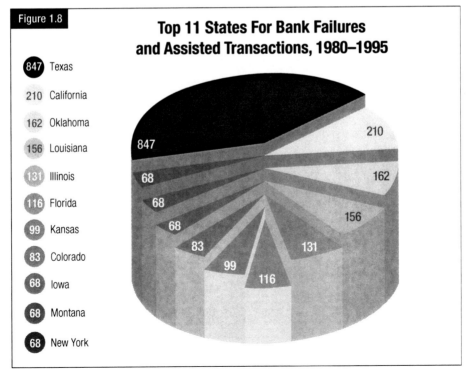

Figure 1.8

Top 11 States For Bank Failures and Assisted Transactions, 1980–1995

847 Texas
210 California
162 Oklahoma
156 Louisiana
131 Illinois
116 Florida
99 Kansas
83 Colorado
68 Iowa
68 Montana
68 New York

Source: FDIC

were home to the majority of the bank failures: 2,008 to be exact. Second, of the 11 states with the most failures from 1980 to 1995, four are repeat offenders in the recent financial crisis: California, Illinois, Florida, and Missouri; three of those states are in the top five for both time periods. And third, note how Texas accounted for the largest percentage of the failures during the 1980s, but is not among the top states in failures during the recent financial crisis.

We are left with more questions than answers at this stage:

1. Why are federal lawmakers and regulators not talking about the repeated pattern of large numbers of bank failures concentrated in a handful of states?
2. If the nation has federal banking laws and regulators overseeing banks, why is there so much variability in bank failure rates among the states? For that matter, why is banking so different state by state?
3. How can three states—California, Florida, and Illinois—have so many bank failures twice in 25 years?
4. What happened to Georgia from 2008 to 2012?
5. Why did Texas—and for that matter, most states—not experience a lot of bank failures during the financial crisis?

We will answer these questions in the pages ahead.

Every good story needs a hero and a few villains. In the next chapter, we will meet our hero, a banker from Winesburg, Georgia. You will walk in "Old Man" Mueller's shoes as he builds his bank, fights to keep it profitable, and ultimately prevails against the forces of evil.

Banking in Winesburg, Georgia, is banking in America. If you understand Winesburg, you will understand why America has a banking problem.

Banking in Winesburg, Georgia: 1939-2012

I f every good story needs a hero and a villain, some cynics might say finding villains in banking is not so hard. But heroes? Now that is a challenge.

Having scoured the country, we meet our hero. He is a banker from Winesburg, Georgia. "Old Man" Mueller has been known as "Old Man" so long in Winesburg that no one today even knows his real first name. At 95, he is the town's oldest citizen.

Even in his thirties, Mueller was known as "Old Man." Back in 1951 as a 34-year-old banker, he formed Winesburg's first bank. As the son and grandson of bankers, he was already an old man in many ways. Taught firsthand the anguish of bank failure when his granddad's bank failed in 1932, he felt burdened to prove the Muellers were good bankers.

1939-1951

With $125,000 in capital raised from local industrialists whose plants produced millions of uniforms for soldiers during World War II, the Bank of Winesburg opened in 1951 with Old Man Mueller as president. Some people in town thought he was too young to have such an important job. Others who knew him best said he'd been preparing for the job for 25 years.

Right out of the University of Georgia in 1939, encouraged by his dad, Mueller ventured north to work in the mail department of one of New York City's big commercial banks. Two years later, he joined the Navy, where for the next four years he served as purser on several ships in the Pacific. By 1946, influenced by what he had learned from his days in the mail department and armed with G.I. Bill money, he applied and was accepted at the Wharton School to study finance. Two years later, he was back in the same New York City bank, now in the bank's prestigious Credit Training Department.

Mueller spent three years soaking in everything he could learn from the "old men" who led the commercial loan training. The old men in the New York City bank survived the Great Depression and never let a day go by without the trainees knowing it. Every hour of the day, they inculcated into their trainees the virtues of sound banking practices.

Mueller and his classmates all had similar backgrounds: military experience, some family banking history, and an MBA from Wharton, Columbia, or Harvard. The "Young Turks" brought to banking a desire to modernize it. Combining their military experience and MBA training, they wove together their bank mentors' training with a push for policies, procedures, manuals, controls, and documentation.

By early 1951, Mueller was itching to get back to Georgia and reclaim his family's position as Winesburg's only family of banking. By year-end, capital and a new bank charter in hand, he was in business.

Mueller knew banking to be an elegantly simple business. In its essence, banking is about trust and being right 99.5% of the time. Trust begins when a banker raises enough capital—back in 1951, $125,000, but today, no less than $10 million—to ask permission of a banking regulator to open a bank. Once approved, the banker builds a branch and opens the doors. If he or she is trusted, people looking for a safe place to store their cash walk in the door.

To maintain the confidence of the banking regulator, the banker must prudently leverage his initial $10 million in capital. Although the definition of a prudent amount of leverage varies over time, as a rule of thumb, a 10 to 1 leverage ratio is considered prudent most of the time.

With a 10-to-1 leverage goal, the banker takes his $10 million in capital and sets out to attract $90 million in deposits. These deposits are essentially IOUs. It is money depositors expect to get back when they need it.

Since the banker knows from experience that not all the depositors will need their money back at the same time, he is able to use the depositors' money temporarily to make a profit. His goal is to make a profit on the $10 million of capital he invested in the bank. To create a profit, he knows he must take risk.

The banker takes risk by investing his depositors' cash. Carefully and prudently, the banker looks for good investments. For banks, investing primarily takes the form of making loans to people who the banker trusts will pay him back.

Another rule of thumb is that the banker seeks a 1% return on assets and a 10% to 12% return on equity. What does this mean? *Return* means profit. *Assets* are the investments the banker creates from his $10 million of capital and $90 million of IOUs known as deposits. *Equity* is the $10 million in capital the banker and investors put in the bank to start it.

A target 1% return on assets (ROA) and 10% return on equity (ROE) means our banker seeks to make an after-tax profit of $1 million. Over decades and decades of banking, averaging out good times and bad, a 1% return on assets and a 10% return on equity are considered normal.

Because there is always uncertainty over whether a loan will be paid back, there is risk. If the banker takes too little risk and invests only in loans almost certain to be paid back, he will fail to achieve his investment return targets.

Mueller the banker is prudent. He realizes that one of his risks is his own fallibility. Rather than manage the money by himself, he believes in the counsel of wise advisors. In 1951, his first order of business is to hire a board of directors. Four respected and financially skilled business leaders in the community agree to help him. Mueller is 20 years junior in age to the youngest member of the new board.

As the bank's directors gather for their first board meeting, Mueller rolls in a cart. On it are five stacks of documents, each more than a foot high. In the most authoritative voice he can muster, Mueller announces, "Gentlemen, today we review the bank's policies and procedures."

January 1989

Mueller is still in charge of the only bank in Winesburg. The year 1988 was tough for bankers in Georgia. The big Atlanta banks are still reeling from some stretch real estate loans they made to keep up with the fast-growing S&Ls. The S&Ls felt the pain of their growth and, as a result, a number of S&Ls and banks failed in Georgia in 1988. Even more appear to be on the brink of failure in 1989.

Mueller's bank felt some bumps and bruises in 1988, but at 0.83% ROA and 9.11% ROE, the Bank of Winesburg did OK. Mueller's bank remains the only one in town. The aggressive S&L two towns over had not inflicted too much damage on the Bank of Winesburg.

Talking to the board about the 1989 profit plan, Mueller proposes the same profit goal that he has every year since 1951: a 1% ROA and 10% ROE. He realizes he could try to target higher returns, but he knows from experience that making loans requires taking on a level of risk that his granddad said was too high to sleep well at night.

He reminds the board that if the bank takes on too much risk, it could actually lose money and, even worse, go out of business like his granddad's bank. A few board members share sly smiles, recognizing that Old Man Mueller issues this same reminder annually. Privately, board members joke among themselves that they could repeat Old Man Mueller's annual planning speech in their sleep.

The board of directors is given the same charge it has been given for the prior 37 years. Although his southern drawl is a bit slower than back in 1951, the words from Old Man Mueller's crusty lips are familiar:

My fellow directors, as your chairman, I urge our esteemed board of directors to consider "Mueller's Five Laws of Banking" as we embark on the 1989 plan.

1. *Trees don't grow to the sky and neither does the return on assets of a bank.*
2. *Gravity pulls objects down to earth at 9.8 meters per second squared and banking revenues grow only as fast as GDP allows; try to defy these two laws of nature and bad things can happen.*
3. *Bankers have a moral obligation and duty to our community to always act in the best interests of those we serve; we must build and protect this bank for the people we serve.*
4. *Never trust an imperial CEO. I am not a king; if I act like a king or you treat me like one, fire me immediately!*
5. *Never, never, never should this board bet the bank, and if any of us says we are doing something because it is strategic, fire me and then fire yourselves.*

Old Man Mueller is just getting warmed up. The directors know what is coming next—"Mueller's Four Imperative Questions":

We're aiming for 1% ROA and 10% ROE in 1989 and we need to answer four imperative questions.

1. *How much risk are we willing to take in order to reach our profit goal?*
2. *Who will help us manage the risk?*

3. *Where will we invest our capital and our depositors' money in order to meet our risk tolerance?*
4. *How will we know if we are taking on more or less risk than we intend?*

As they did in 1951, in answering the first question, how much risk, they decide they want to spread risks across as many good borrowers as possible. After much hot debate, with the bank now at $10 million in capital, they agree to make no loan bigger than $500,000. One director, in particular, expresses concern with this policy.

He reminds his fellow directors that banking is about being right 99.5% of the time. He reminds them of the math: The bank can afford to lose no more than $500,000 in bad loans in a year. If a big borrower cannot pay back his or her loan, every other loan must work as planned. Other board members agree that $500,000 is a lot of risk. As a result, they agree to take on less risk with the big loans, while acknowledging that with less risk comes less profit potential.

On the second question, they know they need help managing loan decisions. They discuss the performance of the bank president they hired three years earlier. All agree he's done a good job keeping the bank on track during a tough time. As a result, they agree to renew his one-year contract with a $60,000 annual salary and the potential for $10,000 in bonus if he meets key performance goals related to the safety and soundness of the bank.

On the third question, where the bank will do business, the board of directors cannot seem to agree. Two of the directors state emphatically that the bank should lend only to borrowers who live and work in the community where the bank is located. They argue that this is the market the bank knows best. They also point out that the bank's collateral is close by in the event a loan goes bad and the bank must secure the collateral to help pay back the loan.

On the other side of the debate are two directors who express concern about concentrating all the loans in one community. They remind their colleagues that two big companies employ 30% of the people living in the community. They ask: What if one of those companies closes down and a lot of people lose their jobs? If that happened, potential borrowers like the grocery store and the ice cream parlor would suffer from a big drop in business.

Finally, Old Man Mueller, who has been quiet, ends the debate by voting with the directors who want to limit lending to just the community in which the bank operates. Mueller acknowledges the risk of over-concentrating loans in one community, but concludes the risk is reasonable given the trade-off of better knowing the borrowers and having quick access to collateral.

The last question discussed is how the board will know for sure that the loans meet their tolerance for risk. The directors quickly agree to a proposal suggested by a director with a long history of successfully investing her own money. She outlines three actions she uses to monitor her own investments. First, the board will receive weekly reports showing the status of all loans. Second, the board will meet monthly to evaluate big decisions; those meetings will be used to approve loans over $100,000 and to evaluate capital decisions, such as dividend payouts and timing for building a second branch office. Third, every monthly board meeting will include an open session to discuss all the things that could possibly go wrong and create more risk than the board intended.

For the next 10 years, the only bank in town grows profitably. Unwilling to take on too much risk and content with a solid 1% ROA and 10% ROE, the bank's profits grow slow and steady. All is well.

1999

No man is an island, entire of itself; every man is a piece of the Continent, a part of the main....

—JOHN DONNE

No bank is an island. Consider the town of Winesburg, Georgia.

All remains well for the Bank of Winesburg, even when a group of investors in town decide they want to start a bank to compete against the one bank in town. The investor group is led by C.V. Crocker, a popular and successful real estate developer who is frustrated that the only bank in town is stifling his growth potential by not allowing him to borrow more than the bank's loan limit, which has just been increased to $1 million.

Together with several rich merchants, C.V. raises $15 million in initial capital to start the bank. Knowing they need a banker, the developer persuades his commercial loan officer at the only bank in town to become president of the new bank. Helped by a consultant and a lawyer who used to work as state bank regulators, the new bank investors submit a plan to the regulators to start a new bank. With $15 million in capital and a strong case showing the community would benefit from more bank competition, the regulators quickly approve the new bank's application.

In the meantime, Old Man Mueller and the directors of the only bank in town continue to meet monthly to discuss what can go wrong. As news of the new bank is confirmed, board discussions quickly turn to the risk that the new bank may not manage risk as prudently as the Bank of Winesburg.

One director points out that C.V. is "full of himself" and "kind of a loose cannon." Another director expresses concern that the commercial loan officer slated to be president of the new bank is not qualified for such a big job. "He has only seen good times," the director warns, offering his own observation that the commercial lender had often seemed overconfident in his own skills.

2002

From day one, Crocker's bank grows fast. By year-end 2002, emboldened by success, the new bank's board agrees to increase leverage to 15:1, up from the 12.5:1 leverage goal set when the bank was formed. The new bank proudly announces 2002 record earnings. C.V. Crocker tells the only newspaper in town that the new bank "now makes as much money as the old bank in town and, at a 1.5% ROA and 21% ROE, is actually more profitable."

Everyone in town is talking about how the new bank is making good money and running circles around the old bank. Community spirit is nearly as high as the record-breaking prices local real estate is enjoying. The tremendous success of the new bank spurs another investor group to start yet a third bank in Winesburg.

Heading the investors is Dr. John Pangloss, a local M.D. (neurology) and Ph.D. (metatheocosmology) who invests $10 million of his own money in the new bank. The other two key investors are hot-shot Atlanta bond traders Al Ranovas and Brian Michael Wallace Sherman. Importantly in the eyes of some investors, Al and Brian Michael Wallace led the local high school football team to the state championship back in 1985.

The regulators approve the bank's application, stipulating that the third bank in Winesburg must stick to the business plan it has submitted as part of its application. Later in the day, waving the new charter before the local public television camera, Dr. Pangloss announces, "I am very optimistic in the future of Winesburg and our new bank." When asked about his experience in banking, the good doctor reminds the reporter with a twinkle in his eye that "banking isn't brain surgery."

Old Man Mueller and his board meet the next day to discuss what they see as the big risk. For two hours they debate whether there are enough people in Winesburg with the skills and experience needed to oversee and run three banks. "When banking seems easy, it's exactly the moment it ain't," Old Man Mueller offers as the board meeting draws to a close.

2003

The third bank in town books twice as much in loan volume as forecast in the original business plan submitted to the FDIC and state banking commissioner. During its annual bank exam, the bank examiners ask Ranovas and Sherman about the pace of growth. When the examiners complete their exam, they issue a CAMELS rating for the bank: 221222. Some of the board members are not quite sure what a CAMELS rating is, so Sherman tells them:

C is for capital adequacy.
A is for asset quality.
M is for management quality.
E is for earnings.
L is for liquidity.
S is for sensitivity to market risk.

Sherman enthusiastically tells the directors a CAMELS score of 221222 is terrific, noting a "1 is like an A in school, and 2 like a solid A- or B+ and so on." After the meeting, the board heads to the local pub to celebrate its CAMELS rating. Sherman buys.

2006

"Old Man Mueller is just an old fuddy-duddy."

Sherman's quip at the annual Winesburg Chamber of Commerce meeting leads to a cascade of guffaws from its members. Sherman, whose four-year-old bank has just received $25 million in new capital for expansion into Atlanta, is just getting warmed up.

"If Old Man Mueller is so smart, why is his bank half as profitable as our bank and a quarter as profitable as the other bank in town? We all love the Old Man, but he's from another era. Bob Dylan is right—the times they are a changin'.

"Sure, maybe trees don't grow to the sky. But I want you to really think about this because it's true: In these modern times with good fertilizer you can grow trees a lot closer to the sky than in the so-called good old days."

As heads nod in agreement, first one chamber member and then another rises to his feet. For a full two minutes Sherman basks in the ovation. Although no one sees it, a tear wells in his eye as the moment conjures up memories of his high school football glory days.

On his way home from the chamber meeting, Brian Michael Wallace Sherman crashes his car. No one is hurt. Two days later, Al Ranovas's home burns to the ground. No one is hurt.

The third bank in town undergoes its third bank exam. CAMELS are 121122. Sherman takes the board members and their spouses to the Ritz in Atlanta for a weekend of celebration. The *Atlanta Courier Press* writes a glowing story on Sherman's "glorious attack on traditional Atlanta banking."

2007

How quickly things change. Midyear the local economy slips. The biggest employer in town closes when foreign competitors sell products under the local firm's cost to manufacture. The plant closure leads to the slow death of several local businesses. The first to fail is the ice cream parlor. The local townspeople no longer can afford such a luxury. By year-end, profits from the past four years at the third bank in town are wiped out completely when their biggest borrower, C.V. Crocker, defaults on the loan for the new Atlanta office tower he was developing.

2008

As businesses board up in Winesburg, the ripple effect leads to even more businesses boarding up. Having peaked at $2.1 billion in assets, the second bank in town is ordered by the FDIC into receivership. As the FDIC liquidates the assets of the now-failed bank, real estate values in town plummet even faster. For the first time ever, Old Man Mueller's bank loses money. Although the bank still has plenty of capital, the regulators downgrade the bank's CAMEL ratings, including management, to 4. "Saddest day of my life" is all Old Man Mueller can mumble to the bank directors when he delivers the news.

2009

Bank of Winesburg reports a small profit in the first quarter. By year-end, the bank's ROA is 0.45%.

2010

In June, the FDIC files a lawsuit against Pangloss, Ranovas, and Sherman for their negligence in overseeing the third bank. According to the complaint, the bank "failed primarily due to the bank's rapid growth and the Board of Director's failure to ensure that bank management identified, measured, monitored, and controlled the risk associated with the institution's lending activities. Specifically, bank management materially deviated from its business plan...." A month later, the FDIC files suit against Crocker for "damages caused by the defendant's failure to use ordinary care and gross negligence."

Motivated and upheld by unknown forces, 94-year-old Mueller joins with an old friend to put into writing a lifetime of banking lessons. His book, *Realism in Lending*, is released in December, "just in time for Christmas gifts," he jokes.

2012

Amazon's list of best-selling business and investing books includes such titles as *The Millionaire Next Door, Strength Finder, Steve Jobs, What Every Body Is Saying, How to Win,* and *Highly Effective People.* Mueller's book is not a bestseller. What a shame.

Why Banks Succeed and Fail: Lessons Learned from the Winesburg Case Study

By now the astute reader has searched on Google and figured out there is no such town as Winesburg, Georgia. Winesburg is just about any town in Georgia or Washington or Nevada or Arizona or Florida from 1995 to 2012.

For every conservative Bank of Winesburg, there were at least one or two new banks determined to deliver rocket-fuel profits to impatient investors. For every seasoned banker like Mueller, there was one or two spit-and-polished bank CEOs who had never seen tough times, never even ran a bank, and, in some cases, never even took their first class in credit training.

Mueller represents the very best in *people risk management.* He represents bank CEOs who want the most-informed and knowledgeable group of advisors they can possibly find. Mueller expects the board to debate. He seeks to be challenged and kept humble. Mueller and the bank board discuss the performance of the CEO and know the performance of bank employees besides Mueller and the CEO.

Mueller is a product of the Depression era, and he has established a consistent, repeatable process to assess risk. His focus on consistently evaluating risk represents the best in *process risk management.* He is alert to danger, careful about keeping rainy-day money, and comfortable forgoing high periodic returns for lower, more reliable returns. Some people think Mueller is too bureaucratic, especially when he wheels a cart of policy books to his first board meeting. The real point here is that he is "by the book." He knows commercial banking is about being right 99.5% of the time and that people are human and make mistakes. Processes are in place as guardrails to keep the bank on the straight path.

Mueller's attention to emerging and external event risk is very important. The board has a formal process to ensure a forward view of risks. When the largest employer in town fails, it is a risk the bank's directors had already identified and mitigated. Is there any more critical function for a board than to look over the horizon for 10X risks that could damage and possibly kill the bank? The Bank of Winesburg board is made up of skilled financial people. They are not business developers. They are not public relations people. They govern the bank, which requires enormous skill and experience when done right.

Mueller has been with his bank 61 years. He represents bankers who care about honor, personal sacrifice, and integrity. When Mueller's bank receives a CAMELS rating with a 4 for management, Mueller tells his board it is the saddest day of his life. Such a

19

statement is the sum and substance of the banker who cares so deeply he cannot separate himself from the welfare of his institution. Mueller's tenure represents all bankers, retired or not, who have spent 25, 30, 35, and more than 40 years with their banks. It is impossible to comprehend the pain and anguish they feel when they see their banks crumble. Such bankers really do exist.

The two new banks in Winesburg are fictional as well. Each represents risk factors that cause banks to fail. Present in the story are the underskilled, overconfident, and inexperienced bankers and directors who see their new banks as personal piggy banks and a source of community stature. Also in the story are the novices who think banking is easy, never having lived through tough days, never having studied bank cycles, and eager to make a quick buck. These "leaders" epitomize people risks and the absence of solid processes to protect banks. The new banks' poor risk management practices created systemic risk to the communities in which they did business.

As for the regulators who supervised the Winesburg banks, did you note how the failed banks received strong to very strong CAMELS ratings not long before failing? As will be discussed in detail later, this was true not only in Winesburg, but across the U.S. in the buildup to the most recent rash of bank failures.

And, yes, there are banks in America like the new ones in Winesburg, although 457 fewer than existed five years ago.

Banking is an elegantly simple business, but it is not easy. This book is about what it takes for banks to be successful. In a sentence, success in banking requires honorable, humble, capable bankers who use reliable, repeatable, proven processes to navigate ever-lurking emerging and existing risks that threaten doom to the bank.

As for Mueller's book, yes, there is a book by a banker named Mueller. He is now 95 years young. Time-tested, the real Mr. Mueller is indeed honorable, humble, and capable.

In fact, P. Henry "Hank" Mueller is still spry enough to write about banking with my University of Virginia Darden School professor, William W. Sihler. Their book—*Realism in Lending*—is a classic. At 50 pages, it can and should be required reading for anyone who sits on a bank board, runs a bank, is part of a risk management function, or lends money.

Believe it or not, the real Mr. Mueller has even more experience than the fictional Mr. Mueller: The real one started at Citibank in 1934 at the tender age of 17. By the mid-1970s, the real Mr. Mueller was chairman of Citibank's Credit Policy Committee. Read his and Bill's book.

Ten Lessons Learned from Winesburg: Parsons Rules of Banking

- *Bankers and banks connect; when one goes bad, and then another, the dominoes fall and bad things happen.* The first rule is the most important. In banking, underskilled and unskilled so-called bankers like Sherman and Crocker can do tremendous damage to local, national, and global economies. Even more dangerous than people like Sherman and Crocker are bankers and directors like Dr. Pangloss, who combine inexperience with overconfidence. Banking is different. More than any other industry, a bad banker and unskilled director can not only damage their own financial institution, but poison the neighborhood wells from which prudent bankers drink. Like John Donne's observation that no man is an island, no bank is an island.

- *When bankers do not appreciate the precious nature of capital, it flows too easily to wrong places and bad things happen.* Capital is good. Like the air we breathe, capital can be taken for granted. When the investors' capital seems abundant, it can be protected inadequately. When capital is taken for granted, it is underappreciated.

- *When bank investors think banking is a high-growth investment, bad things happen.* Natural laws govern banking. Like corn, bank assets and profits can grow only so fast. Over time, the growth rate of the economy and growth rate of bank assets and profits should be in sync. The natural laws of banking can be cheated for a short time by a few people, but can never be cheated over a long time by a lot of people.

- *When a lot of bankers and bank directors think they are all smarter than the average banker, bad things happen.* Gathering deposits and making loans is a banker's job. Lending is investing, investing brings risk, and risk brings potential for profit and loss. Like achieving a .300 career batting average in baseball, beating the market over a career is very rare. Bankers and bank directors are really investors. Very, very few investors are like Warren Buffett, who has proven he can beat the market. In good times, when the stock market goes up, most of us think we are smarter than the market. In bad times, we are reminded of the truth.

- *When bankers and bank directors do not understand the risks they are taking, bad things happen.* A bank's tolerance for risk must be understood and measured. Neither is easy. History proves that many bankers do not measure risk well. Untrained and inexperienced bank directors lack the know-how to independently understand and assess bank risks.

- *When banks that need to be right 99.5% of the time turn out to be right only 95% of the time, really bad things happen to the bank.* Bankers who are wrong more than 1% of the time must be paid more money and get more fees to compensate for being wrong more often. The problem is that good borrowers do not want to pay more money to compensate for the bankers' errors.

- *When a bank lacks skilled and experienced advisors, bad things happen to the king, his court, and his investors.* Imperial CEOs are dangerous. Absolute power cannot be trusted. Wise leaders see themselves as servants, not kings. They seek the counsel of skilled and experienced advisors.

- *When bankers are too confident, they assume more and more risk, and when they take on too much risk, bad things happen.* Better humility than pride, as pride leads to overconfidence. Overconfidence is the banker's enemy. Prudent bankers worry a lot. They are never confident in their ability to see all the risks facing the bank.

- *When bankers do not have several ways to skin a cat, bad things happen.* Prudent bankers plan well. They constantly ask, "What can go wrong?" Good bankers and bank directors have a Plan A, a Plan B, a Plan C, and sometimes even a Plan D. When they make loans, they carefully consider "what-ifs."

- *When bankers think this time is different, you know what happens.* The final rule: The practice of banking goes back thousands of years. The fundamental truths of good and bad banking are immutable and timeless.

Bankers and Directors: It's Time to Raise the Bar

10X Risk Kills Banks

The term "10X" was used by former Intel CEO Andrew Grove in a book he wrote in the mid-1990s called *Only the Paranoid Survive*. I thought the book so important back then that I gave a copy of it to my bank's CEO. A year ago I read that Grove's book was among the 25 most important books on the "must-read" list of JPMorgan Chase's chairman. In Grove's book, he described a "10X force" as an event or invention that radically alters the playing field, leaving companies at risk of losing control of the future.

I define "10X risk" as risks that cause banks to fail. In contrast, "X" risks are real risks, but they cannot result in bank failure. Bank directors and executives must conduct operational risk assessments with the goal of discovering 10X risks that can kill or seriously impair the bank's earnings or reputation. The topic of 10X risk will be developed further shortly.

Often directors and bankers confuse cause and effect when it comes to bank failure. Too often bad loans are cited as the cause of a bank's failure. Yes, banks fail when bad loans eat up capital. But bad loans are the effect, not the cause; deeper underlying problems cause banks to fail. Years of regulator examinations of failed banks show banks actually fail for one of three reasons:

- The bank has unskilled and inexperienced *people* on its board of directors and in management.
- The bank's management, directors, and regulators supervising the bank have inadequate *processes* and *systems* to identify risk early enough for the risk to be mitigated and controlled.
- The bank's management and directors are unable to foresee and control for *external event risks* like big swings in oil prices.

These four factors—people, processes, systems, and external events—constitute operational risk management. The true cause of repeated bank failures in the U.S. is weak operational risk management. When two or more of these four factors fail, the potential for 10X risk increases.

The best bankers and directors are like Old Man Mueller, an expert in operational, strategic, and credit risk management. Successful banks understand they need skilled and experienced people to develop and oversee the processes and systems to manage risks. When skilled bank management is not in place, effective risk management processes and systems provide directors with a counterbalance to the talent gaps. Over time, however, if weak bank risk management is not replaced with skilled risk management, capable processes and systems atrophy.

Finally, the banks with the best risk management people and capabilities are ever-vigilant in identifying emerging external risks. Although not all external event risks can be prevented, bankers and directors can significantly reduce risks common to bank failure by building appropriate controls. Capable and strong operational risk management requires banks to have five specific capabilities:

1. **Scenario analysis**: Directors and managers invest valuable time and energy in "seeing around the corner" and preparing for "what-ifs." Chapter 16 and Appendix 2 focus on this critical risk management process.
2. **External failure and loss analysis:** Bankers study the failures and losses of other banks, past and present, in an effort to learn how to avoid making the same mistakes.
3. **Internal loss analysis:** Losing money, be it from a bad lending decision or a broken process, is never OK. When losses occur, each must be studied to determine lessons learned and which processes broke down that allowed for the loss.
4. **Risk and control assessment (RCA):** Banks effectively identify risks inherent to their businesses and then build needed controls. Banks that have capable risk assessment processes and controls make fewer mistakes and lose less money than banks that do not.
5. **Strategic risk management**: Bringing together the four prior capabilities, banks must assess strategic opportunities with discipline and rigor. Directors must ask the tough questions to ensure appropriate strategic risk management.

The Root of All Bank Failures: Operational Risk Failures That Combine as 10X Risk

We are told the root of all evil is the love of money. So what is the root of all bank failures? The root of all bank failures is not a credit problem. It is not liquidity. It is not even bad strategy. These are symptoms.

Recently I asked my personal physician about something my octogenarian dad has said throughout his life. My dad says, "Pneumonia is the disease that kills old people." When I asked my doctor if this is true, he shook his head and said, "Back when your dad was growing up, just about every old person died of pneumonia, so everyone in the 1930s and 1940s just assumed it was the cause of death." He explained that pneumonia is a symptom of an underlying but undetected disease like cancer or something else.

Banks that fail do not die of pneumonia, nor do they die from bad credit. They die from an underlying disease always tied to one of four other failures. Often these failures are combined into a perfect storm leading to bank failure. The four are risks associated with people failures, process breakdowns, systems problems, and external events outside the bank's direct control. These four risks constitute operational risk.

Unlike the credit and market risk management disciplines, operational risk management is a much less mature risk science and discipline. There is increasing appreciation among bank experts that operational risk management skills are foundational to effective credit, liquidity, market, and strategic risk management. Despite this growing recognition, many banks of all sizes in the U.S. still lack a capable and sound operational risk management program. U.S. regulators, especially the Federal Reserve and the Office of the Comptroller of the Currency (OCC), are leading the effort to heighten industry awareness of this shortcoming. Regulators in Australia have been at this task longer. Not surprisingly, banks in Australia generally are viewed to have more advanced operational risk management programs and skills.

In some ways, regulators have been their own worst enemy when it comes to advancing the operational risk discipline. The first challenge is the simple fact that most bank examiners have no personal experience running a community or regional bank and, consequently, do not always have credibility with bankers and directors. Second, operational risk management is new not only to bankers, but to examiners, too. As the banks take their guidance from regulators, the regulators take their guidance from an international collection of bank regulators known as the Basel Committee.

U.S. regulators rely on internally developed "how to" checklists to supervise a bank's operational risk management program. Some of these lists are quite good and can be very helpful. The big challenge, however, is that these checklists often do not adequately discriminate between run-of-the-mill risks and material ones. What's the difference between a run-of-the mill risk and a material one? Answer: One can hurt you; the other can kill you.

Effective operational risk management can be compared to an effective physical examination. Doctors can perform physical exams ranging from a 10-minute checkup with some blood work to an eight-hour exam with multiple tests and multiple specialists who evaluate each organ, muscle, and bone in the body. Certainly not every patient needs the eight-hour exam. On the other hand, if not done correctly, the 10-minute exam may be too cursory. A good doctor must evaluate the patient and determine the best type of physical exam.

As regulators wisely push the operational risk management agenda on banks, many bank risk managers try to push back. These bankers see operational risk management as the construction of long lists of potential problems and the development of process maps showing highly detailed pictures of possible external event, system, and supplier risks. As each risk is identified, additional work is required because each risk must be documented with steps for mitigation, measurement, monitoring, and control.

These risk managers believe their bank's risk profile—which is a description of the risks facing a bank—requires something less than the identification of hundreds if not thousands of potential problems. Further, and importantly, they fear that long checklists lead to a new risk: failing to see the forest for the trees. Therefore, the stiffest challenge to successful implementation of a robust operational risk management program is a focus on form over substance.

To advance the operational risk management discipline, regulators and bankers would be better served if they focused on forward-looking material operational risks. I call these 10X risks. Distinguishing between X and 10X risks requires highly skilled bankers using effective processes. The most critical process is what is known in bank risk management language as the "three lines of defense."

The first line of defense is the bank executive who is responsible for the P&L of a line of business; his or her job must include risk identification, mitigation, monitoring, and control. The second line is made up of people who are completely independent of the business executive; this is the risk management organization, which must independently challenge and verify the line of business's work. The third line of defense is the bank's audit function, which must independently challenge, review, and validate the work of the first two lines.

Banks with a strong risk culture and experienced banking professionals should be able to identify 10X risks and challenge each other when certain risks are in the gray zone. My view is that any one of the three lines should be able to independently identify a risk as 10X and override the objections of the other lines.

Banks must conduct periodic and comprehensive operational risk self-exams. The frequency is a function of the bank's risk profile; quarterly and semiannually are most common. The more difficult decision for risk managers and the board is to determine the scope of the operational risk assessment. At least annually, banks should conduct thorough, detailed operational risk assessments that capture *all* operational risks.

Too few U.S. bank directors and executives appreciate how operational risk management skills are essential to effective bank oversight. Partly because current operational risk practices remain immature, some community and regional bank directors do not even have operational risk issues on board agendas. In contrast, much more board time is spent discussing credit risk management.

Board time must be devoted to debating and challenging management about operational risks—that is, people, processes, systems, and external events. The problem with this board imperative is that it assumes directors have the necessary skills and experience to debate and challenge management regarding these risks. Lacking necessary banking skills and experience, the boards of many banks today are the bank's "people risk."

Directors will discover that, when banks fail, the regulators almost always identify the primary root cause to be the directors' failure to hold management accountable for identifying, mitigating, monitoring, and controlling for risks. Here is the main point of this chapter: Banks fail because of operational risk failures, and skilled directors can prevent 10X risk.

Returning to Winesburg, Georgia, we see that 10X risk killed Crocker's and Sherman's banks. As the next chapter will show, when new banks and S&Ls enter a market, the probability of 10X risk increases enormously.

Community Bank Failure, 2008-2012: A Shortage of Skilled Bankers and Directors

S ince the beginning of 2008, we have seen 457 banks fail. Why? My data and analysis show two root causes. Neither is like a new strain of a deadly disease. Neither should have killed banks in the 21st century.

The first reason is tied to an external event risk that may surprise people. Bank failure appears to be highly related to the entry of new bank competitors into markets. Specifically, the likelihood of failure—10X risk—rises significantly when new banks are chartered and led by inexperienced directors and so-called bankers like C. V. Crocker and Brian Michael Wallace Sherman. In addition, industry profitability appears to be highly correlated to new bank formation rates. Not only are the new chartered banks at risk of failure, but existing banks in the market, like Old Man Mueller's Bank of Winesburg, are put at significantly higher risk as well.

The second reason relates to the need for capable people and processes in banking. Bank failures and problem banks lack experienced and skilled directors and management. There are a finite number of talented people capable of running and overseeing America's banks. Skilled bankers and directors are trained to know which processes are critical to success. Over the past 20 years, the industry has actually cut back on the kind of training needed to develop general bankers like Old Man Mueller. Consequently, the talent issue in banking is worse today than it has been in more than 50 years.

The first reason does not seem to get any attention. Maybe no one knows that bank failure and entry of new banks into a market are correlated, or maybe it is known but not made public. The second reason was learned less than 20 years ago when 3,000 banks and S&Ls failed, but it was forgotten.

Root Cause #1: Déjà Vu All Over Again

My analysis began with a simple question: Is it possible the U.S. did not learn from the banking crisis of the 1980s and early 1990s? To answer this question it is necessary to go back 30 years ago. In 1982 the U.S. economy was beginning to heal from years of high inflation. As any banker knows, inflation is terrible for the lending business. Assets and liabilities are hard to match if inflation drives up the short-term cost of funds. S&Ls in the 1970s were in a terrible predicament as deposit costs eclipsed the rates earned on fixed-rate residential loan portfolios.

Enter into the picture well-meaning federal legislation. Intent on helping the S&Ls, the Garn-St. Germain Depository Institutions Act of 1982 allowed S&Ls to start making certain types of commercial loans that could float with the cost of deposits.

The Garn-St. Germain Act almost overnight altered the landscape of U.S. banking. Out of nowhere, it seemed desperate S&Ls became quasi-commercial banks. Although often lacking the people and processes to oversee commercial lending, these new bank competitors jumped into markets like the Tampa Bay region where I worked. They had capital to lend. The capital had to find a place to go. As more loans poured into the region, capital seemed to get cheaper, and more and more projects were funded. Exacerbating the problem was that the regulator for the S&Ls lacked the skills to supervise commercial lending activity. At some magic point, the tide turned and banks and S&Ls started to fail.

My research shows that a substantial majority of the 457 bank failures seen in the United States from January 1, 2008, to October 2012 have as their root cause two operational risks. Like the banking crisis experienced in the four to eight years after Congress passed the Garn-St. Germain Act, some of the current failures can be traced to an external event risk. My extensive analysis of FDIC data shows the rate of new bank formation in a state from 2000 to 2007 to be a critical factor in influencing whether a state had high or low performing banks from 2008 to 2012.

To begin with, banking varies a lot across the country. As shown in Chapter 1, some states have hundreds of banks headquartered in the state and some have only a few. It comes as no surprise to learn that some states added many new banks over the seven years building up to the financial crisis, while others experienced little or no growth in newly chartered banks.

Let's return to the Bank of Winesburg case study. Recall that one of the most critical decisions Old Man Mueller and the board made every year was to establish the bank's profitability target. At the Bank of Winesburg, the directors set a profit target every year of a 1% return on assets (ROA). The profit target is perhaps the single most important determinant of a bank's risk appetite. The lower the profit target, the less risk a bank must take.

One big challenge faced by a bank when setting its profit target is the influence of external forces, like competitors and their behaviors, on the bank. Setting the annual profit goal requires a bank's directors to make certain assumptions. The Latin phrase *ceteris paribus* means "all other things being equal or held constant." Setting the profit goal and risk appetite requires the bank to assume that certain conditions are likely to hold constant.

Of course, nothing is ever constant in life. For bankers in certain states in the years from 2000 to 2007 (like Georgia, where the fictional town of Winesburg is located), the addition every year of more and more new banks made setting profit targets and risk appetites problematic. We will work backwards to prove this point. Table 5.1 shows the ROA of commercial banks by state for year-end 2009 and as of September 30, 2011. First, compare 2009 to September 30, 2011; note the improvement in ROA across the country, which gives evidence of the healing of the industry. Second, take a look at the wide variation in profitability by state; Alaska is the best in 2009 at 1.17% and Nevada the worst at -2.87%. Third, 10 states in 2009 actually showed respectable ROAs of 0.75% and higher; on the other hand, nine showed the average bank in those states actually lost money. In the 10 states where the average bank showed a 0.75% ROA or better, there appears to be little evidence of a banking crisis in 2009.

Table 5.1						

Bank Profitability by State for 2009 and 9/30/2011 (%)

	State ROA 2009	State ROA 3Q/11	Change in ROA 2009–11		State ROA 2009	State ROA 3Q/11	Change in ROA 2009–11
Alaska	1.17	1.05	-0.12	Illinois	0.44	0.75	0.31
Oklahoma	1.07	1.34	0.27	Maine	0.43	0.61	0.18
New Mexico	1.05	1.12	0.07	Colorado	0.42	0.70	0.28
Louisiana	0.98	1.07	0.09	Massachusetts	0.38	0.56	0.18
Iowa	0.90	1.31	0.41	Tennessee	0.37	0.79	0.42
Arkansas	0.87	1.10	0.23	Hawaii	0.34	0.82	0.48
Texas	0.86	1.06	0.2	Utah	0.32	1.39	1.07
Nebraska	0.81	1.14	0.33	Connecticut	0.28	0.40	0.12
North Dakota	0.81	1.29	0.48	New Jersey	0.27	0.51	0.24
South Dakota	0.75	1.33	0.58	Michigan	0.23	0.68	0.45
West Virginia	0.73	0.71	-0.02	Virginia	0.18	0.67	0.49
Montana	0.72	0.95	0.23	Rhode Island	0.18	0.37	0.19
Wyoming	0.70	0.96	0.26	Alabama	0.17	0.73	0.56
Mississippi	0.70	0.89	0.19	North Carolina	0.09	0.24	0.15
Kentucky	0.68	0.87	0.19	Maryland	0.08	0.42	0.34
Kansas	0.65	1.01	0.36	Delaware	0.02	0.51	0.49
Missouri	0.59	0.94	0.35	South Carolina	-0.06	0.31	0.37
Vermont	0.59	0.67	0.08	Oregon	-0.40	0.31	0.71
New York	0.58	0.73	0.15	California	-0.61	0.66	1.27
Minnesota	0.54	0.93	0.39	Washington	-0.84	0.43	1.27
Ohio	0.48	0.73	0.25	Idaho	-0.91	0.12	1.03
Wisconsin	0.47	0.84	0.37	Georgia	-0.96	0.26	1.22
Pennsylvania	0.47	0.76	0.29	Florida	-1.46	0.23	1.69
Indiana	0.45	0.75	0.3	Arizona	-2.36	0.42	2.78
New Hampshire	0.45	0.60	0.15	Nevada	-2.87	0.74	3.61
				AVERAGE	0.24	0.76	0.52

Source: www.fdic.gov/bank/analytical/stateprofile/SanFrancisco/Az/AZ.xml.html

From the FDIC's website, the return on assets (ROA) is calculated as the median ratio of net income (including gains or losses on securities and extraordinary items) divided by average total assets during the listed period for all FDIC-insured institutions headquartered in the state. Quarterly figures are annualized (multiplied by four).

Table 5.2 is compiled from FDIC data as well. It shows by state the rate of new bank formation from 2000 to 2007 compared to the total number of banks headquartered in each state as of the year 2000. Once again, variability jumps out. Led by Arizona, 15 states chartered 25% or more new banks from 2000 to 2007 over the baseline number of

Table 5.2	

New Bank Formation Compared with Total Bank Numbers, 2000–2007

State	# New Banks Chartered by State, 2000–2007 as % of Banks in 2000	State	# New Banks Chartered by State, 2000–2007 as % of Banks in 2000
Arizona	93	New Mexico	11
Nevada	75	Montana	10
Rhode Island	57	Wyoming	9
North Carolina	51	Texas	9
Utah	46	Kentucky	8
Florida	45	Minnesota	8
California	43	Massachusetts	7
Connecticut	39	West Virginia	7
New Jersey	37	Mississippi	7
Oregon	36	Illinois	7
Washington	34	Missouri	7
Georgia	32	Maine	7
Idaho	28	Indiana	6
South Carolina	27	Ohio	6
Hawaii	25	Wisconsin	5
Tennessee	22	Louisiana	4
Delaware	21	Kansas	4
New York	20	Arkansas	3
Virginia	19	Iowa	3
Alabama	17	South Dakota	3
Pennsylvania	15	Nebraska	3
Maryland	15	North Dakota	3
Michigan	14	Oklahoma	2
New Hampshire	13	Alaska	0
Colorado	13	Vermont	0

Source: www.fdic.gov/bank/analytical/stateprofile/SanFrancisco/Az/AZ.xml.html

banks in those states as of 2000. In contrast, almost half the states saw a very modest jump in newly chartered banks—less than 10%—during this same seven-year period.

Is there a relationship between a state's rate of new bank formation from 2000 to 2007 and its ROA in 2009? To answer that question, it is necessary to run a statistical analysis comparing the numbers by state. The correlation coefficient (r) between the 2000-2007 state new bank chartering (formation) rate and the median 2009 state ROA is -0.835. This number suggests a strong negative correlation (*higher* new bank chartering rates from 2000 to 2007 correlate strongly with *lower* 2009 state ROA). Statisticians would commonly use the "r squared" statistic to clarify this point. Squaring our correlation shows us that 69.7% of the variation in 2009 state ROA is explained by the variation in state new bank formation from 2000 to 2007. While the statistics cannot guarantee that higher new bank charter rates cause lower ROA in subsequent years (and vice versa), they can confirm the effectiveness of new bank charter rates as a predictor of ROA for the period studied.

Let's take a look at just one more table drawn from my research. Table 5.3 shows the number of banks that failed by state between January 1, 2008, and February 29, 2012. Is there a relationship between new bank formation rates from 2000 to 2007 and the fail-

Table 5.3

Number of Failed Banks (1/1/2008 to 2/29/2012)

State	# Banks in State	FDIC # Bank Failures, 2008–2012	Failed Banks 2008–2012 as % of Banks in State	State	# Banks in State	FDIC # Bank Failures, 2008–2012	Failed Banks 2008–2012 as % of Banks in State
Nevada	25	11	44%	Arkansas	127	2	2%
Arizona	33	13	39%	Ohio	237	5	2%
Georgia	246	78	32%	New York	187	4	2%
Florida	233	61	26%	Indiana	143	3	2%
Washington	73	17	23%	Texas	600	9	2%
Oregon	34	6	18%	Oklahoma	242	4	2%
California	261	38	15%	West Virginia	63	1	2%
Utah	57	6	11%	Mississippi	89	2	2%
Michigan	133	13	10%	Tennessee	188	2	1%
South Carolina	80	7	9%	South Dakota	83	1	1%
Colorado	109	9	8%	Kentucky	195	1	1%
Illinois	585	49	8%	Nebraska	221	3	1%
Maryland	85	6	7%	Iowa	348	2	1%
Idaho	18	1	6%	Louisiana	150	2	1%
New Mexico	50	3	6%	Massachusetts	160	1	1%
Minnesota	395	19	5%	Hawaii	9	0	0%
Alabama	142	6	4%	Montana	73	0	0%
North Carolina	98	4	4%	Alaska	6	0	0%
Virginia	112	4	4%	Delaware	27	0	0%
Missouri	333	12	4%	Rhode Island	14	0	0%
Kansas	320	8	3%	Connecticut	52	0	0%
New Jersey	116	4	3%	North Dakota	92	0	0%
Wyoming	36	1	3%	New Hampshire	23	0	0%
Pennsylvania	209	6	3%	Maine	29	0	0%
Wisconsin	271	6	2%	Vermont	9	0	0%

Source: www.fdic.gov/bank/analytical/stateprofile/SanFrancisco/Az/AZ.xml.html

ure of banks in those states between 2008 and 2012? Again, when the two sets of numbers are subjected to correlation analysis, we find a 0.729 correlation coefficient and an r square of 53.1%. By removing the four states with fewer than 15 banks (Hawaii, Vermont, Rhode Island, and Alaska), the correlation coefficient increases to 0.791 and to an r square of 62.5%, suggesting the effectiveness of using a state's new bank charter rate as a key risk indicator of future bank failure rates.

Appendix 3 provides additional statistical insights into the relationship between new bank chartering rates, bank profitability, and bank failures and problems. When problem bank data is added to failed bank data, as shown in Appendix 3, the statistical significance increases for key metrics.

There are at least two serious implications to the statistics here and in Appendix 3. First, investors in community banks would be well served to pay close attention to new bank formation rates in the markets where their banks compete. As a corollary, bank investors will want to continue to study bank consolidation rates as the number of banks inevitably declines in the coming few years. In theory, bank consolidation should lead to improved industry profitability. However, it can also lead to unintended consequences that bank CEOs, CROs, and directors should monitor closely.

The second implication is to those regulators who are in the position to approve new bank charters. My research should give them solid ground for denying or delaying charter approval in cases where new bank formation rates are so frothy as to create systemic risk to local markets (such as a town or city) and regions (like the Atlanta metropolitan area). By the way, other industries are accustomed to this rationale. For example, the number of hospital beds in a community is carefully controlled based on adverse-impact studies that consider the short-term implications to existing hospitals operating in the community.

Does correlation prove causation? No. But meaningful correlation provides a smoking gun for why so many banks failed in some states and not in others. Common sense suggests that fast growth in a business stretches people and resources. Major League Baseball and the National Football League carefully regulate new team formation. They know that new teams can dilute their product as teams stretch to find qualified athletes. The same is true in banking. Communities and states that charter new banks run the same risk MLB and the NFL do when they add new teams. To build on that analogy further, the NFL and MLB worry not only about the quality of players on the field, but also the quality and skills of the referees and umpires. Expanding the number of teams means hiring more officials to referee and umpire games. Without a doubt, the same is true in banking. States that added significant numbers of new banks needed to have qualified state and federal regulators to oversee those banks. What are the chances that the states with the fastest new bank formation rates between 2000 and 2007 were truly able to keep up with the demand for such regulatory talent?

Root Cause #2: "Second Verse, Same as the First"

When I was in the fifth grade, I studied guitar for all of six weeks. The practice part of playing guitar was not my thing. I did learn one song during my brief career as a guitar player, "Mrs. Brown, You've Got a Lovely Daughter" by the inimitable Herman's Hermits. Back then, I was a big Hermits fan. Among their hits was the song, "I'm Henery the Eighth, I Am."

Yes, it is "Henery," not "Henry." Herman's Hermits released the song in 1965, and it climbed the Billboard 100 chart to number 1. What few non-Brits knew at the time was that the song actually dated back to 1910, when it was a popular tune in English music halls. Perhaps one reason for its popularity was this clever phrase: "Second verse, same as the first." Mark my words—anyone who knows this catchy little tune is now humming it to himself or herself.

When it comes to America's latest round of bank failures, it is indeed "second verse, same as the first." The other major root cause of the recent financial crisis comes from the 1980s' songbook: a lack of managers and directors with banking skills and experience. Said another way, there are too few Muellers, and it is too easy for the Crockers and Panglosses to become bankers and directors.

Material loss reviews (MLRs) are conducted by the Office of Inspector Generals of the FDIC, OCC, and Federal Reserve. MLRs are required anytime the U.S. government experiences a financial loss from a bank closure over a certain amount. An inspector is essentially a pathologist who performs an autopsy on the bank corpse. His or her job is to identify the reasons the bank failed. In addition to MLRs, regulators also file enforcement actions against problem banks. Virtually every MLR and enforcement action letter done by the FDIC and other regulators repeats the same themes.

- Board governance is weak because directors lack bank skills and experience.
- Management lacks skill in identifying, mitigating, monitoring, and controlling risks.
- Controls are inadequate.
- The bank does not have a strategic plan, and if it does, it is inadequate.

Noted below are verbatim comments taken from several different MLRs written by the FDIC about banks that have failed in the past couple of years:

- The bank's "failure can be attributed to inadequate oversight by the Board and management."
- "Examiners particularly noted that none of the Board members, with the exception of the CEO, had any banking experience…."
- "Ultimately, the economic downturn exposed" the bank's "risk management weaknesses and contributed to the rapid deterioration of asset quality."
- The bank "failed primarily because the Board and bank management did not effectively oversee the bank's operations…. The institution grew rapidly…. As a result of inadequate controls…."
- "Management and the Board pursued a business strategy that deviated from the original business plan without having the appropriate management expertise and internal controls in place…."

Noted below are verbatim comments from several different enforcement actions of problem banks at risk of failure:

- "…the board of the Bank shall submit to the Reserve Bank and the Bureau a written plan to strengthen board oversight of the management and operations of the Bank."

- "As of the effective date of this ORDER, the board of directors shall increase its participation in the affairs of the Bank, assuming full responsibilities for the approval of sound policies and objectives for the supervision of all of the bank's activities...."
- "The Bank shall have and maintain qualified management."
- "Each member of management shall have qualification and experience...."
- "...the Board shall develop ... a written Strategic Plan for the Bank ... covering at least a three-year period." And another read "The Strategic Plan shall establish objectives for the Bank's overall risk profile, earnings performance, growth ... and shall, at a minimum, include: (a) a mission statement that forms the framework for the establishment of strategic goals ... (b) a description of the Bank's targeted market(s) and an assessment of the current and projected risks and competitive factors...."

A couple of Texas boys named Seals and Crofts sang a forlorn ballad in 1979 lamenting "we may never pass this way again." Perhaps you remember it? Unlike Seals and Crofts, I will lament if we *ever* pass this way (of bank failures) again due to inadequate oversight and governance by directors and management. The next three chapters describe actions bankers and directors can take to avoid passing this way again.

Developing Strong Community and Regional Bankers: The Need for a Paradigm Shift

Midway in our life's journey, I went astray from the straight road and woke to find myself alone in a dark wood. How shall I say what wood that was! I never saw so drear, so rank, so arduous a wilderness! Its very memory gives a shape to fear.

The Inferno by Dante Alighieri begins with those fateful words. Bankers in 2013 are in their own inferno. It is called The Public Utility Era of Banking. Like Dante, bankers went astray. As Dante discovered, there is an exit.

Paradigm Shift

The banking system in America is broken. By now it is apparent that the patchwork of U.S. bank regulation cannot solve the problem alone. No greater evidence is needed than 3,400 bank and S&L failures during the past 30 years. Bankers must step up and fix banking.

Visionary community and regional bankers are needed to build a new banking system that works for all of America. Government cannot solve the problem. Banking problems have plagued this nation for 200 years. Dodd-Frank is fraught with the same risk of unintended consequences experienced 30 years ago with the Garn-St. Germain Act and 13 years ago with the Gramm-Leach-Bliley Act.

For good reason, bankers are in the penalty box. Getting out will take time, disciplined management processes, unswerving evidence of integrity, and a commitment to balance competing interests. Can community and regional bankers do anything to accelerate the industry's exit from the penalty box? Yes, but it requires bankers to think differently about the industry. Bankers need to acknowledge that the system is broken and small tweaks will not fix it. What is needed is a paradigm shift.

What is a paradigm shift? The term was coined by Thomas Kuhn, an American academic who taught history and philosophy at Harvard, Berkeley, and Princeton. A paradigm is a model or pattern for how we see and understand the world around us. Life is full of paradigms.

An example will illustrate the point. When I was in college in the 1970s, I took a course in COBOL, one of the oldest computer programming languages. I absolutely hated the course. I was particularly frustrated with the huge amount of time I wasted "punching" cards. Simple programming tasks required mounds of punch cards. Each represented one step in the overall program. Heaven help me when I made a typing error, which unfortunately was frequent. Inevitably I would find myself in the computer lab well past midnight trying to figure out which of my 552 punch cards had errors.

While I was up late punching cards in an effort to develop some elementary program, a guy a year older than me named Bill was also up late working in a computer lab. But Bill was not mindlessly punching cards with the goal of formulating a simple program. He was trying to figure out how guys like me would not have to stay up all night developing programs. He figured he could save people like me a lot of time and energy if he could create programs that made our lives easier. Eventually Bill succeeded, and his company, Microsoft, was formed and made some money.

So what is the paradigm and what is the shift in this example? People like me saw computer programming as a pain. It required lots of tedious work. Everyone knew punching cards was the way to create a program; there was no way around it. Along came Bill Gates, and he had a better idea. His idea was the foundation of a shift in how the rest of us saw the world of computers. He introduced the paradigm shift, and the rest is history.

The banking system in America is broken. Bankers can improve banking. Visionary community and regional bankers are needed who can address the industry's most pressing challenges.

In banking, a new system is needed to address three deep-rooted, multigenerational problems. None is easy to address. All three require bankers to join forces and take control of the industry. First, bankers must establish that they have a duty to society, and with duty comes responsibilities. Second, bankers must self-police the industry by requiring all bankers to have appropriate training and licensing. Third, bankers must put in place safeguards to protect the industry from systemic risk.

The Banker's Duty to Society

If we return to Old Man Mueller, do you recall his motivation to start a bank in Winesburg in 1951? "Taught firsthand the anguish of bank failure when his granddad's bank failed in 1932, he felt burdened to prove the Muellers were indeed good bankers." And do you recall the profound pain he felt when his bank was downgraded to a 4 management rating in the 2009 regulatory CAMELS exam? Mueller built his bank with the intention of it living forever. He saw it as his duty to build and preserve a bank that protected the interests of all he served.

What if all of America's banks were built to last? How would bankers, directors, and investors in banks behave differently? First, corporate decisions would be made with a long-term perspective. Second, and even more important, building and sustaining enduring corporate cultures would become an overarching priority for bank directors. Finally, and most difficult because it costs hard dollars, banks built to last would invest in training the people who run and work in the banks. Combining the second and third points, is there any greater imperative than to build a culture where bankers demonstrate knowledge of their unique role in society?

If the past five years have taught bankers anything, it is that bankers have a special role in society. The capital bankers protect and allocate is critical to growing commerce

CHAPTER 6 • Developing Strong Community and Regional Bankers: The Need for a Paradigm Shift

and the nation's economy. But do bankers really understand their role in society? Certainly some like Old Man Mueller get it, but evidence suggests many do not.

We bankers must understand our duty to society. Duty connotes honor and integrity. Duty speaks to moral virtue and the moral commitment bankers have to the communities and constituents we serve. Bankers who understand duty have a framework for understanding how to balance conflicting priorities. They know how to think through competing needs of clients, employees, investors, and directors.

A sense of duty establishes and defines the banker's responsibility to a greater good than just our own happiness. Although our individual happiness—and compensation for that matter—is important, it is important only in the context of the greater good created by the bank. Some may scoff at this notion, but it is true. Ask to see the paychecks of former leaders of banks that have failed. No one gets paid when a bank fails.

Honor and integrity require bankers to ask tough questions. How profitable can and should our bank really be if we intend to preserve and protect it for future generations? How much money do we spend and invest to ensure our employees have the appropriate skills to do their jobs? Where do we draw the line when the government requires bankers to make certain loans when we know those loans are risky for the borrower and bad for society in the long run? What do we do when we see another bank in town exercise bad judgment that may not just increase financial risks for that bank but bring further reputational damage to the banking industry? How do we evaluate marketing spending—especially when we may personally benefit from it—that does not create a clear-cut return on investment for the shareholders?

A moral commitment to serve our many constituents brings enormous challenges. Often what is good for one may not be good for another. As one constituent pushes for the bank to have more capital, investors may push for more dividends. Although potential borrowers may disagree, not every loan should be made. Sometimes teller lines get long because bank management strives to find the right balance between staffing costs and the client's need not to waste time in line. And while local charities in town expect to receive bank contributions, perhaps banks should not be donating their shareholders' money.

Although at times constituents' needs vary, what must never be lost is the common interest all constituents have in the bank's ultimate measure of purpose: to make a profit. It is a moral imperative for the bank to make a fair profit and to grow responsibly. No constituent benefits when the bank fails in this moral imperative. Quite simply, America needs profitable, healthy banks.

Bankers and Directors Must Have Certain Verified Skills to Do Their Jobs

It is time for a reality check. Some bankers probably have read the last couple of pages and said "poppycock" (or possibly something a whole lot worse). Some will be turned off by the idealistic tone of "duty." Others will argue that banks are not and should not be built to last. On this point I partially concede.

Over the next eight years, more bank boards will sell banks than buy banks. Few new banks will start up. Many smaller community banks will consolidate into larger, midtier community banks. Large regional banks will continue to have enormous opportunities to grow. Their management teams and directors will ask themselves whether they want to be a SIFI (systemically important financial institution) subject to greater regulatory scrutiny. Chapter 16 and Appendix 2 will include an overview of the consolidation issue facing community and regional banks.

Why will the industry experience substantial industry consolidation over the next eight years? The answer in two words is *talent shortage*, and the talent shortage has three dimensions. The first is that too few directors and bankers have the skill and expertise to do their jobs; for proof, go back and read the FDIC's material loss reviews. The second is because more community banks cannot find CEOs and directors; read the FDIC lawsuits and ask who in their right mind would want to be a $6,000 to $45,000 a year bank director and risk being sued by a plaintiff that prints money? The third reason is because the industry stopped training bankers 20 years ago.

On this third point, it is worth relating a story I heard from a former CEO of a community bank. Prior to selling his bank several years ago, the CEO did a formal assessment of the talent in the bank. He found good news and bad news. The good: deep talent across the bank with strong credit and risk skills. The bad: no one was under 40 years of age. The CEO decided the bank needed to fix the problem. He and his people went out looking to hire future bank management. To their surprise, they could find very few "real" bankers under the age of 40 who were trained in commercial lending and the basics of how banks operate.

Over the last 20 years, not only have the big banks significantly cut back their traditional general management and credit training programs, but many of the community and regional banks have done so as well. Some cut back training to save money, some to prop up earnings, and some in anticipation of selling the bank. The director of a highly respected banking school told me attendance in his program has fallen as low as 50% from the peak days. The drop in this program as well as in other bank schools and risk management programs even predated the financial crisis. The good news is that banking schools are now reporting some improvement in attendance.

MBA programs like the one I attended in the late 1970s included a commercial lending and commercial banking curriculum. I took three different second-year elective courses on banking. However, even back then the handwriting was on the wall: Those classes had fewer than 10 students in them. In contrast, courses on capital markets and investment banking were just beginning to boom. By the early 2000s, traditional commercial banking courses had disappeared from the curriculum of many undergraduate and graduate schools. Students today have little interest in general commercial banking, a situation probably not helped by the industry's terrible reputation. Ironically, now is probably a great time to study banking since the industry is on the brink of a serious talent shortage. Are community and regional bank CEOs thinking about who will run their banks in 2035?

I can hear the critics now. They say: "What an idealist! Who is worried about 2035 when my bank has trouble earning enough profit to cover my cost of capital in 2013?" I concede the point. The truth is, community and regional banks need to invest in skills building in 2013 and for 2035. It is not an either/or. Banks that want to sell today or in the next few years do not care about 2035, but they should care a lot about the state of industry skills in 2013.

There are two reasons why sellers and potential sellers should push the industry training agenda. The first has to do with the directors' obligation to maximize the value of the bank when it is sold. If it is true that a lot of banks will sell over the next few years, sellers can expect buyers to be in the preferred negotiating position. What will determine the price the buyer is willing to pay? Obviously, buyers will consider the projected discounted cash flow of the acquired bank. Some sellers' banks will have more certain cash flow projections and some less certain. The more or less certain, the higher or lower the price the buyer is willing to pay.

But another factor may influence the price a buyer is willing to pay: access to talent. If it is true that there is a talent shortage and likely to be one for years to come, banks with certified talent are worth more than ones without such talent, all other things being equal. It behooves directors to make sure their bankers are certified experts in banking.

The second reason goes back to Chapter 2, when two new banks began to compete with Old Man Mueller's bank. Do you recall the reaction of Mueller's bank when the first of the two banks was formed in 1999?

> *In the meantime, Old Man Mueller and the directors of the only bank in town continue to meet monthly to discuss what can go wrong. As news of the new bank is confirmed, board discussions quickly turn to the risk that the new bank may not manage risk as prudently as the old bank in town.*

Good banks and bad ones drink from the same community well. Let a bad banker poison the well, and good banks suffer, too. Whether a bank wants to sell tomorrow or is built to last, all bankers and directors have to protect their wells. History has proven a minimum of 3,400 failures later that bankers cannot rely on nonbankers to protect their wells. Bankers should require industry-wide standards for anyone who is a banker or director.

It is the last issue—the need for industry standards—that bankers can do something about in 2013. Unlike just about any other profession, banking lacks a definition of minimum standards of ethics, skills, and experience. Anyone can be a banker. No schooling is required. No training is needed. All one has to do is work at a bank. The term *banker* must mean something.

Unskilled and inexperienced so-called bankers damage this industry. The recent failure of 457 banks and the identification of nearly 1,000 banks in the United States as problem banks reveal two clear facts:

- America lacks enough qualified directors to govern 7,246 commercial banks and savings institutions.
- America does not have sufficient numbers of skilled and qualified managers to run 7,246 banks and savings institutions.

The industry today is paying a high price for failing to invest sufficient time and resources in training and educating the banking workforce. In 2013 the industry finds itself short of bank executives with the broad experience and skills necessary to run banks. Likely the problem will get worse before it gets better.

Leading community and regional bankers can develop a clear course of action to prevent future epidemics of bank failure. Through an unprecedented cooperative effort of The American Bankers Association (ABA), The Risk Management Association (RMA), and The Consumer Bankers Association (CBA), leading bankers should promptly engage in their own independent assessment of the root causes of the 457 bank failures and the nearly 3,000 failures from the 1980s. The industry must self-regulate.

The industry must design standards for bankers. Standards must be established for risk-takers and risk-protectors. It is critically important that standards apply to senior members of management as well as bank directors. Yes, even directors. If the industry is able to cooperate, it will want to learn how other professions have worked with lawmakers and regulators to ensure needed checks and balances are in place. The assessment process should develop a plan for standards and certifications for bankers.

It may surprise many that consumers are better assured of a competent barber or hair stylist than they are of a competent banker. Why? In just about every state a barber must have 1,200 to 1,600 hours of classroom and apprenticeship training before qualifying to be tested for a license. One may wonder why the state regulates barbers and hair stylists. How bad can a bad haircut really be?

By establishing industry standards, the banking industry can block corrupt, incompetent, and unskilled bankers from entering the business. As the data about bank failures show, bad bankers make banking bad for everyone. Good bankers should push for banking to have the highest ethical and professional standards. By doing so, they not only help consumers and small business owners who need advice, they protect themselves. Beyond standards, bankers in risk-taking and risk-protecting roles should have licenses or professional designations awarded after completing industry-defined training, testing, and, when applicable, apprenticeship. Licenses should require annual continuing education similar to what actuaries, CPAs, and lawyers require in their profession.

Bankers can leverage their industry associations to develop cooperative and broad engagement of the nation's community and regional bankers; the ABA, CBA, and RMA are already in place to move much of this work forward. Also, bankers can leverage industry training organizations to help develop and deliver curriculum. Organizations like The Risk Management Association, The Graduate School of Banking at LSU, Pacific Coast Banking School at the University of Washington, the ABA Stonier Graduate School of Banking, the North Carolina Bankers School at the University of North Carolina, and Southwest Graduate School of Banking at SMU can play critical roles in developing needed banker and director training.

The Bankers' Collective Accountability to Protect Against Systemic Risk

I must admit it troubles me to acknowledge that I have been profoundly wrong about something for most of my career. I wish I had been wiser.

As a banker I believed for a long time that banking was a zero-sum game. According to my simplistic model, if another bank wins, I lose. Sometimes there was a grain of truth in my view: If the bank down the street got a big loan from the fast-growing business in town and my bank did not, then clearly we had lost. But I realize now that I did not see the world quite right. Banking is not a zero-sum game.

I was not looking at the big picture. What I was missing is what Old Man Mueller's bank learned in 1999 when Crocker started the new bank. Communities must be protected against bad banking. You will recall Crocker's and Sherman's community banks grew like wildfire and received high marks from bank examiners until months before their failures. With all due respect to regulators, the past 10 years suggest bankers must protect themselves from bad bankers in the same way other professional groups protect their industries.

What examples are there of other industries that protect themselves and how do they do it? I will cite three. Having sat on boards for both a college and a kindergarten-through-12th-grade private school, I witnessed firsthand how those two industries self-regulate. Each was subject to rules established by the industry that covered curriculum reviews, teacher selection processes, financial oversight, board engagement, and so on.

Every three years, assuming all was well, the industry examiners from other schools conducted on-site reviews, including, in the case of the K-12 school, interviews with parents and assessments of teachers and principals. Most interestingly, the examiners were actually academic deans, college presidents, and school headmasters who left their full-time jobs at their respective schools to conduct the on-site reviews. No one questioned their experience and qualifications.

Another example comes from serving as the volunteer chairman of a not-for-profit organization with a $10 million budget. A big budget brings privileges and burdens. Contributors expect the not-for-profit to ensure their contributions are spent and invested wisely. Not-for-profit board members, on the other hand, often lack expertise in managing and overseeing budgets. To address this gap, some not-for-profit organizations participate in an industry-wide consortium that independently evaluates the not-for-profits' fiscal management. The consortium has a professional staff that reviews financial and governance material, conducts on-site interviews with the organization's staff and volunteer directors, and provides budget comparisons on key metrics like compensation. Reports are issued that identify gaps requiring staff and director attention. When the consortium's representatives are satisfied a not-for-profit has no gaps, the not-for-profit is approved for inclusion on the consortium's public list of approved, responsible charities.

A final example is one from an industry that shares many of the characteristics of commercial banking. The American Academy of Actuaries may be the best model for the banking community to study. Independent of the U.S. government, but cooperative with it, the Academy sets and controls the standards for the actuarial profession. Actuaries are required to pass a series of exams before they are able to work in the industry. In addition, continuing education requirements ensure that actuaries are up to date with best practices. Interestingly, like banking, there are multiple levels of actuaries, including an associate designation used to describe new actuaries. Importantly, the Academy is serious about the conduct of actuaries; it has the power to expel, suspend, and publicly reprimand members. Go to www.actuary.org to learn more about a rigorous process that bankers would be wise to adopt.

Bankers can learn from barbers, schools, and actuaries. The industry needs to establish standards. Certification and licensing should be required of bankers who serve in certain jobs. The term *banker* must stand for a person who has passed certain tests, understands duty and ethics, and has specific experience. Special training and testing should be required of bankers who are performing such roles as risk management, commercial lending, balance sheet management, and compliance. When bankers pass tests and demonstrate on-the-job skills, they should receive a designation, such as the Credit Risk Certification (CRC). The CRC is awarded by RMA to bankers who study and complete a rigorous credit risk training program.

Similarly, *director* must mean something; directors must have certain documented skills. Today, other than the special qualifications required to sit on an audit committee, there is great variability in what the word *director* means in practice. Community and regional bank investors should expect independent directors to be sufficiently expert in bank governance. Whether it is reasonable to expect all directors to be certified is worthy of debate. However, at a minimum, the banking industry should make it possible for individual banks and directors to choose to be certified. Directors would be wise to push for certification. Such a designation not only would equip them to govern effectively, but also act as a strong potential deterrent against lawsuits.

In addition to certifications, the industry should form peer reviews. As with private schools, peer reviews should be conducted by the industry's respected leaders and subject-matter experts. Every bank with qualified personnel should be expected to contribute time to peer reviews. One of the big advantages regional and especially community banks have is that they do not compete across the country. It is possible for a banker from Iowa to review a bank in New Hampshire. The industry should either leverage an existing entity (like ABA, RMA, etc.) or form a consortium to develop criteria to identify when banks should be subject to peer reviews. Although those details should be worked out by an industry group, it is important to highlight three examples of the kind of criteria the industry could use.

First, using quarterly FDIC data, it would be easy to identify banks and regions of the country where banks are growing at a rate worthy of industry scrutiny. If such a mechanism existed in 2003 in Georgia, it is possible banks there could have avoided much pain. Second, and surely to be controversial, banks that intend to grow through rapid acquisition deserve added industry scrutiny. Peer reviews should focus on the depth of talent (directors and bankers) in the acquiring banks and the strength of operational risk management. And third, new banks should be required to undergo a peer review before receiving regulatory approval. Peer reviews of new banks could include expert directors and CEOs independently assessing the qualifications of the new bank's directors and management team.

Another clear-cut benefit of industry-wide self-policing is the ability that community and regional banks would gain to oversee key suppliers. Today it is highly probable that few smaller banks have the management expertise to fully evaluate suppliers and vendors who provide such mission-critical activities as cyber security, online banking, ATM maintenance, data processing, privacy protection, and so on. The consortium could work together to independently evaluate the contingency planning and backup resiliency capabilities of vendors who provide the systems backbone to so many community banks.

Investors should be interested in certification. Community and regional banks that file 10-Ks should be required to identify the certified qualifications of their bankers and directors. Over time, as the industry demonstrates the risk mitigation associated with testing, certification, and licensing, community and regional banks should press Congress, the FDIC, and bank supervisors to reevaluate FDIC fee schedules and supervisory oversight charges.

The Need for Bank Directors Who Know How to Govern Banks

A story about a bank director from Georgia appeared in the *South Florida Business Journal* of March 15, 2010. Joe Ernest is CEO of Ernest Communications, a Georgia company in the telecom industry. Seven years earlier he had joined the board of Integrity Bank of Georgia.

"Most guys that go on a bank board say, 'Wow, this is prestigious. This sounds like the safest investment I could ever make,'" Ernest said. "Wow, it turned out not so good."

"I was the lamb led to slaughter," he continued. "I wish I had never heard of it."

When news of my decision to retire became public, I received a phone call from a bank consultant who had retired a few years earlier after a long and distinguished career as a senior bank regulator. Knowing of my pending retirement, he asked if I had any interest in going on a bank board. He told me many banks needed directors, and he thought my 31 years of industry experience could be helpful to one of them. I thanked him for his idea, but told him I still had a couple of months to work with my employer and that I was not prepared to make any new commitments.

His call got me to thinking about bank boards. Unlike Joe Ernest, who apparently had no idea what a bank or a director did, maybe my problem is that I know too much. I got to wondering about the nation's bank directors. If you assume there are roughly 7,246 banks and saving associations, and each has 10 to 11 directors, it means there are approximately 75,000 directors. How many of them completely understand their duties? How many have the skills and experience necessary to discharge those duties?

When I think about bank boards, I think about Potemkin Villages. In the second half of the 18th century, Russia's Czarina Catherine the Great faced a problem. In the early 1760s Russia secured the Crimea, a region of present-day Ukraine that sits at a strategic entry point into the country. Russian leaders throughout history sought to control the Crimea, believing that by occupying the region, they could dissuade the Turks (back then the Ottoman Empire) from attacking Russia via the Black Sea, on which the Crimea sits.

Around 1787 the Turks and Russia declared war on each other. Catherine appointed Prince Potemkin, one of her reputed former lovers, to command the troops. Early in the war, Catherine decided she wanted to tour the recently annexed region and confirm that transplanted Russians were living in the region. Historians debate the details, but the story goes that Prince Potemkin constructed fake villages, complete with pasteboard walls, up and down the Dnieper River. His goal: to fool the czarina into thinking that, under his able leadership, these new villages constituted a strong defense against a Turkish attack.

Sadly, this is what comes to mind when I think about some bank boards. As recently filed FDIC lawsuits and material loss reviews attest, too many bank boards proved to be elaborate, flimsy models of independent governance. In too many cases, the board is populated by fine people who are not prepared or trained to govern a bank. And like a Potemkin Village, they appear to be a strong and sturdy defense until adversity hits.

Exacerbating the problem, too many regulators went along with the ruse, either knowingly or blindly unaware. Evidence can be seen countless times in a detailed examination of MLRs written by the FDIC. Details such as prior CAMELS ratings results are reported in every MLR. In case after case of failed banks, the CAMELS ratings showed good to superior scores (typically all 1s and 2s) up to a year or so prior to bank failure.

Imagine yourself living in Anytown, Georgia. You own a successful small business that builds and replaces roofs. You participate in the local chamber of commerce, are active in your church, and volunteer as the local United Way chairman. A respected banker in town comes to you and says he is starting a bank and wants you to be on the new board of directors.

You are flattered, while acknowledging that you don't know the first thing about being a bank director. The bank president tells you that's not really a problem because he and his new management team will actually run the bank.

He tells you the board is there to help drum up business and make sure the bank is involved in the community. He fails to give you regulatory documents that spell out the duties and responsibilities of a bank director. The bank president informs you that for your services you will be paid $500 for each meeting you attend, and that you should expect no more than 12 meetings a year, each lasting no more than an hour or so. Wow, sounds like a terrific opportunity!

But before you sign on the dotted line, you ask who else in town is going to be on the board. The bank president proudly informs you that the board will be composed of community leaders. He rattles off their names and what they do:

- A urologist who was on a bank board in Troy; he has agreed to be board chairman.
- The owner of the three movie theaters in town.
- Two real estate developers.
- A real estate lawyer.
- An administrator at the local hospital.
- The owner of a grocery store.
- The retired CEO of a textile company.
- An appraiser.
- The director of a local not-for-profit agency.
- An accountant.
- And, of course, the bank president, who is very experienced in banking.

You know many of these people and hold several in high regard, but you ask one more question: "Does anyone actually have to approve of my appointment to the board?" The president congratulates you for asking such a good question. He says the

Georgia Department of Banking and Finance and the FDIC must approve the new bank's application as well as the new board. He assures you it's a formality—very rarely do the regulators quibble about board appointments. You agree to join the board and within a few days wire over $25,000 from your IRA to buy stock in the new bank.

Three months later, just as the bank president predicted, the new bank's charter is approved by the regulators. The charter is granted with no comments about the board composition. The bank opens and for four years everything seems to go quite well. Even though you acknowledge, "I don't really understand all these numbers," the bank president dumbs down the information so that you think, "I'm really starting to get the hang of this."

Every year bank examiners come into the bank just like they did in the movie *It's a Wonderful Life*. You are not part of the exam process. You don't know much until their report is issued. You and the board are delighted when the president reports that the CAMELS scores are 112312. One board member asks about the rating of a "3" for earnings. The president says not to worry because 3 is a high score for a new bank. A year goes by and the new scores come in at 112312. Another year goes by and the scores get jumbled up: 222222. The board is confused by the drop in capital and asset quality. The president says it's not a big deal because it reflects a different examiner's opinion, and, more importantly, the improvement in the earnings rating is a "really big deal."

One year later, bank earnings are suffering. You don't quite understand it, but you know past-due loans are going up, including loans to two board members. Bank examiners are back and the CAMELS ratings fall to 433422. You start to feel nervous. The board meeting, which usually consisted of 30 minutes of business and 30 minutes of chitchat, is running long. Two hours into it, it is clear the accountant on the board is not happy. When he announces that he feels too much in the dark and resigns, you get a sick feeling in your stomach.

You like the bank president and you want to protect your $25,000 investment, so you decide to stick around. So do most of the others. But nine months later the examiners are back, and now they deliver terrible news: CAMELS ratings are 555533. Seven weeks later the board receives a problem bank memorandum from the regulator. Exactly two months later, at 3:35 p.m. on a Friday, an emergency board meeting is called. The president delivers devastating news: The bank has been ordered by the FDIC into receivership, effective immediately. You go home and throw up in the toilet.

How have bank boards changed in recent years? Consider the evolution of the board of directors at a megabank, Citigroup. The 2007 proxy (pre-crisis) for Citigroup showed a list of individuals with the following backgrounds:

- Former chairman and CEO of a major telecommunications company with board experience on notable charitable and large for-profit public companies.
- Current chairman and CEO of a large public company that manufactures aluminum.
- Current chairman and CEO of a large public diversified manufacturer.
- Recently retired chairman and CEO of a large public oil and gas company.
- A professor from MIT.
- Chairman of a Mexican bank.

- President and CEO of a large public German technology manufacturer.
- Chairman and president of a large public chemical company.
- Chairman and CEO of a large public technology company.
- Chairman and CEO of a large public entertainment company.
- Chairman and CEO of Citigroup.
- President of a large private foundation.
- Chairman of the Executive Committee of Citigroup.
- A consultant.

Like many banks at the time, Citigroup's 2007 proxy did not include a description of the skills required of its directors. Three years later and now in the heat of the financial crisis, some banks' proxies added language describing director qualifications. Citigroup's 2010 proxy included a section entitled "Director Qualifications." It reads in part:

> *The nominees for the board of directors each have the qualifications and experience to focus on the complex issues confronting Citi and the financial industry in the most challenging economic environment since the Great Depression. Citi's board of directors consists of individuals with the skills, experience and backgrounds necessary to ensure that Citi is taking the right steps to solve problems arising in connection with the current economic environment and the complex financial and regulatory issues that Citi faces. The nominees listed below are leaders in business, the financial community and academia because of their intellectual acumen and analytic skills, strategic vision, their ability to lead and inspire others to work with them, and their records of outstanding accomplishments over a period of decades. Each has been chosen to stand for election in part because of his or her ability and willingness to ask difficult questions, understand Citi's unique challenges and evaluate the strategies proposed by management, as well as their implementation.*

This is really a remarkable document and evidence of the industry's intensifying focus on bank governance and directors. Let's highlight some key messages that can be drawn from Citigroup's list of director qualifications. First and foremost, note the emphasis on the words "experience" and "skills." It is clear that Citigroup recognized that the financial crisis required the bank to have directors with the skills and experience to deal with very difficult problems unique to banking and bank oversight. Next, examine the words about *how* Citigroup directors are to act: they must "ask difficult questions" and analyze "complex" issues. The choice of words is meaningful; Citigroup is telling its stakeholders that its directors have the know-how and temperament to oversee Citi during one of banking history's most difficult times.

Just one year later, in March 2011, the updated proxy reflected a material change to the qualifications. The first sentence in the qualifications section of the proxy reads: "The nominees for the board of directors each have the qualifications and experience to approve and guide Citi's strategy and to oversee management's execution of that strategic vision."

The 2011 proxy is similar in many respects to the 2010 proxy; however, the first sentence change is significant in several ways. The 2011 proxy makes it quite clear that Citigroup directors are responsible for the bank's strategy. The directors have gone from "evaluating" the strategies management designs to "approving and guiding" strategy.

The list of qualifications by itself is a profound statement by Citigroup to its shareholders. By placing the emphasis on the board's strategic guidance, Citigroup is setting a very high bar for bank director qualifications. Since 2007, Citigroup's board of directors has been revamped completely.

Of the 14 independent directors in 2007, only three were still on the board when the 2012 proxy was sent out to shareholders. The new directors all have substantial banking backgrounds. Three new members once held regulatory positions. Four new members are former bank and investment company CEOs. Two of the other three worked in financial institutions prior to joining the Citi board.

My educated guess is that Citigroup's board is one of very few in the country consisting of directors capable of *guiding* versus *evaluating* strategy. Should all banks adopt Citigroup's approach? What messages can directors of America's 7,245 other financial institutions take away from the evolution of directorship roles and responsibilities at Citigroup?

First, experience and a strong working knowledge of the financial services industry are a high priority. Second, skills to not just evaluate but approve and guide strategy are essential; being a CEO of a big public company seems to no longer sufficient to qualify for the Citigroup board. Third, being a director is hard work: it requires time and the acumen to understand complex, challenging banking problems. Fourth, directors with hands-on financial institution management experience ask the toughest questions.

What are the chances America's banks could round up a board of even five people per bank that qualify for the higher standards established by Citigroup's board? Some will argue that Citigroup is a special situation. It is a megabank with offices all over the world and made up of highly complex business processes. That is a fair point. Not every bank board in America requires the qualifications of Citigroup.

Here is the dilemma. Does a bank have any choice but to transform its board from the old model of community directors to a new era of experts in banking and financial markets? Some community and regional bank CEOs will argue, yes, they have a choice. Furthermore, they will adamantly say, "We do not need to go overboard and load the board with banking experts."

OK, go there at your own peril, but make sure your board is part of the decision. The question of board composition is a board decision led by the board committee assigned accountability for board selection. Ultimately, the decision belongs to the shareholders.

How many community and regional CEOs and directors have examined closely the material loss reviews (MLRs) conducted by the FDIC or OCC or Board of Governors of the Federal Reserve System when a bank fails? The MLRs and the FDIC's lawsuits against bank directors reveal a clear theme: Directors must oversee their banks and must have the requisite skills to do the job. Of the 98 MLRs written by the FDIC through the third quarter of 2012, 97 cited bank director ineffectiveness as a leading factor behind bank failure. Below are verbatim excerpts from the MLRs of seven failed Georgia banks. Note the consistent message about director accountability.

1. **American United Bank**, $114 million assets, founded 2004, failed 2009. "AUB failed primarily because the *Board and bank management* did not effectively oversee the bank's operations, particularly, by failing to ensure there were adequate

risk management controls over CRE and ADC lending activities. The institution grew rapidly after opening...."

2. **Appalachian Community Bank**, $1.04 billion assets, founded 1995, failed 2010. "Appalachian's failure can be attributed to losses associated with its ADC loan concentration that were the center of the *Board's and management's* growth strategy. Although initially profitable, Appalachian's *Board and management* failed to provide appropriate oversight...."

3. **Community Bank and Trust**, $1.2 billion assets, founded 1900, failed 2010. "Inadequate oversight by the *Board of Directors*.... After his (CEO) death in 2005, it became apparent that the bank lacked management depth and an effective succession plan, as the *Board and management* were unable to demonstrate sound management practices."

4. **Crescent Bank and Trust**, $980 million assets, founded 1989, failed 2010. "Crescent failed primarily because its *Board* did not effectively manage the risks associated with the institution's aggressive growth and heavy concentration in ADC loans.... Specifically, the bank exhibited weak ADC loan underwriting, credit administration, and related monitoring practices."

5. **First Piedmont Bank**, $115 million assets, founded 1998, failed 2009. "FPB's failure can be attributed to a high ADC loan concentration, weaknesses in underwriting and credit administration practices, and poor *management and Board of Directors* (Board) oversight... *Board and management* failed to adequately identify, measure, monitor, and control emerging risks...."

6. **Freedom Bank of Georgia**, $176 million, founded 2004, failed 2009. "Freedom failed primarily due to the bank's rapid growth and the *Board of Director's* failure to ensure that bank management identified, measured, monitored, and controlled the risk associated with the institution's lending activities. Specifically, bank *management* materially deviated from its business plan...."

7. **Georgian Bank**, $2.1 billion in assets, founded 2001, failed 2009: "Georgian failed because its *Board and management*, led by a senior bank official, pursued an aggressive growth strategy focused on ... ADC lending that coincided with declining economic conditions in the Atlanta metropolitan area.... The bank added several new directors and officers to its management team in 2003 to guide its expansion and implement its new strategic direction. The change in strategic direction was predominantly led by one senior banking official, a veteran banker in Atlanta who joined Georgian in 2003....[T]his official dominated decision-making and had a strong influence over other board members.... [A] director expressed concerns that this individual did not allow the Board to openly discuss bank business at the Board meetings.... [I]ssues were not allowed proper debate.... In response to those allegations, examiners reviewed Board minutes and concluded that the Board discussion did not appear to be dominated by this one individual...."

The material loss reviews noted in the list represent just seven of 83 Georgia bank failures and 457 overall failures in the U.S. The seven are representative of the MLRs conducted on other failed banks in Georgia. A number of observations can be drawn from this small sample.

First, boards and executive management need to analyze other banks' failures. A bank failure is the ultimate material loss. Boards should use valuable meeting time to discuss specific root causes of bank failures. Lessons from the failures should be noted and board members should formally assess whether such risks exist in their own institutions.

Second, most of the MLRs written by the FDIC's Office of Inspector General (or the consultants selected) do not provide sufficient insight for true and effective root-cause analysis. It appears many of the MLRs conform to a checklist or template rather than being a thorough and factual assessment of the root causes leading to failure. Go back and scan the comments. Note how often the same words are repeated. Rare is the MLR, such as the one conducted for Georgian Bank, where the writer of the MLR explores fundamental weaknesses in people, processes, and systems as drivers of failure. Effective root-cause analysis requires a much deeper examination of the facts. Being told of "lax oversight" is insufficient: *Why* was there lax oversight?

Question: Is it possible that the FDIC, OCC, and Federal Reserve are conflicted when they write MLRs for the very same banks over which they once supervised? Are the examiners in charge of the reviews truly independent and willing to identify specific failures of the FDIC's supervision of the failed bank? Some MLRs are actually written by consultants presumably hired by the FDIC. Those MLRs outsourced to consultants are less critical of the FDIC than even the MLRs written by the FDIC. Too bad, because the industry needs to know exactly why banks failed, including gaps in regulator performance. It would be helpful if the FDIC went back and updated two or three of the MLRs that could be especially instructive to bank directors.

A third observation can be drawn from the fifth bank on the list, First Piedmont. Rare for an MLR, this one actually pinpoints a specific root cause for failure: The board and management lacked effective processes to "identify, measure, monitor, and report emerging risks." Is there any issue as pressing for a board than discussing emerging risks? Routine and meaningful discussions about emerging risks should be a standing agenda item for boards. However, back to Citigroup: In the absence of directors who are skilled and experienced in banking, can an effective discussion about emerging risks really take place?

The fourth observation is related to Georgian Bank, the last one listed. Note the size of the bank: $2.1 billion. Note the year the bank was founded: 2001. Those two numbers make it clear the board had a tiger on its hands, but what is really interesting about this particular MLR is the discussion related to board and management dynamics. The writer of the MLR shows a lot of insight by his or her willingness to identify the dominant executive as a leading cause of failure. Unfortunately, the MLR fails to go deeper in its analysis. What is the evidence? What exactly did he do? What specific CEO behaviors give proof to this statement? What did the board do or not do to exacerbate the problem? Such information could help other boards evaluate their own relationship with bank management.

The Bank Director's Duty

Lessons Learned from the Royal Bank of Scotland

Although the U.S. regulators' MLRs do not provide thorough root-cause analyses of failed banks, fortunately the Financial Services Authority (FSA) in the United Kingdom has given the world a broad and deep analysis of the near failure of one of the country's largest banks.

By far the best publicly available evaluation of a bank's failure or near failure is the FSA board report *The Failure of the Royal Bank of Scotland (RBS)*. RBS was on the brink of failure in 2008 when the government stepped in with $60 billion to rescue it. Today, RBS is 82% owned by the government. This document is extraordinary in many ways.

First, in sheer size (452 pages), the FSA left no stone unturned in its analysis of RBS's near failure. Second, FSA's analysis of RBS's board and executive management's failure to evaluate adequately the strategic risk of acquiring ABN AMRO has implications for every banker and director who serves in a bank that plans to acquire another bank. Third, the FSA report is remarkably candid; apparently the writers of the report did not intend for it to become public, which may explain the candor. And last, the section of the report entitled "Management, Governance, and Culture" should be required reading for every bank executive and director in the U.S.

To the last point, directors of banks of all sizes really must read pages 220 to 240 of the report. It is a wonderful and painful case study of how boards, even ones with the most respected CEOs in the country, can fall short in their exercise of governance duties. There are so many precious insights to draw from the FSA report. We will focus on four that are germane to a bank board of any size bank in America:

1. "The quality of critical interactive discussion among board members."
2. The need for a "critical mass of deep experience in both core banking and investment banking activities."
3. The board's ability and willingness to raise "informed challenge to executive assumptions, explanations, and proposals" regarding strategic risks.
4. The challenge of serving on a board where the CEO is a superstar.

Quality of Interaction among Board Members

The FSA study goes into considerable detail to highlight its inability to identify cases or occasions when the board or management disagreed. While acknowledging the potentially debilitating nature of disagreement, the FSA points out that a bank board's healthy, productive challenge should be a natural by-product of effective analysis and debate. "Group-think"—which is how one former RBS board member described RBS board meetings—is dangerous.

Companies, like people, have their own traits and characteristics. From the FSA report we learn that "RBS was unique among major banks in having many 'hill climbers' and almost no 'hill finders.'" Climbers are executors; finders are strategists. The board is heavily criticized in the report for failing to challenge the climbers' assumptions about revenue, asset, and profit targets. Consistent with a company more focused on execution than strategic analysis, the board failed to think adequately about emerging risks and the aggregation of risks.

Boards have a duty to challenge management just as a trial jury must challenge the evidence before them. RBS repeatedly failed to demonstrate evidence that its board exercised such a challenge function. Perhaps it was because the company's culture attracted people with an execution mind-set and not strategic analytical thinkers.

The Board "Lacked a Critical Mass of Deep Experience in Both Core Banking and Investment Banking"

No one outside of a few federal regulators and the Citigroup board really knows what happened to trigger an 80% change-out of directors. What is clear, however, is that Citigroup's board was transformed from a hall of fame of Fortune 50 chairs and CEOs to a stellar collection of some of the nation's most prominent senior bankers and regulators.

In the case of RBS, the FSA is transparent in its expression of concern regarding the board's lack of banking knowledge, skills, and experience. The FSA poses the question: Is greater "industry-specific expertise than is typically considered necessary" required for banks than for other industries? As further evidence of the integrity of its work, the FSA acknowledges that the presence of more banker types would not have necessarily assured a different outcome. It cites as evidence the number of banks that made similar, but not necessarily as egregious, decisions during the 2005-08 time period. However, the FSA clearly seems to have arrived at the same place in its thinking as Citigroup has.

For banks that are not RBS and Citigroup, there is the question whether it is realistic for them to acquire the necessary "critical mass of deep experience" needed for director positions. This question will be explored shortly.

The Board's Ability to Issue Informed Challenges to Management's Strategic Plans

RBS took several paths to the canyon of failure. Like one of America's great banks, Wachovia, RBS's decision to acquire another bank proved to be the death blow to the firm. The FSA analysis of RBS's strategic framework for analyzing the ABN AMRO decision is a must-read for any bank director. Especially interesting is the list of four attributes of risk the FSA identifies as the keys to RBS's blunder: 1) size and complexity; 2) use of debt, not equity, to buy the bank; 3) inadequacy of due diligence; and 4) the unique nature of the consortium structure.

The FSA does not allow the board of RBS off the hook for its failure to properly assess the risks associated with the ABN AMRO acquisition. In essence, the board, knowingly or not, bet the bank when it made the decision to acquire ABN AMRO in the manner it did. The FSA's contention is that a board does not have the right to bet the bank; the board holds a sacred duty to all constituents to exercise the highest standards of risk analysis before making a final decision. In the FSA's words, greater strategic analysis is imperative, which would include a full description of the "nature and scale of the risk that the board is prepared to take." In particular, the RBS board comes up especially short in its ability to evaluate "what-if" scenarios that could have challenged management's strategic thinking.

Imperial CEO: Special Organizational Dynamics When the CEO Is a Superstar

In 2004, RBS was such a stunningly successful bank that its 45-year-old CEO, Fred Goodwin, was dubbed a knight by Queen Elizabeth II. Fred became Sir Fred. He remained Sir Fred until early 2012 when Queen Elizabeth II "cancelled and annulled" his knighthood for having "brought the honors system into disrepute." It is difficult for Americans to imagine the significance of the Queen's action.

Until the global banking crisis and the ABN AMRO acquisition, Sir Fred came as close to an imperial CEO as any bank executive in the world. As a relatively young man of 45, he had been knighted and recognized as one of the nation's leading citizens. Prior to ABN AMRO, everything he touched seemed to turn to gold. The FSA report includes this comment about the CEO: He "is and was an optimist and he tended to take an optimistic view of what was likely to happen and had often in his life been proved right." In other words, success blinded Goodwin to the potential for failure.

The FSA raises the question of whether his confidence tipped into overconfidence and even hubris. Although Sir Fred had "an excellent grasp of detail and skill in forensic analysis, it was difficult to raise more general questions or concerns that were not readily supported by detailed, objective facts and evidence." There are further questions raised in the report as to whether Sir Fred was so capable of dealing in the minutiae of the bank that he ran the risk of doing other managers' jobs. This tendency was especially seen in his relationship with the chief financial officer. Implied is the issue of whether a high-energy, imperial CEO can crowd out emerging talent who learn over time not to challenge the boss.

For bank boards, the question is how to deal with the CEO who has a strong record of success. Sir Fred may be an extreme example of the CEO whose track record is so good that no one thinks himself worthy of challenging such a great man. In a perverse way, the CEO's great strength ultimately became his undoing. By not challenging the CEO, RBS's board fell into the one trap that could lead to bank failure.

Wachovia Bank

I worked at Morgan Guaranty Trust Company as a summer intern in 1979. This may sound corny, but I felt like a member of the Pittsburgh Steelers when I walked into the 15 Broad Street building each day. In the 1970s, the Steelers had the best talent in football at just about every position: Hall of Famers Terry Bradshaw, "Mean" Joe Greene, Jack Ham, Lynn Swann, Jack Lambert, and on and on. Like the Steelers in football, Morgan Guaranty took great pride in its deep bench of talent. Morgan Guaranty bankers were made to feel like they were part of something special. When I was offered a permanent position at the end of the summer, I was extremely thankful.

Despite the draw to work in New York with Morgan, I felt the need to talk to some other banks before making a final decision about permanent employment. As a result, I headed to Winston-Salem, North Carolina, in December of that same year to interview at Wachovia Bank. I sensed during my visit that Wachovia was a southern "blue-blood" bank. In many ways, it reminded me of the culture at Morgan: proud, cultured, conservative.

After my visit to Wachovia, my wife and I drove to Charlotte, North Carolina, to interview with NCNB. Contrary to later reports out of Texas that NCNB stood for "no cash for nobody," the acronym actually stood for North Carolina National Bank.

NCNB was an upstart bank with a chip on its shoulder. Throughout my day of interviews in Charlotte, I heard NCNB bankers tell me that banking was going the way of the "buggy whip." In contrast to Wachovia and Morgan bankers, who seemed to bask in their successes, the NCNB people talked like underdogs who had something to prove. A chief goal for NCNB was to get bigger and more profitable than the much more prestigious Wachovia. To NCNB, Wachovia bankers were the enemy who every day stole food off the dinner tables of NCNB families.

You get the point. I chose to join NCNB and drank the Kool-Aid. From the day I joined the bank in June 1980, Wachovia was public enemy number one as far as I was concerned. You would think with such a mind-set I would have relished the news of Wachovia's near failure and shotgun wedding to Wells Fargo. The truth is, I found Wachovia's demise a source of profound disappointment. I felt great anguish for friends who worked there whose lives were in turmoil. Many North Carolina families for generations had come to rely on Wachovia dividends to sustain grandma in her twilight years. On their dying beds, family patrons would admonish their children to "never sell those Wachovia shares." I am not exaggerating.

How did a megabank of Wachovia's stature come so close to failure? Although there are few public records chronicling Wachovia's downward spiral, insights can be drawn from the Financial Crisis Inquiry Commission findings. Page 305 of the FCIC report states that the Federal Reserve "bluntly criticized the board and senior management for 'an environment with inconsistent and inadequate identification, escalation and coverage of all risk-taking activities...little accountability for errors....'" The report adds:

- Management "had not completely understood the level of risk across the company...."
- The board "had not sufficiently questioned investment decisions."
- "The OCC noted that the Board had 'acknowledged that the Golden West acquisition was a mistake.'"

■ "And, like the Fed, the OCC approved of the new management and a new, more hands-on oversight role for the board of directors."

Wachovia was a good bank—no, not just a good bank, but a great bank with great people—that nearly failed.

The FCIC report on Wachovia is important for bank directors in two ways. First, it cracked open the door to show the Federal Reserve's concern with the board's failure to adequately identify risks, especially strategic risks associated with acquisitions. The message is clear: Directors must identify risks. Second, and arguably of even greater significance to directors of banks today, the FCIC used the phrase "more hands-on oversight" to describe the active role directors at Wachovia had begun to play after the bank encountered problems. The implication to all directors is that governing a bank is a "hands-on" role.

Board Governance at Large Regional Banks

It will be interesting to see how the large regional banks' boards evolve over the next eight years. A close examination of the directors of regional banks reveals that many are current and retired senior officers in nonfinancial companies and not-for-profit organizations. However, few are banking experts. Rare is the regional bank director with banking or bank regulatory experience. If the U.S. banking industry consolidates like many expect to see between now and 2020, likely the regionals will be among the acquirers. Stakeholders need to ask whether these directors are sufficiently skilled to exercise a well-informed independent challenge when "bet the bank" strategic decisions come before the board. Better to ask this question too soon than too late. Board nominating committees must work hard to find the most capable director talent.

Bank CEOs often make the case that it is important to have access to advisors who are or have been CEOs themselves. True, but it is the rare chemical company CEO, college president, or horticulture expert who has the banking experience required to independently assess the wisdom of the very tough decisions that will come before them in the years ahead. Some directors and CEOs of regional banks will take offense at these comments. Please be assured that no offense is intended. If you are on a regional bank board, ask yourself these questions:

■ Are you aware of the FSA study of the RBS directors' role in the near-failure of RBS? What about the failure of WaMu and the role of the board?

■ Has your board discussed the lessons learned from the Citibank director changes?

■ Did you read the Financial Crisis Inquiry Commission report, and, if so, how much time did your board devote to this subject in 2011?

■ If you are on the risk management committee of your regional bank, have you been trained in any aspect of banking, such as credit, liquidity, market, compliance, or operational risk? If your answer is "no" to two or more of these questions, what does that say? Have you attended serious training provided by industry experts or a professional risk organization like The Risk Management Association?

Directors must evaluate how much time they are willing to invest in learning how to become a highly skilled bank director capable of governing the bank and exercising the challenge role. The expectation for training is not high in many banks. Here is what the 2012 proxy of one large regional bank says about "Director Continuing Education": "Each director is *encouraged* to obtain the requisite training or education to fulfill his or her responsibilities ... the director is *encouraged* to obtain director training ... a director is *encouraged* to obtain director training.... Each director is *expected* to attend a director training or education session every three calendar years...."

Do not be surprised if bank shareholders press banks to move beyond *encouraging* directors to *requiring* directors to invest time in becoming expert in banking and bank governance. It is worth noting that the typical director on a large regional bank board earns a good living: about $140,000 to $280,000 per year for their part-time work. For that kind of money it would seem fair for shareholders to expert their directors to do more than attend training every three years or so.

Except for lead director compensation, it is difficult to find any banks that truly differentiate director pay. The equal pay for all directors is surprising for two reasons. First, clearly not all directors are equally qualified; some have more skill and experience to govern a bank than others. And second, even though virtually every bank claims to pay its personnel based on performance, there is little evidence that individual directors are paid based on individual performance. Maybe that should change. A great director can be worth a lot of money to investors.

Joe Ernest, Bank Directors, and Lambs

Joe Ernest and the boards of Wachovia and RBS have a few things in common: bank failure, public scrutiny, and personal investment losses. In Joe's case, he carries the added burden of having to defend himself in the FDIC lawsuit against him and several other bank directors of Integrity Bank. Although I have absolutely zero compassion for directors who committed bank fraud, my heart goes out to directors who had no business being on a bank board in the first place and now find themselves in the crosshairs of FDIC lawsuits.

What can America's 75,000 or so bank directors learn from Joe Ernest's experience? Here are 10 specific actions directors can take to more effectively exercise their duties:

1. *Be strategic and challenge, challenge, challenge.* And then document, document, document. Make sure the meeting minutes reflect the directors' challenge questions and comments. Be on guard especially for decisions that bet the bank. Review Old Man's Mueller's counsel. Strategic risk management is the ultimate responsibility of board governance. Is the bank growing too fast? Is it growing slowly or actually shrinking and, if so, why? Directors should never bet the bank. If management proposes a strategic acquisition or major initiative, be particularly on guard. Do not be afraid of a reasonable level of management-board tension; remember, you work for shareholders.

2. *Set a risk appetite.* Just like the Bank of Winesburg, discuss as a board how the bank's risk appetite and tolerance for risk relate to profit and performance targets. Make sure you agree with the risk appetite. If it seems too risky to you, say

so. Go back to Chapter 2 and review Old Man Mueller's Five Laws and Four Imperative Questions.

3. *Identify emerging risks.* Require management to identify emerging risks. At least quarterly, if not monthly, formally discuss these risks in board meetings. Do not rely only on management. One of the most effective means for a board to evaluate emerging risks is to conduct a formal scenario analysis or war games discussion with senior management at least semi-annually. Such discussions are best conducted through formal facilitation and direct board engagement. An outcome from the scenario analysis should be a written document that overviews the issues identified in the meeting as well as the plan to measure, monitor, and control these risks. Pay special attention to competitors.

4. *Study external failures and losses.* Read the FDIC's material loss reviews and determine if there are key lessons your bank can learn. At least quarterly, discuss in board meetings the root cause of bank failures and big losses of other banks. Challenge the board to evaluate whether the lessons learned from other banks exist or are emerging risks at your bank.

5. *Risk and controls system.* Require management to create a process for identifying, measuring, monitoring, and controlling key operational and reputational risks. Expect management to have 10 to 15 key risk indicators (KRIs) that summarize those risks. Be prepared to discuss and review KRIs monthly at board meetings. If such a report does not currently exist, focus on the processes and systems most often linked to bank failure. Those include key talent assessments, underwriting of loan processes, and credit administration. Ask questions about key suppliers, especially in relation to the redundancy of their systems. Look for changes in numbers that indicate potential stress to operating systems, people, and processes. Key metrics that illuminate the velocity and volume of change and complexity are especially critical to watch. Boards need to understand which numbers are material. For example, double-digit growth in customers or fees or loans should always be a yellow flag indicating caution. Often it is important to look not just at the total numbers, but a layer or two down to examine particular lines of business. For back-room operating systems, seemingly small numbers can actually suggest significant growth in risk. For example, if online banking "uptime" is usually .9997% but drops to .9910% for a week, the board would be wise to inquire into which factors are driving the drop in performance.

6. *For larger community and regional banks, directors should work directly with internal audit and risk management.* In the Financial Crisis Inquiry Commission report, there is a story on pages 182-183 about Fannie Mae's slow death. As Fannie Mae faced greater financial pressure, the CEO felt the understandable pressure to cut expenses. According to the FCIC report, the cuts were applied across the company, including the risk management organization. At the time, the chief risk officer protested to the CEO. He reminded the CEO that Fannie had the "weakest control processes" and that the organization was "not even close to having proper control processes for credit, market, and operational risk." Furthermore, he warned that "reducing expenses" and "scraping on controls" prove that "people don't care about the (risk) function or they don't get it." Apparently the board of

Fannie did not know of the chief risk officer's concerns. According to the FCIC report, "Management told the Board that Fannie's risk management function had all the necessary means and budget to act on the plan." Directors should always work directly with chief risk officers. If the CEO objects, which is unlikely, the board needs to have a heart-to-heart discussion with him or her. When directors hear directly from the chief risk officer, the CEO almost always understands that it is in everyone's best interests to ensure directors have as full a view of risks and controls as possible. On a related note, cost-cutting creates its own challenges that directors do not always fully appreciate. Strong chief risk officers should be expected to raise concerns to the board when cost-cutting jeopardizes controls.

7. *Assess talent and ensure the bank has a talent pipeline.* Conduct a serious and effective assessment of your CEO and management team. As the financial crisis reveals, lack of talent may be the single most critical root cause of bank failure. Make sure management has effective, reliable, and unbiased tools to conduct assessments. Assign two or three board members, including the independent chair or lead director, accountability for coaching and developing the CEO. Hold the CEO accountable for having an effective process for ensuring the management team is properly and accurately coached. Your talent assessment must extend beyond the CEO. Evaluate the skills and experience of executives assigned to key P&L, risk, and control functions. Be sure they bring proven records of performance and expertise to their positions. Be alert to cronyism; it can be best detected by observing patterns of executive assignments based more on CEO loyalty than proven demonstration of deep subject-matter expertise. As long as the banking industry avoids certification and licensing, boards may want to consider using technical tests to gain a better understanding of the competency of the bank's executives. Boards lacking banking experts must ask themselves whether they require an independent view of the bank's talent if there is any question about the accuracy or candor of management's account of the talent assessment process. Bank boards should expect management to clearly identify succession plans for key roles. Challenge assumptions. Boards lacking directors with substantive bank experience and skills are at a distinct disadvantage when it comes to evaluating bank talent. Bank directors whose field of expertise is not banking must rely on bank experts to help them evaluate their bank talent. If you are the board chairman, be sure you know a search consultant who specializes in filling community and regional bank jobs. These individuals usually have a good handle on the state of industry talent. Some boards may rely on a bank consultant for advice about bank talent. This is not a bad idea, but beware of the risk that the bank consultant is likely to bring an unhealthy bias if that person does work for the CEO or other members of the bank's leadership team.

8. *Ensure roles and responsibilities are clear.* Examine current bank policies and procedures to ensure that all roles, including the board's, clearly define accountability and responsibility. Whether directors want to or not, the reality is they owe it to themselves out of a need for self-preservation to have a strong working knowledge of the duties and responsibilities of a bank director. There are two must-read documents. The first is *The Director's Book,* which can be found on the OCC's website

(www.occ.treas.gov/publications/publications-by-type/other-publications-reports/ director.pdf). The cover of the 124-page book says it is about "the role of a national bank director." Even directors of state banks would be wise to read it since the duties of state bank directors and national bank directors are not all that different. The other document worth reading is *Principles for the Sound Management of Operational Risk* (www.bis.org/publ/bcbs195.pdf). It is only 19 pages. Some bankers might say it is "overkill" for directors to read Basel guidance. I disagree, especially guidance regarding culture and risk management governance. An informed director is a better director.

9. *Be smart.* The bad news is that being a bank director is one of the most challenging jobs in America. Commit to and invest in training. Require your bank management team to be certified as experts in key banking functions. If you are a bank director and all your training has been on the job, you would be very wise to seek formal training. Some professionals in banking education candidly complain that bank director education programs tend to be short on real education and long on golf. Directors must insist on classroom time over tee time.

10. *Be honest.* This one may be the toughest. Just because someone is CEO of XYZ company does not mean he or she is qualified to be on a bank board. If a director has no experience in banking other than being a customer, is it really possible to be anything more than window dressing for the first year or two on the job? Is it possible the bank CEO chose an inexperienced bank director precisely because of the lack of real banking know-how? Directors need to ask themselves if they have the experience and skills to discharge the duties of a bank director. Your bank should consider bringing in an independent expert to evaluate the board. There is a severe shortage of prospective directors available who have the requisite skills and experience. Some banks may wish to consider a new model for bank governance that calls for professional bank directors who are completely independent of management and invest considerable time and energy staying current with banking issues and best practices. It is conceivable that a large regional bank could have two or three full-time directors supported by eight to 10 part-time directors. Another variation might be to have five to seven higher-paid expert directors instead of a board of 10 to 14 directors with less knowledge. A word of advice: If the board does not have people on it with real banking experience, get such people on the board or sell the bank. As a final thought, if your bank requires directors to retire at a certain age, seriously consider revising this rule or moving the retirement age. Some of the nation's very best bankers and potential bank directors are over 70 years of age. If I started a bank, I would load my board with every Old Man Mueller I could find! Like the real Mr. Mueller, the ideal banker and ideal director never stop learning, teaching, and raising the bar.

PART

3

Apple Pie, Chevrolet, and Bank Failures

Congress's Favorite Question: How Did We Get in This Mess?

I grew up in a small town in Ohio. The town next to mine is Bay Village. Bay has an odd law on its books: "It is illegal to walk a cow down Lake Road." This is clearly a good law because Lake Road is the busiest road in town. Besides, Lake Road runs parallel to Lake Erie and cows can't swim. Over the years, I drove on Lake Road hundreds of times, and I can say with certainty that I never once saw anyone break the cow-walking law.

I went to school near Culpeper, Virginia, where it is illegal to wash a mule on the sidewalk. This law really seems unnecessary; I don't think Culpeper even has sidewalks.

Do U.S. lawmakers understand how their banking system evolved? It is likely most would be surprised to know the current system is saddled with problems dating back to the 1700s.

Banking in America has been a political and economic hot potato ever since the 1st United States Congress met in 1789. Almost every Congress since has wrestled with banking issues. Financial panics usually kick Congress and the president into high gear. Every panic is an opportunity for new laws. Banking has made for great politics, especially in 1791, 1811, 1816, 1832, 1837, 1841, 1857, 1863, 1873, 1893, 1907, 1913, 1932, 1981, 1999, as well as the most recent few years. Our financial crisis just as easily could be called the Panic of 2008, which would fit in well with the six panics of the 19th century and the Panic of 1907, 1930-1934, and 1985-1992. Do you notice a pattern?

Voters who think Barack Obama is the first president to make banking a key political issue would be wrong. President Andrew Jackson made banking his number-one issue when elected to his second term of office in 1832, arguing that small state banks were much better for the country than a large U.S. bank. George Washington faced difficult decisions about banking when two of his key advisors, Thomas Jefferson and Alexander Hamilton, disagreed strongly about the need for a U.S. central bank. Jefferson was no fan of banks, as evidenced by this quote: "I believe that banking institutions are more dangerous to our liberties than standing armies." He obviously knew a few bankers in his day!

The Founding Fathers wrestled with the weighty issue of which rights belonged to states and which belonged to the federal government. The states' rights advocates, led by the Virginians Thomas Jefferson and James Madison, distrusted a powerful central government. On the other hand, New Yorker Alexander Hamilton advocated strongly for a central bank based largely on the model used successfully in England. Supporters of states' rights saw Hamilton's creation of the First Bank of the United States as a dangerous manifestation of federal power. The 1st U.S. Congress sided with Hamilton, however, and voted in favor of the First Bank of the United States by a vote of 39-20; of the 25 southern legislators, only six voted in favor. Without Hamilton's strong stand on the need for the bank, President Washington, as a Virginian, would have vetoed it.

The U.S. had only three banks in the entire country when the First Bank of the United States was chartered. By 1800 that number had increased to 28 banks, and by 1811 it had swelled to 117. Four years later the number more than doubled to 246, and by 1818 there were 338 banks. All were chartered as state banks. Like America in 2000, starting new banks in early 19th-century America was not difficult. States' righters throughout the 1800s made the case that a big federally controlled bank was not necessary, especially in a country with a growing number of state banks.

When the 1st Congress approved the charter of the First Bank of the United States in 1791, it limited its operation to 20 years. As a result, in 1811 Congress had to decide whether the charter should be extended another 20 years. The bill to extend the charter was defeated by one vote in both the House of Representatives and the Senate. Five years later with the same president, James Madison, and many of the same lawmakers, Congress voted for the creation of the Second Bank of the United States. What changed their opinions? The country in 1816 faced high inflation and problems paying bills from the War of 1812 with England. Lawmakers believed the Second Bank could solve problems state banks could not. The Second Bank was given a 20-year charter set to expire in 1836.

In the nation's first 25 years, lawmakers could not agree on how banking in America should be conducted. Banking votes were close. Emotions ran high. Debates were heated. Nothing has changed. The U.S. Congress throughout history has struggled over banking issues. Congress has tried new and different solutions for over 200 years. The issue facing the 1st Congress—the role of state banks versus a big national bank—remains a hot issue. Voting down the First Bank in 1811 and approving the Second Bank in 1816 highlights the vagaries of political judgment when it comes to banking laws in America. And the rapid growth of state banks, from three in 1791 to 338 a little more than 25 years later, is characteristic of how easy it has been to form new banks in the United States.

Three threads run through U.S. banking history. The first is that nearly every Congress has dealt with banking issues. The second is that every 20 or 30 years, Congress seems compelled to put its fingerprints on yet another design for how banking in America should be conducted. The third thread is bank failure. Pick the century—19th, 20th, or even the first decade of the 21st—and banks have failed. Judging only by the history of bank failures, it is reasonable to ask if Congress really knows how banking should best be conducted in this country.

Part of the problem is that banking makes great politics. Like other weighty issues facing lawmakers, this one is rich in nuance and controversy: state power versus federal, big versus small, laissez-faire versus centrally planned, and the real honey pot, rich versus poor. Perhaps until recently, no politician in U.S. history has better milked the banking issue than a North Carolina-born backwoodsman turned Tennessee lawyer.

Andrew Jackson was elected the seventh president of the United States in 1828. Jackson distrusted bankers almost as much as he distrusted federal power and a big U.S. bank. Jackson preferred a banking system of state banks, "hard" gold-based money, and

100% reserve banking, which he believed would curb inflation. No one in Washington questioned Jackson's opposition to the Second Bank of the United States, including the president of the bank.

When Jackson came up for reelection in 1832, the president of the Second Bank started politicking early to ensure Jackson's opposition did not stop renewal of the bank's charter in 1836. Jackson's opponents supported renewal of the charter, which only hardened the president's view. The national bank became the key issue of the 1832 presidential election. In the end, Jackson prevailed, winning a stunning 219 of 223 electoral votes.

Once back in office, mandate in hand, Jackson took immediate action to dismantle the Second Bank. By the time Jackson was out of office, in 1837 and later in 1841, the economy went sour and more than a few politicians called for the creation of a new central bank to coordinate the flow of money needed during the 1837 financial panic. But Jackson's legacy was firmly in place when his successor, Martin Van Buren, held tightly to Jackson's position.

U.S. banking history is not well understood in 2013. Evidence suggests it was not well understood in 1928, either, when the Treasury Department decided to place Andrew Jackson's portrait on the $20 federal bill, replacing President Grover Cleveland. Jackson might have turned over in his grave when his visage graced a national currency that he never supported. Jackson's influence lasted into the early days of the Civil War and arguably into the 21st century. Today he would oppose the Federal Reserve and clearly favor state banks over large national banks.

Some historians argue Jackson was a libertarian and suggest his support of the Free Banking Era from 1816 to 1863 as evidence. Not to be confused with free banking as it is known today, free banking then meant banks were free of any federal oversight and, for a while, free of state supervision as well. It was not until the late 1830s and early 1840s that "radical" bank depositors pushed states to have bank regulators oversee banks.

Like today, the historical record of the 19th century shows that some states supervised banks well and some not so well. Supervising banks was certainly no easy task in the days of horse-drawn carriages and Morse code. Compounding logistical issues, each bank actually printed its own currency. Less like cash as we think of currency today, the banks' currencies were much more like personal checks. The banknotes were only as good as the writer of the note. Prior to the Civil War, the United States had more than 7,000 banknotes and another 5,000 or so fraudulent notes in circulation.

Keeping track of the relative value of each bank's notes was quite a chore for merchants and saloon operators. Newspapers across the country actually employed banknote reporters to track the relative value of each bank's notes. Once a week, newspapers would publish the values of the various banks' notes. There is a modern equivalent to this practice: Media today report the value of the U.S. dollar compared with the relative value of other nations' currencies.

Bank panics were triggered when banks lacked the credibility or gold to stand by their notes. The term "wildcat banking" became common across the country in the mid-19th century. Historians are divided about the origin of the term. One view is that it evolved in Michigan when a bank with the picture of a wildcat on its note went out of business. When banknotes became worthless, merchants would say it was "good as a wildcat," meaning it was no good at all.

Another view suggests that the term is associated with a dastardly practice of unscrupulous bankers to set up banks in small towns with the full intention of causing a panic. Local townspeople would be persuaded by the banker to leave their gold in the bank's vault. With the gold protected in its vault, the bank would then print its own banknotes backed by the gold. Over time the banknotes became the currency of the local community. When enough banknotes were in the community, the conniving banker would relocate his bank to a remote part of the state where note redemption was nearly impossible. This practice was known as wildcat banking because the banks were so remote that only the howl of wildcats could be heard at night. No surprise, then, that trust in the banking system was not always high.

When Abraham Lincoln took office on March 4, 1861, he inherited not only a potential Civil War, but also a dysfunctional banking system. Five weeks into his presidency, the Union Army's Fort Sumter in South Carolina fell after 34 straight hours of Confederate bombing. At war with the South, Lincoln faced countless challenges. At the top of the list were questions of how to finance the war and pay troops and suppliers. He turned for answers to his Treasury Secretary and one-time rival for the Republican nomination, Salmon P. Chase.

Chase went to work immediately. As a new nation, the U.S. had limited access to debt; in fact, many eastern banks had better credit than the U.S. government. To address the need for cash, Chase designed and promoted the National Currency Act, which Congress passed in early 1863; Senate debate was particularly acrimonious as evidenced by the body's razor-thin 23-21 vote. A year later Congress passed the National Bank Act.

The legislation created the first national banks as well as the Office of the Comptroller of the Currency. Newly approved national banks were required to set aside one-third of their capital for the purchase of U.S. government bonds issued by the U.S. Treasury. Ingeniously, the bonds were then held as security for the new currency created and controlled by the OCC. Each national bank received a "greenback" that bore the name of the bank on it. For the first time, the U.S. had a national currency backed by faith in the U.S. government and a promise to redeem the currency for either gold or silver coins. Unlike bank currencies, the greenback was soon viewed as risk-free and not subject to relative value markups and markdowns.

By 1865 the future of state banks seemed bleak. Intent on the U.S. having a single national bank system, Congress imposed a stiff 10% tax on notes issued by state banks. The tax was a back-door attempt to force state banks to convert to national banks. It nearly succeeded. In 1866 national banks outnumbered state banks, 1,634 to 297. However, in a nation of clever people, the states' righters found a loophole in the law. Rather than issue banknotes, the state banks began to issue a new form of payment, the checking account. Emboldened by their success, states began a full-court press to convert banks back to state banks through more lax regulation and lower reserve requirements. Some states allowed their banks to enjoy more liberal branch banking rights, which Congress had restricted to combat wildcat banks. By 1873 the number of state banks grew to 1,330. Not until 1927, with passage of the McFadden Act, did national banks enjoy the same branch banking rights as state banks.

To highlight how history shapes the industry, one of the states with the least restrictive branch banking for many years was North Carolina. As a result, Wachovia and predecessors to NCNB, First Union, and BB&T became accustomed to running large branch networks as early as the 1800s. Unlike states such as Florida, Texas, and Illinois, where state laws restricted branching well into the 1980s, North Carolina banks' experience with running far-flung networks of branches became a competitive advantage when interstate banking laws fell. North Carolina banks capitalized on this experience to quickly acquire banks in states that were unprepared for the new era of national banking. It is no accident that North Carolina banks—not banks in Texas, Florida, or Illinois—were early winners when banks were allowed to branch outside their states.

If necessity was the mother of invention of the OCC, then the Panic of 1907 was the mother of invention of the Federal Reserve System. The Panic of 1907 is known by some as the 1907 Bankers' Panic. The Panic started when speculators tried to control the stock of the United Copper Company. Using borrowed money, the investors' plans backfired and creditors demanded repayment. Unable to meet the margin call, a bank panic ensued when lenders stopped lending each other money.

Not unlike what happened 101 years later with the failure of Lehman Brothers, the financial system locked up. In the absence of a lender of last resort, the most powerful banker in New York City, J.P. Morgan, called all the other bank and trust presidents to a meeting in his home. Locking the doors from the outside in, he told them no one could leave until they hammered out a deal to inject liquidity into the system. Morgan committed sizable personal wealth to the cause. Panic gradually gave way to calm, only to be lost temporarily when yet another speculative deal went awry.

Twice burned, powerful bankers and industrialists—notably J.P. Morgan and John D. Rockefeller—worked with Rockefeller's father-in-law, Senator Nelson Aldrich of Rhode Island, to persuade Congress to pass the Federal Reserve Act of 1913. In addition to its official mission of managing the nation's monetary policy, the Federal Reserve was charged with maintaining the safety of the financial system. As witnessed in 2008, the Federal Reserve in practice became the nation's lender of last resort, but the Federal Reserve of 1913 hardly resembled what it would evolve into over the next 100 years.

In the remarkable story of the global financial system from 1914 into the Depression years, author Liaquat Ahamed's *Lords of Finance: The Bankers Who Broke the World* describes the inner workings and mission of the early Federal Reserve. As the title of the book suggests, certain bankers "broke the world." The book describes the lives and failings of the central bankers of England, Germany, France, and the United States. Whether contributing to the Great Depression or not preventing it from happening, the Federal Reserve proved insufficient to manage the massive failure of the U.S. banking system. As a result, Congress passed the Banking Act of 1933, which authorized creation of the Federal Deposit Insurance Corporation.

The FDIC was actually established in 1933 to provide insurance—and, more importantly, confidence—to bank depositors. The FDIC also picked up responsibility for regulating and supervising state banks that did not have national charters. Going back to the time of Lincoln, states continued until the Depression to control and oversee all banks not chartered as national banks. The FDIC's accountability for co-regulating state banks was landmark legislation. Just as in 1791 and 1864, not everyone in America in 1933 wanted to see the federal government wield too much influence over rights traditionally possessed by the states.

If politics is the art of the compromise, bank regulation is the art of compromise incarnate. In return for the federal government's insurance, the FDIC was allowed to oversee and regulate the state banks, but not independently of the states. So a dual system was approved. In other words, the states continued to enjoy the right of supervising banks even though the federal government held all the liability through the insurance fund if a state bank failed. Who knows if Jefferson and Jackson would have supported such a structure, but it was clear evidence of their lasting influence. State banks were then and still are jointly overseen by both the FDIC and the state banking commissions.

How does this work in practice? Putting politics aside and judging only by the historical record of facts and data, the dual system is broken and does not work well. In addition to being inefficient, the central problem of the dual system is the lack of accountability of state regulators and the FDIC. When investors seek to charter a new bank in a state, its founders must gain approval from both the FDIC and the state. If the new investors' board of directors turns out to be unqualified, as happened in scores of cases over the past decade, is the FDIC or the state regulator responsible for failing to screen directors effectively?

Once the new bank is chartered, supervision of the bank is shared by the state regulator and the FDIC, or, in a small percentage of cases, by a Federal Reserve Bank. Of the 457 banks that failed in the U.S. since 2008, roughly 80% were state banks, the majority supervised by the FDIC and state regulators. For those failed banks, it is impossible to pinpoint whether the FDIC or the state dropped the ball in supervision. However, given the widely disparate bank failure rates by states during the past two crises, the question must be asked whether the FDIC has developed and executed consistent supervisory processes across all 50 states? Results suggest the answer is no. The topic of regulatory oversight of state banks will be further developed in Chapter 13.

An overview of financial system oversight would not be complete without highlighting the life and death of the Office of Thrift Supervision. In the early 1980s, Congress tried to breathe new life into the dying savings and loan industry with the passage in 1982 of the Garn-St. Germain Act. Some 3,000 bank and savings and loan failures later, Congress realized it had to do something. Rather than rely on any of four existing bank supervisors (the OCC, the Federal Reserve, the FDIC, or the state banking commissions), Congress did what Congress is prone to do—it created yet another agency to oversee and regulate financial institutions while abolishing two others (the Federal Home Loan Bank Board and the Federal Savings and Loan Insurance Corporation, whose duties moved to the FDIC).

The result was the authorization for the Department of Treasury to form the Office of Thrift Supervision. The OTS was assigned accountability to charter, supervise, and regulate federal and state chartered S&Ls. If it all sounds familiar, it's because Congress keeps creating regulatory oversight rules that change, but not really. In fact, until 2011 both the OTS and OCC reported into the Department of the Treasury.

The OTS charged out of the gate in 1989, baring its teeth, snapping and growling, and closing down weak and failing S&Ls. Fast-forward less than 20 years, and the once ferocious OTS had lost its teeth and apparently been transformed into the S&L industry's lapdog. In 2006, Countrywide Financial actually converted to a thrift charter; Countrywide management apparently made it known that it preferred the more reasonable OTS over its former regulator, the OCC. By 2007 problems began to pile up on the OTS as Washington Mutual, IndyMac, and AIG hemorrhaged red ink.

Before its failure in September 2008, it might be interesting to know Washington Mutual's CAMELS ratings in the years leading to failure. In 2005 and 2006, the OTS gave CAMELS ratings of 222222/2, reflecting a view that WaMu was "fundamentally sound." On September 18, 2007, WaMu received from the OTS CAMELS ratings of 222212/2. The score of "1" was for liquidity, meaning "sound in every respect." The high liquidity score connoted the OTS's confidence in WaMu's perceived strong deposit base.

One month later WaMu received a cease and desist order related to its failure to comply with the Bank Secrecy Act and anti-money-laundering regulations. To receive a cease and desist order indicates substantial and prolonged failure of compliance. It is puzzling how the compliance failure was not factored into the exam that had been completed 30 days earlier. If the compliance problems were known, it seems reasonable that the "M" for management rating would have dropped a notch or two, from 2 to 3 or even 4. Stunningly, almost one year from the day WaMu received its September 2007 CAMELS ratings, the institution failed. Its failure could be tied to one overarching issue: a liquidity crisis. In other words, just like in the Depression era, a good old-fashioned bank run took WaMu under.

Two years later, in 2010, the U.S. Senate Permanent Subcommittee on Investigations' hearing on "Wall Street and the Financial Crisis" convened to review the role of the regulators in the buildup to the crisis. The committee revealed what it called a "shared cooperative relationship in regulating Washington Mutual." A turf war had apparently developed between the OTS and the FDIC as WaMu deteriorated. The FDIC-OTS cooperative relationship included an agreement that the FDIC would not get involved with WaMu supervision unless the CAMELS ratings deteriorated to 3 or worse. Either by intention or wishful thinking, the OTS's "fundamentally sound" CAMELS ratings kept the FDIC off OTS turf. (Similar machinations allegedly occurred with the supervision of AIG.)

Born in the 1980s crisis, the OTS died when the Dodd-Frank Wall Street Reform and Consumer Protection Act merged it into the OCC under the Treasury Department in 2011. But as Congress taketh away, Congress giveth. Not satisfied that the existing regulators paid sufficient attention to consumer protection, the financial crisis killed one agency and gave birth to another—the Consumer Financial Protection Bureau (CFPB). To some industry experts, the role and function of the CFPB is a bit fuzzy. Imagine that.

What Would Abraham Lincoln Do?

Give me your tired, your poor, your huddled masses…

The words engraved on the Statue of Liberty are from Emma Lazarus's 1883 poem "New Colossus."

America is unlike any other nation. It is a sum of the parts of people from all over the world. It is constantly evolving, blending cultures and experiences, yet preserving fundamental truths like justice and liberty. America's banking system is the sum of the parts, too.

Abraham Lincoln is now revered by many as America's greatest president. This was not always so. He holds the distinction of being the only president elected to office with less than 40% of the popular vote. To suggest he was off to a tough start would be the ultimate understatement.

As a 30-year-old Illinois Whig politician, Lincoln pressed hard to develop a national banking system, a position resolutely contrary to that of President Andrew Jackson and his followers. Lincoln delivered a speech to the Illinois Legislature on January 17, 1839, railing against the irresponsible fiscal management of his opponents who opposed national banking. Nearly 20 years later, in Springfield, Illinois, Lincoln delivered one of his most stirring speeches. Quoting from the Bible as he was apt to do, Lincoln prophetically stated, "A house divided against itself cannot stand."

What would Lincoln think about the nation's current banking system if he were alive today? Is it possible his banking speech might go something like this?

> *A house added onto itself cannot stand. I believe this bank regulation cannot endure, permanently, one part Federal Reserve, one part OCC, one part FDIC, one part 50 states' banking commissions, one part CFPB, one part NCUA. I do not expect the banking system to be dissolved—I do not expect the house to fall—but I do expect it will cease to be added on. It will become all one thing or all one of the other things.*

The nation's current banking system is a house added onto itself. What does that mean? Have you ever been to one of those 18th-century houses where it is evident each generation of owners has added on a room or two every 20 years or so? By 2012 the house has had so much work done to it that the basic floor plan is a maze. Corridors sometimes lead to nowhere. Some rooms can be accessed only from outside doors. And one part of the house is heated by fireplaces, another by old radiators, and still another with electricity.

Our banking system is that house. Each Congress is like a new generation of homeowners who hire architects—or worse yet, practice architecture without a license—to modify the home to make it more livable. Consider all the rooms that have been added over the years to the foundation the 1st Congress formed in 1791.

Bank Village, U.S.A.

Congress built the first Main Banking House in Bank Village, U.S.A., in 1863 and 1864. At the time there were already other bank houses in Bank Village. In fact, each state had its own bank house. And as new states were formed, each built its own bank house. But the federal government did not want to share space with the states, so in 1863 its architects, Abraham Lincoln and Salmon P. Chase, designed and built the first big house called the Office of the Comptroller of the Currency (OCC). Truth be told, if Lincoln had his way, all the other houses occupied by states would have been razed and the occupants forced to move into the big federal house. But he did not get his way. All those houses are still in Bank Village; some have been kept up quite nicely, while others are termite-infested and can barely stand.

Bank Village suffered through some stormy weather in 1907, convincing a number of influential Americans that the Main Banking House needed an update. It took a few years for them to persuade the architects to agree, but in 1913 the Federal Reserve was added on to the Main Banking House. That addition seemed perfect until an earthquake struck Bank Village in 1929 and tremors were felt for another 10 years or so. New architects were now on the job. They saw fixing up the Main Banking House as one of their highest priorities.

So another room was added in 1932 and 1933 called the Federal Deposit Insurance Corporation (FDIC). To make sure none of the occupants of the state houses in Bank Village were upset with this addition, the owners of the Main Banking House promised not to evict them from Bank Village. In fact, over time the architects struck a deal that the state houses could keep doing exactly what they always had done in Bank Village, but with the added bonus of not having to pay for insurance if their house burned down; since the insurance money was actually not coming out of the architects' pockets, everyone was delighted with the solution.

Since tremors continued to rock Bank Village, architects continued to work on the Main Banking House in 1933 and 1934 and added several new rooms for special purposes since it was not clear the Main Banking House was suitable for all. In 1933 the Federal Home Loan Bank Board (FHLBB) was affixed. The architects got real busy in 1934 hammering in the Bureau of Federal Credit Unions (BFCU) and tacking on the Federal Saving and Loan Insurance Corporation (FSLIC). Some architects questioned the need for the BFCU addition, since by 1934 each of the states had actually built their own little credit union houses in Bank Village.

More than 20 years later, new architects looked at the Main Banking House and decided it needed a big new addition in the form of the Bank Holding Company Act in 1956. This addition expanded the room occupied by the Federal Reserve so it could do some of the work that the occupants of the OCC's room either could not or would not do. As the Fed's room got bigger, it became even harder to navigate the growing house, where visitors often got lost trying to figure out how the Fed and OCC and FDIC rooms connected.

Architects being architects, by 1970 they were determined to make some more changes just to keep their skills sharp. So they cobbled together a new room for the exclusive use of the now independent National Credit Union Administration (NCUA) and repainted the insurance fund walls by creating a new shade called the National Credit Union Share Insurance Fund (NCUSIF).

In 1979 the newest architects in Bank Village got so lost in the Main Banking House that they convened a meeting of all the occupants. Some joked that the house was less a house than an English garden maze with hedges so high no one could see over them. No problem, because in that year another room was added. This one was called the Federal Financial Institutions Examination Council (FFIEC). This new room was a smart addition because it was built for the sole purpose of giving the various occupants of the Main Banking House a new room to meet and talk about how to make navigating the Main Banking House less confusing. Some occupants questioned the need for the room since they saw no reason for the occupants of the Main Banking House to talk with each other anyway.

A series of devastating tornadoes touched down in Bank Village in the mid-to-late 1980s and early 1990s. The tornadoes created a real mess because no one living in the Main Banking House saw the storm coming. Although the entire house was rocked by the tornadoes, the room occupied by the tenants responsible for savings and loans was obliterated; the architects replaced it with a spiffy new room called the Office of Thrift Supervision (OTS). Also in that same year they added yet another new room, this one called the Federal Housing Finance Board (FHFB) to oversee the Federal Home Loan Banks.

By 1992 the weather in Bank Village was fair and sunny; however, a few architects started worrying about a neighboring village where Ms. Fannie Mae and Mr. Freddie Mac lived. These architects went to work on the Main Banking House and added a new room called the Office of Federal Housing Enterprise Oversight (OFHEO). This was an odd addition because Ms. Fannie and Mr. Freddie helped write the blueprint, and for the longest time they made sure only their friends had keys to enter the room.

Just as some architects had been saying for a long time, it turned out that the neighboring village where Ms. Fannie and Mr. Freddie lived was actually located on a major earthquake fault line. Sure enough, an earthquake hit in 2006 and eventually Ms. Fannie and Mr. Freddie lost everything except their ability to sue the workers who helped build Fannie's and Freddie's palatial homes. After working hard to find out who among Fannie's and Freddie's architect friends actually had keys to the old room, the architects sprang into action in 2008 and built a new room to the Main Banking House called the Federal Housing Finance Agency (FHFA).

The 2006 earthquake was followed by aftershocks for five more years. No problem, because the architects were led by two chief architects who knew for certain how to fix the problems plaguing Bank Village once and for all. The other architects agreed and a series of room fix-ups and room additions were completed in 2011. The first change was a decision to force the occupants of the OTS room to move into an expanded OCC room. Also, because the chief architects had personally seen ugly rats scampering free in Bank Village, they made sure to add another room to the Main Banking House for the Consumer Financial Protection Bureau (CFPB) to meet and talk about killing rats.

The chief architects' best idea was to kind of agree that maybe, arguably, possibly the Main Banking House is unlivable and should be condemned. Well, they didn't say that in so many words. And to prove that modern architects do indeed know their Main Banking House architecture history, the architects in 2011 went back to 1979 and dusted off the blueprint used to create the FFIEC room. They added the Financial Stability Oversight Council (FSOC) room. However, this new addition has a clever wrinkle to it: the new FSOC room is big enough for only 10 thrones. Unlike the FFIEC room that apparently did not work but is still attached to the Main Banking House, the fancy new FSOC room is set up for just 10 bigwigs to meet and talk with each other. The architects are pretty sure—actually, not quite certain but they have a good feeling about it—that this FSOC room is the answer. But what is the question?

By the way, what was described is just a partial blueprint of the U.S. financial regulatory house. The list did not even touch on the CFTC, SEC, HUD, etc.

Does this not conjure up memories of the "Dry Bones" song? You remember: "The toe bone connected to the heel bone, the heel bone connected to the foot bone, the foot connected to the leg bone...." The only problem is our banking system is not all that connected.

How dare those bankers complain about the 2,319 pages of the Dodd-Frank bill!

America's maze of bank regulatory oversight does have its advantages. One clear example is the opportunity regulators have to learn "best practices" from each other.

What Can the Nation Learn from Texas?

When I was a banker in Texas, I struggled to comprehend what I called the Texas paradox. One side of Texas projects an image of rugged individualism and "Remember the Alamo" toughness. Texas leaders, including a former governor who went on to become the 43rd president of the United States, claim less government is better government. On the other hand, Texas has a paternalistic side, especially coming out of the Texas banking depression of the 1980s. Going back for years, Texas's homestead laws limited homeowners from any kind of mortgage except a purchase money loan. The homestead law was a convenient excuse for much of the 1990s for Texas lawmakers to prevent Texans from tapping their homes for home equity loans.

As a banker in the state from 1990 to 1995, I was frustrated with this attitude. For the longest time, Texans were the only Americans blocked from taking out home equity loans. Despite doing my share of fruitless lobbying, the law was never changed during my tenure as a Texas bank executive. Time proved Texas lawmakers were right in rebuffing the bankers' efforts to completely do away with the highly restrictive homestead laws.

Texas lawmakers eventually came around to allowing Texans access to home equity loans, but not until 1998, and even then not nearly as liberally as other states. When Texas lawmakers passed the Texas equity law, also known as the A6 law, the state built in a lot more consumer protections than other states. For example, in Texas the A6 law stipulates:

- Origination fees capped at 3%.
- No prepayment penalty.
- A 12-day disclosure process so borrowers could not rush into a loan.
- Texas home equity loans can be refinanced only once per year.
- Most importantly, borrowers could borrow only up to 80% of the home's value.

Several years after the state made it possible to have a home equity loan, it permitted Texans to have a home equity line of credit (HELOC). But again, the state lawmakers imposed a number of hurdles to prevent borrowers from harming themselves:

■ Again, 12-day disclosure, a cap on origination costs, and no ability to borrow over 80%.

■ A special requirement that the borrower had to review the settlement statement one day before actually closing on the loan—a further effort to ensure borrowers had "cooled off."

■ Most interesting, the state would not allow a HELOC borrower to draw less than $4,000 at any one time; the idea was that the state did not want the home to be a credit card.

Was Texas correct by imposing much more stringent conditions on home borrowers? The answer appears to be yes. The results speak for themselves. At the height of the financial crisis in 2009, Texas banks at year-end 2009 had a median return on assets (ROA) of .86%. Nine states actually had negative median bank ROAs, including the five at the bottom of the list:

■ Nevada -2.87%
■ Arizona -2.36%
■ Florida -1.46%
■ Georgia -0.96%
■ Washington -0.84%

The Case-Shiller index by major metro area provides additional insight. The data below shows the price of a typical home in June 2011 compared to January 2000. By going all the way back to 2000, the comparisons smooth out the effect of the big growth in home prices in some states between 2001 and 2006.

■ Dallas   115.9%
■ Atlanta   104.3%
■ Las Vegas   95.7%
■ Phoenix   100.7%
■ Miami   139.5%
■ Tampa   128.9%

On an 11-year basis going back to 2000, the results are not disturbing. As everyone knows, from 2002 to 2006 some states experienced a big spike in home values. And as Sir Isaac Newton might have said had he been a mortgage lender, "What goes up a lot must come down a lot." Recent home price trends remain discouraging in some states. According to Case-Shiller, the November 2011 to November 2010 home value comparison looks like this:

■ Dallas   -0.8%
■ Atlanta   -11.8%
■ Las Vegas   -9.1%
■ Phoenix   -3.6%
■ Miami   -4.4%
■ Tampa   -6.1%

Whether Texas home equity laws helped stave off home devaluations is difficult to say. However, it would appear that, based on home price stability and lower foreclosure rates, Texans have weathered the mortgage debacle as well as or better than other states.

Not only does Texas appear to have better public policies protecting homeowners, it also advertises how much more efficient it is than the OCC at supervising banks. As of January 1, 2011, according to the Texas Department of Banking (DOB) website, a bank with $1 billion in accessible assets would be charged $230,000 by the OCC for supervision. In contrast, the Texas DOB would cost the same $1 billion bank only $101,400, a savings of than $128,000 or 56%. That is a lot of money.

Outsource to Canada?

Although outsourcing bank supervision to Canada is pure folly, U.S. policy makers can learn about banking supervision from our friends north of the border, where bank failures are rare. The success of the Canadian banking system is not lost on the rest of the world. The 2012 appointment of Canada's chief central banker as head of the Bank of England is strong evidence of Canada's standing in global banking circles.

The U.S. banking system has not fared as well as Canada's during the past century. Contrary to some Internet hype, however, Canadians have not been spared problems with financial institutions. In fact, what is important to know is that Canadian lawmakers revamped their regulatory system in direct response to the bank failures in the mid-1980s. Before describing those changes, I will turn to the factors that drove the redesign.

The most recent significant challenge to Canada's banking system was back around 1985. Two moderate-sized banks failed for reasons similar to what was happening in Texas at the same time. The oil boom led to the rapid growth of two western Canada banks formed in 1975. However, by the early 1980s, as oil prices fell, recession hit the region. As in Texas, asset values fell, loans went bad, and deposits fell substantially. Several banks in addition to the two that failed suffered enough that the Bank of Canada needed to provide some temporary liquidity support. Canada eventually weathered the storm.

In addition to the bank failures, between 1980 and 1996, 24 Canadian trust companies and 10 mortgage companies failed. Since the mid-1990s, Canada has not experienced failures of any members of the Canada Deposit Insurance Corporation, in contrast to 505 financial institution failures in the U.S. during this time. The U.S. number does not include mortgage companies.

Although Canada has not been spared banking crises, it is clear the damage over the past 25 years is minimal compared to the U.S. experience. In fact, several of Canada's large banks are today among the most respected in the world. *Bloomberg Markets Magazine* lists four Canadian banks among its top-10 strongest banks in the world: "CIBC (CM) was No. 3 in Bloomberg Markets' second annual ranking of the world's strongest banks, followed by three of its Canadian rivals: Toronto-Dominion Bank (TD) (No. 4), National Bank of Canada (NA) (No. 5) and Royal Bank of Canada (NA) (No. 6), the country's largest lender." Two others are in the top 25. However, success breeds its own risks.

Frankly, Canadian bankers may want to ask whether their recent success is producing too much confidence in their own good judgment and sense of superior banking skills. History has a way of humbling bankers. The reality is that a large portion of Canada's economy remains tied to natural resources. As China's economy has grown dramatically over the past decade, Canada and Australia have benefited directly. China's demand for natural resources has created a boom for the Canadian economy. With it comes a stronger Canadian dollar. A strong local economy has produced well-capitalized banks.

Well-capitalized Canadian banks with a favorable exchange rate can buy banks in the U.S. cheap. However, a strong currency does not necessarily translate into superior returns on capital from U.S. investments. Canadian banks have a spotty history with their U.S. bank investments. The best-performing Canadian investment is Bank of Montreal's 1984 acquisition of Harris Bank in Chicago. More recent acquisitions like Royal Bank of Canada's $2.3 billion purchase of North Carolina-based Centura Bank in 2001 did not go well. RBC's sale to PNC is a partial exit from U.S. banking. It also may be a reality check that Canadian banking skills do not transfer easily to the U.S.

For Canadian banks doing business in the U.S., they earn substantially higher returns on equity in Canada than in the United States. For example, TD Bank, the only Aaa-rated bank in North America, earned in Q3 2012 a 45.2% ROE (not a typo) in Canadian personal and commercial banking compared to an 8.1% return on common equity in U.S. personal and commercial banking. Only time will tell whether Canadian banks' high ROEs on domestic business activity are challenged when the Canadian consumer chooses or is forced to pull back. Perhaps the bigger question is whether TD will improve its U.S. ROE anytime soon since 2012 shows little improvement over 2011.

With that said, there is significant evidence that Canada has designed a banking regulatory system with several advantages over the U.S. version. Some will argue Canada's banking system is too different from the U.S. system to offer much value for comparison. Clearly, Canada has fewer banks. In addition, the big Canadian banks do not rely heavily on trading and investment banking like the largest U.S. banks. Acknowledging these facts, it is reasonable to suggest Canadian banks' business models resemble the models of U.S. regional banks.

There are specific and material aspects of Canada's bank regulatory environment that U.S. lawmakers would do well to understand. Perhaps the most critical difference is the accountability Canada has given one regulator. In 1987, after two bank failures, Canada created the Office of the Superintendent of Financial Institutions (OSFI). It supervises the activities of federally chartered banks, with the exception of the broker-dealer subsidiaries that are regulated by provincial regulators. In addition to the banks, OSFI supervises all credit unions, insurance companies, and pension funds. Having such a broad purview gives OSFI a greater ability to monitor system-wide financial risks.

The other significant difference between U.S. and Canadian regulators is the OSFI's principles-based approach to bank supervision. Although not every regulator across the globe agrees with the direction, it appears more nations are adopting Canada's approach, which emphasizes seven principles. Three are worth highlighting.

First, OSFI is a "big picture" regulator; it focuses on material risks that have the potential to cause bank failure as well as system-wide failure. Second, Canada's financial regulator is forward-looking in its risk and bank analysis; this approach is unlike the U.S. CAMELS ratings, which represent a look-back analysis. Third, Canada's regulator places heavy emphasis on the external environment as well as *how* banks oversee risk management.

OSFI majors in the majors, or in its own language, it pays attention to material risk. It is set up to supervise big risks. By focusing on material risk, OSFI is less distracted by immaterial or secondary or tertiary risks that do not threaten the safety and soundness of the banking system. In Canada, the purpose of the regulatory "Mounties" is to oversee systemic and idiosyncratic risks that cause banks to fail.

Most Americans are not familiar with Canada's unique mortgage lending model. It is a good example of how the OSFI operationalizes its oversight of material systemic risk. Banks must abide by the lending guidelines established by OSFI. Key features of the mortgage lending business in Canada are as follows:

- Until 2008, lenders were prevented by law from making a mortgage that exceeded a 75% loan-to-value (LTV). In 2008, banks were permitted to take the LTV to 80%, provided the borrower qualified for government-backed mortgage insurance. Government insurance will only be issued subject to the bank's conformance to very specific requirements for documentation, disclosure, and credit analysis of the borrower.
- In certain rare cases, a mortgage is permitted to be greater than 80% LTV; in those cases, 100% of the mortgage must have government-backed mortgage insurance.
- Mortgages can be a fixed or variable rate.
- The term of a mortgage is one, three, or five years. Mortgages are underwritten in recognition that rates could move up in five years.
- In contrast to those in many states in the U.S., borrowers are responsible for full repayment of the mortgage even if the home is foreclosed and the bank cannot pay off the loan from the proceeds of the home sale. Further, unlike in the U.S., Canadian banks can garnish a borrower's wages if there is a shortfall.
- Canadian banks make about two-thirds of the country's mortgages and brokers make the other third. In the U.S. during the past decade, brokers accounted for as much as 70% of the production.

Also worth highlighting is OSFI's approach to identifying future or emerging risks. OSFI appears vigilant in using its regulatory tool chest to mitigate systemic risk. In a way, the U.S. Federal Reserve plays this role in its capacity of managing monetary policy. However, OSFI is much more explicit in its exercise of very specific policy actions to curb bank risk.

Evidence of this forward-looking risk management process can be seen as recently as March 2012, when the OSFI issued draft guidelines for more stringent mortgage underwriting. Fearful that Canadian mortgage activity is too frothy, the regulator is using underwriting standards and policies to throttle back mortgage lending and reduce the industry's overall risk profile.

In the U.S., the newly created Financial Stability Oversight Council (FSOC) was created as a forward-looking watch guard for emerging risks that threaten the financial system. It is a step in the right direction. Membership cuts across the Treasury, the Federal Reserve, the OCC, the SEC, the Commodity Futures Trading Commission, the National Credit Union Administration, the Federal Housing Finance Agency, and the newly formed Consumer Financial Protection Bureau. Time will tell if powerful political appointees can share information and avoid turf battles. Judging by the acerbic tone of the book written in 2012 by Sheila Bair, the former FDIC head, likely the FSOC is seen by many as just one more futile attempt to get political appointees to work well with each other.

Back to OSFI; Canada uses a composite risk rating (CRR) for banks. It is equivalent to, but not the same as, the U.S. regulators' CAMELS rating. On the OSFI website (which is uncluttered and easy to navigate), the Canadian regulator acknowledges something one would never see on the website of a U.S. regulator. The "Guide to Intervention" indicates that the composite risk rating was "developed in consultation with the industry." The statement suggests that OSFI actually engages Canadian banks in developing exam practices.

Another example can be found in the May 2009 *RMA Journal*. In it was an interview with the chief risk officer of one of the large Canadian banks. When asked why Canadian banks fared so well in 2009 as banks around the world did not, the CRO had this to say about OSFI:

> *The Canadian regulators, specifically the OSFI, deserve some of the credit. They've worked closely with the Canadian banking system since the crisis began to ensure that the rules worked as they should. OSFI also held banks to a well-capitalized minimum ratio of 7%. In mid-2008, Canadian banks had a tier-one capital ratio of 9.8%, which was well above that of many countries, instilling confidence in our banking system. Further, OFSI has always held us to a leverage covenant, commonly known as the TAC multiple (total assets divided by capital).*

When was the last time you heard a U.S. banker give regulators credit for something good? Notice, too, how OSFI pre-crisis held Canadian banks to higher tier-one capital requirements at the very time other regulators around the world were backing off.

Is Canada's banking and regulatory system perfect? Of course not. Over the past few years, consumer debt has been rising there at a faster rate than in the U.S. Also, it will be interesting to see how the housing market and OSFI adjust in the years ahead as record-low mortgage interest rates disappear. The one-, three-, five-year balloon structure could put a strain on many Canadians. What happens if today's 3.5% mortgage converts to a 7% rate five years from now? How many Canadians can afford a mortgage payment doubling overnight? Once rates rise in Canada, is there anywhere for home prices to go but south, at least in the short term? And if so, what happens to the banks that hold the mortgages? Is one of the reasons Canada's mortgage system has worked so well because of 25 successive years of declining long-term interest rates?

One final thought: Canada has far fewer banks than the U.S. Some will argue that far fewer banks means more too-big-to-fail banks. Maybe they are right. What cannot be denied is that it is far easier to find highly qualified bank directors for 76 banks (of which only 25 are "Schedule 1" true domestic banks) versus 7,246 financial institutions in the U.S.

By the way, my guess is that Abraham Lincoln would have taken a trip to Canada to learn more about their system of bank oversight.

It is time for a short ride to the 1980s, an interesting decade from two perspectives. First, of the top-10-selling music artists of the 1980s, only one was not a solo act: the duo of Hall and Oates, who finished fifth behind Michael Jackson, Phil Collins, Whitney Houston, and Madonna.

The second reason the 1980s are so interesting has to do with banking, of course. (What did you expect? This is a book about banking.)

Unintended Consequences of Bank Legislation

He got what he wanted but lost what he had.

—LITTLE RICHARD, 1962

You may not remember Richard Penniman. Better known to the world as "Little Richard," Penniman took the music world by storm in the 1950s with such classic hits as "Tutti Frutti," "Good Golly Miss Molly," and "Long Tall Sally." Like his contemporary, Elvis Presley, Little Richard's fame led to Hollywood movies. In the early 1960s, Richard experienced a faith conversion. For a while his life and music changed. In 1962 he penned an autobiographical gospel song capturing his new spirit. His message: "He got what he wanted but lost what he had." Like Little Richard, banking is full of unintended consequences.

A Banker's Life in Florida: 1983-1989

When I worked in Florida throughout most of the 1980s, S&Ls were in the early stages of entering the commercial loan business. Inflation and high interest rates in the 1970s and early 1980s had taken a heavy toll on S&L profitability. The reality was that S&Ls had gone the way of the buggy whip by the late 1970s. Their primary mission, making and holding home loans, suffered on many fronts. Fannie Mae and Freddie Mac were building up steam. Inflation, along with perniciously high interest rates, led to S&Ls going underwater on their fixed, low-rate mortgages.

Despite a questionable future role for the savings and loan industry, in 1982 Congress passed the Garn-St. Germain Depository Institutions Act. Intended to revive the sinking S&L industry, the act made it possible for S&Ls to use a portion of their balance sheets to make commercial loans. Expanded lending powers, in theory, would enable the S&Ls to tap into new revenue sources and ultimately improve the industry's long-term profitability.

As a banker competing to make consumer and commercial loans at that time, I observed firsthand the unintended consequences of the Garn-St. Germain Act. The biggest problem with the legislation, although it was not really known at the time, was just how difficult it would be for the S&Ls to attract top commercial lending talent.

The talent shortage did not deter hundreds of S&L boards from diving head first into commercial lending. Not having been in the business, the S&Ls needed to build commercial lending departments. Almost overnight, commercial lenders—skilled and not so skilled—became hot commodities. A hiring boom ensued. I had no interest in joining an S&L, so the hiring spree really did not matter to me at the time.

However, by the mid-1980s, I began to see signs that the S&Ls' entry into traditional commercial lending was headed in the wrong direction. By then, many were aggressively ramping up commercial lending activities. I began to see more evidence of unhealthy competition from the S&Ls. Some of our clients with real estate projects pressured us to cut pricing on our loans. They threatened to take their loans to the local S&L "banker" who promised to make the same loan at a lower rate. Sometimes we lowered our pricing to keep the business. At other times, when we felt we were not getting paid fairly for our risk, we let the customer walk.

More troubling than pricing pressure, some clients told us the S&L was willing to make loans with lighter covenants—that is, the terms and conditions of a loan—and sometimes even without personal guarantees. It was clear to me, especially in my Tampa Bay region, that the S&Ls' entry into commercial real estate lending was leading to a breakdown in credit standards and in disciplined, risk-based pricing.

In addition to lending money, my job in Florida in the second half of the 1980s included management responsibility for 50 of my bank's branches in the Tampa Bay region. Unlike today, back then bank competitors in Florida freely shared quarterly deposit data at the county and branch-office levels. Using this data, I was able to construct a reasonably useful deposit market share analysis for each of the 50 branches. My analysis evaluated dozens of factors that I speculated influenced bank-branch market share.

My first task was to define each of the 50 branches as independent markets. My analysis revealed that one factor, above all others, influenced which bank in any market held first or second position in deposit share. That factor: when the branch was built and opened. The key to success, according to my data, was to own the bank that entered a market first.

The first bank to enter a market in 48 of 50 cases, regardless of the name of the bank, held in the 1980s either first or second position in deposit market share. This came as no surprise. Knowing each of the 50 markets well, I could see that the first entrant almost always secured the prime piece of real estate.

The first entrant almost always had the most visible branch, as well as easy flowing ingress and egress from the intersection of the two busiest streets in the market. In addition, in most cases, the first entrant had locations highly convenient to the big grocery stores. And although people are slow to change banks, first entrants used their early entrance advantage to draw customers seeking convenience.

The data were clear: Market share for bank deposits was highly correlated to the order in which bank competitors entered a market. However, I saw something that troubled me. In the two cases where the first entrant did not have first or second market share, the leader was actually a fast-growing S&L.

As some S&Ls pursued hot loan growth, they needed deposits to fund the loans. Those growing fastest paid the highest CD rates in the Tampa Bay region. As I dug deeper into this phenomenon, I noticed that these same S&Ls were quickly gaining share in other markets, too. Based on the S&Ls' deposit growth trends, I concluded that the fast-growing S&Ls would move inevitably into top market share positions across all the markets.

Sometime around 1986, I sensed we had a serious problem. I saw many of the S&Ls as plain dumb competitors. Their aggressive growth appetite and high risk tolerance had created an undisciplined "Wild West" of lending for many financial institutions.

In looking back, it seems so obvious that the era introduced by Garn-St. Germain would not end well. In my view, the root cause of more than 3,000 bank failures between 1985 and 1993 was not the legislation itself. The root cause was a dearth of skilled and experienced bankers and directors for S&Ls. With Congress's blessing, eager S&L lenders and directors quickly got back on their feet by making commercial loans. Given their historical experience with consumer real estate, the S&Ls directed most of their capital to commercial real estate projects. Making a bad situation worse, most S&Ls were small, and therefore, were left with little alternative but to concentrate their commercial real estate loans in confined, nondiversified markets.

The rest of the story is now history. The failure rates in the late 1980s were especially painful in Texas, Florida, and the Baltimore-D.C. corridor, where S&Ls had been especially active. Although S&Ls were not the only cause of the banking crisis, their ill-managed entry into commercial lending was a major contributing factor. As witnessed during the post Garn-St. Germain era, once a market bust takes hold, even the highly skilled lenders who refused to compromise credit standards get pulled into the downward-spiraling credit vortex as real estate values in a community deflate.

My experience in Florida turned out to be a course in Bank Failure 101. By 1990 I was working in Dallas, Texas, where I found myself in the next course, Bank Failure 201.

Lessons Learned

The first lesson is what one banking industry leader calls the "Little Richard Lesson": Be careful what you ask for. Little Richard sang: "He got what he wanted but lost what he had." The S&Ls got what they wanted from Senator Garn and Congressman St. Germain. But in the end, they lost what they had.

Lawmakers need to tread carefully when it comes to resuscitating dying industries. The S&L business was flawed and could not be revived. As Henry Ford said, "If I asked my customers what they want, they simply would have said a faster horse." Leave it to the Henry Fords of the world to pick business winners.

The nation needs lawmakers to perform more effective risk analyses when introducing significant new banking legislation. Garn-St. Germain and later Gramm-Leach-Bliley each introduced unintended consequences with grave outcomes. Dodd-Frank is a case study of unintended consequences yet to be known.

The scenario analysis or "what-if" tool is always helpful in evaluating unintended consequences. It is unlikely the bank regulators who oversaw implementation of the Garn-St. Germain legislation used scenario analysis to evaluate downstream risks. In the future, it will be quite helpful if the Federal Reserve and OCC take full advantage of scenario analyses as they help lawmakers evaluate potential new legislation.

A Brief History of Risk Management in Commercial Banking: 1945-2010

Competition has been shown to be useful up to a certain point and no further, but cooperation, which is the thing we must strive for today, begins where competition leaves off.

—FRANKLIN D. ROOSEVELT, 32ND PRESIDENT OF THE UNITED STATES, 1936

The philosopher George Santayana is credited with the observation that "those who do not learn from history are doomed to repeat it."

With two goals in mind—to learn from banking history and make sure the unseemly parts of its history are not repeated—this chapter provides a brief history of the banking industry in the United States since 1945. The year 1945 was chosen since it marks a definitive time of change in the United States. In the 15 years prior, two catastrophic events rocked humanity: the Great Depression and World War II. America's new spring commenced in 1945.

American banking history since 1945 can be delineated into five distinct eras:

- Era 1: The Public Utility Era of Recovery and Stability (1945–1965)
- Era 2: An Era of Innovation and Inflation (1965–1980)
- Era 3: The Unintended Era of Bad Public Policy, Bank Failures, and Coast to Coast Banking (1980–1995)
- Era 4: The "4 D" Era of Digitization, Deregulation, Debt, and Dismay (1995–2009)
- Era 5: The Second Public Utility Era (2009–?)

Era 1: The Public Utility Era of Recovery and Stability (1945–1965)

Era 1 represented a time of recovery and stability for the U.S., its economy, and the banking industry. The Great Depression and the devastating aftershocks of 9,000 bank and S&L failures continued to cast a long shadow on banking practices.

Influenced by the colossal failure of the banking system, in 1933 Congress imposed the Glass-Steagall Act and with it tight bank rules. America had been burned by banks. President Roosevelt and Congress sought cooperation over competition. In recent years some pundits have expressed a desire to return to Glass-Steagall. Almost always what they really are saying is they want to block commercial banks from the securities business, especially trading and investment banking activities.

Today's pundits seem unaware that the Glass-Steagall legislation meant more than the separation of commercial banks from those higher-risk activities. Glass-Steagall effectively allowed banks to operate cartels. The laws prevented banks from competing on price. Banking was kept as simple as possible. Rules required all banks to pay the same price for deposits, and S&Ls could pay exactly one-quarter of a percentage point more than commercial banks. Profit margins were locked in. Governance required boards to meet paint-by-numbers rules and regulations. Risk-taking was out.

Bank governance was turned over to local business owners who held a vested interest in the success of their local economy. Era 1 bank boards were dominated by skittish bankers who had barely survived the Depression. Once burned, boards sought out conservative bankers who had a complete mastery of loan policies and procedures. During this time, the banking industry created credit schools and loan departments where the "five Cs of lending" (character, cash flow, capital, collateral, and conditions) were drilled into young bankers.

During Era 1, virtually none of the nation's 20,000 financial institutions failed. As banks matured, profits climbed steadily. Bankers agreed implicitly not to engage in brash competition and the industry made steady but unspectacular profits. In the second half of Era 1, times were so good that bankers gained a reputation for enjoying a "9 to 3 job." New country clubs popped up across America filled with thousands of bankers who needed a place to go when the workday ended at 3 p.m. For many years, country club membership was one of the most common perks enjoyed by bankers. (This is no longer true and, because it is not, the game of golf has suffered.)

Era 2: Innovation and Inflation (1965–1980)

Profoundly influenced by two phenomena, Era 2 brought a bold surge in innovation and a paralyzing bout of inflation. Era 2 began in 1965 and ended in 1980 with the introduction of new public policies and federal bank laws that would unleash a torrent of change in Era 3.

Era 2 looked a lot like Era 1 for most bankers. Profit margins were still locked in. The nation had thousands of banks and S&Ls. Banks were essentially given fenced-in markets where they could do business. A few states allowed for statewide banking, but most blocked banks from expanding outside their county of business. Bank failure was as rare during Era 2 as it had been in Era 1, despite an unhealthy combination of inflation and economic stagnation by the late 1970s.

Led by a few West Coast banks, farsighted, tech-savvy bankers realized during Era 2 how innovation could translate into greater bank profitability. Bankers in fast-growing California contributed to the state's reputation as the place where all the new trends first took hold.

Two notable innovations stood out, each introducing new opportunities as well as risks to the industry. The first was the BankAmericard, the ingenious precursor to the ubiquitous Visa credit card. The BankAmericard revolutionized commerce and consumer lending. It also prompted the development of sophisticated consumer-lending credit skills. The second major innovation was the advent of the reader-sorter. Leveraging computers, the banking industry quickly adopted new technology to pave the way for breakthrough improvements in back-room productivity. And with the advent of new technology emerged the risk of managing it.

For the most part, the banking industry remained tranquil during Era 2. Three issues cropped up in the 1970s, however, foreshadowing challenges ahead. Perhaps owing to the retirements of the post-Depression bankers, the first issue to emerge was a gradual ramping up in the amount of risk-taking by commercial lenders.

During Era 2, New York money center bankers cautiously began lending money to developing countries. Encouraged by early success, money center banks in New York, Chicago, and San Francisco aggressively expanded lending activities throughout the world, most notably into developing countries where the banking industry's understanding of risk was in its infancy. Also at this time, especially in southern banks, real estate lending accelerated. Lending to REITs (real estate investment trusts) became quite popular. REIT lending led to the first wide-scale boom-and-bust cycle seen in the industry since the Depression.

The old-timers in the industry worried about the new tolerance for risk. Although losing influence in the 1970s as a new generation stood at the helm of most banks, the old-timers continued to preach the basics of the five Cs and push their banks to update credit policies and improve credit schools, based on the lessons learned from the real estate and developing-country loan losses.

The second major challenge to the industry developed when inflation soared in the mid-1970s, escalating pressures on interest rates. Smart nonbanks, most notably Merrill Lynch, met their clients' needs for earning higher interest rates on idle cash by inventing the cash management account. Unable to compete with Merrill because of the Depression-era bank laws that locked in interest rates, bankers began in the late 1970s to clamor for new rules to allow them to get back the deposits they were losing to the investment management companies.

The third major issue confronting the banking industry in Era 2 manifested itself when Congress passed the Community Reinvestment Act in 1977. CRA was a product of landmark Great Society laws passed in 1965 during the Johnson administration. Although the 1977 legislation lacked teeth, it paved the way for policy makers to drive social policies through bank legislation and regulation. Over the next 30 years, astute lawmakers came to realize the personal power they gained by leveraging banks for social engineering. And as banks became instruments of social policy, lawmakers also came to see banks as an extension of law enforcement. The CEO of one community bank told me he considers these responsibilities to be unrecognized and unmeasured taxes on the banks.

Background for Era 3 (1980–1995) and Era 4 (1995–2009)

Christopher Columbus not only discovered America, he discovered Jamaica. By the mid-17th century, the British ruled the island. In the 18th century, Brits relocated to Jamaica to start sugarcane plantations. The plantation owners amassed great wealth. For a while, business went sour when a snake infestation made it nearly impossible for the slave labor to work. For several years, the plantation owners failed in every effort to rid themselves of the pests. Snakes plagued the sugarcane business until one plantation owner, probably prompted by the advice of a slave working his plantation, decided to import mongooses from Africa to eat the snakes. Living on a teeming diet of snake, the mongoose population grew heartily and solved the snake problem. Today Jamaica faces a new challenge: an out-of-control mongoose population.

Banking in America is like Jamaican snakes and African mongooses; sometimes the best answer to a problem leads to yet another problem.

Era 3: Bad Public Policy, Bank Failures, and Coast to Coast Banking (1980–1995)

Era 3 began ominously with 14% inflation and a 21.5% prime lending rate. Such conditions were the seedbed for the Reagan revolution, which brought not only a new president but also a new spirit to America. Underpinning this spirit was a philosophy that big government stifled private enterprise and slowed economic growth. Riding an anti-big-government wave, bankers exerted strong pressure on public policy makers to revamp banking rules. Virtually all the bank and S&L presidents across the country lobbied Congress to rewrite interest cap rules and allow them to compete with Merrill Lynch and other nonbanks. Congress responded with new laws modifying interest rate caps as well as the Garn-St. Germain Act, which, as already noted, dramatically altered the competitive landscape of U.S. banking.

By the early 1980s, the bankers who remembered the Great Depression were now happily retired. A new generation of bankers who had grown up in the "9 to 3" era ran the banks and credit risk organizations. Two prominent external event risks emerged at this time. First, alarmed by the entry of new S&L competitors, some banks let down their credit guard and matched S&L underwriting practices. In many markets across the U.S., most notably in Texas, Florida, California, and the D.C.-Baltimore corridor, the combination of bad S&L and bank lending triggered a catastrophic collapse in real estate values.

Second, the oil boom of the late 1970s and early 1980s pumped billions of petrodollars into the southwest U.S. economy. The influx of new money was largely redirected into Texas real estate. Texas got hit by a double whammy. Not only were the S&Ls particularly aggressive there, but Texans faced the added challenge of a 75% collapse in the price of a barrel of oil. In a stunning development, by the early 1990s only one of the state's top 10 banks (Frost Bank) was still in business. The final count saw Texas lose 847 financial institutions. By the end of Era 3, roughly 3,000 banks and thrifts had failed.

A large number of banks, desperate to survive, sold off businesses. During this time, MBNA (from Maryland National Bank) and Capital One (from Signet Bank of Virginia) emerged as highly focused monoline credit card companies. Each had become independent as their parent banks sold off credit card businesses to raise capital. In the early 1990s, almost all the banks' credit card businesses earned 35% to 45% returns on equity. Rates were 18% or higher everywhere except for banks doing business in Arkansas and eventually South Dakota. The monoline credit card banks exploited the banks' failure to differentiate card terms based on customer segmentation. Using breakthrough processes and systems to identify more affluent customers with good credit records, the monoline banks steadily gained a greater share of industry profitability.

Also at this time, Fannie Mae and Freddie Mac, both Era 2 government innovations, became major players as they stepped into the breach left in the home lending business by the failure of the S&Ls. Rising alongside the two government-sponsored enterprises were home mortgage originators like Countrywide. Armed with big lines of credits from commercial banks and the rising tide of mortgage securitization, the mortgage industry rode the steady decline in 30-year Treasury rates and began in the late 1980s a nearly 20-year run of astonishing profits.

Unprepared initially to respond to the crushing wave of bank failures, regulators learned on the job and developed on the fly what proved to be successful new strategies. The Texas crisis in particular challenged bank regulators and public policy makers to think creatively. The unprecedented scale of failures in Texas led to a policy that put failed banks and S&Ls out to bid. The regulators came to count on healthy banks to buy failed banks. A few of the nation's banks were only too willing to accommodate the regulators. Led by executives who had tried for years to break down legal barriers blocking interstate banking, Texas opened the door for what would inevitably prove in time to be borderless coast to coast banking.

By the early 1990s, the banks acquiring the failed institutions grew so quickly that a few farsighted public policy makers for the first time began to raise concerns. The "too big to fail" issue was on the table. However, like Jamaican plantation owners, the regulators were left with no better options. The FDIC and newly formed Resolution Trust Corporation continued throughout the banking crisis to rely on the bigger banks to help the federal government stabilize the banking industry.

By the end of Era 3, several key developments in risk management began to emerge. Most grave in the minds of the long-retired Era 1 bankers, commercial and consumer credit training in banks was disappearing. Three factors stood behind this change.

First, as a result of so many bank failures, the industry had a talent surplus. Banks could save money by hiring experienced commercial bankers and cutting out the cost of training new bankers. Many banks shuttered or seriously shrank their commercial and consumer credit schools starting around 1993; as a result, it is rare today to find a highly trained credit expert under 40 years of age. The industry today finds itself facing a severe shortage of well-trained commercial and consumer lenders over the next decade.

Second, largely influenced by a small California company named Fair Isaac, by the late 1980s bankers increasingly turned from judgmental lending to computer-driven statistical credit scoring models. The model used an algorithm known as a FICO score to determine creditworthiness. The automation of the credit decision proved especially useful for consumer lending. Banks could save the cost of teaching bankers how to do consumer lending. In addition, the computer-generated credit decision created much more consistent loan approvals and declines when compared to the judgment of individual lenders. Eventually the credit scoring model worked so well that it was carried over to small business lending under the theory that small business lending risk was more akin to consumer lending than commercial lending.

Third, banks started doing away with credit departments. By the end of Era 3, the credit department began to evolve into the risk management department, which oversaw not only a bank's credit risks, but market, operational, reputation, and compliance risks. Along the evolutionary change from credit to risk management, bank risk managers gained greater confidence—sometimes correctly and sometimes misplaced—in their ability to manage all aspects of risk through highly centralized organizations. These high-powered centralized risk groups not only set policies, but in many banks actually controlled all risk decisions.

In the capital markets and trading businesses, risk management evolved as well during Era 3. J.P. Morgan Bank adopted value at risk (VaR) in the early 1990s to get a daily handle on how much risk it was taking in its trading and hedging activities. The idea behind VaR is straightforward: Past experience allows risk managers to calculate probabilities of future events. In time, banks and regulators would come to learn VaR's limitations.

It was also during Era 3 that so-called free checking entered the picture, and with it came bankers' first post-Great Depression industry-wide reputational risk challenge. Like many bank trends, this one started on the West Coast, in California. By 1991, most of the indigenous Arizona banks had failed and been acquired by out-of-state banks. Arizona banking was up for grabs in the early 1990s as aggressive, presumably savvy competitors fought for market share.

Two California banks entered Arizona chomping at the bit to grab big market share. Having dabbled with free checking in the 1980s in California, these two institutions fought tooth and nail to out-do each other with freer and freer checking. Over a matter of a few months, as experts in game theory would expect, almost all the other Arizona banks matched the two California-based banks.

Most bankers hated the idea of free anything, including free checking. Smart retail bankers viewed the free checking movement as a potential plague of locusts, knowing it was only a matter of time before free checking would sweep the nation as it moved from west to east. Sure enough, that is exactly what happened. Texas was the next state to see free checking, beginning in 1992. Again, a California-based bank introduced free checking to Texas when it entered the state through the acquisition of a failed S&L. As in Arizona, in order to protect market share, most other large Texas banks almost immediately fell in line and matched the California bank.

The economics and risks of free checking evolved over time. In the early 1990s, the California banks' strategy was based on a fairly simple notion that "scale"—meaning bigger and bigger numbers of checking customers—would translate into lower and lower unit costs for the bank. At the time, interest rates were still reasonably high, and therefore, deposit "net interest margin spread" income (i.e., the income banks earn when the cost of deposits is subtracted from the earnings from loans and investments) from all but the smallest depositors could arguably justify the strategy. Over the years, as the free checking movement swept across the country, the economics of the strategy changed.

Era 3 was also when banking truly went global for the megabanks. Regulators across the globe began for the first time in Era 3 to coordinate their oversight of credit risk. They chose the beautiful city of Basel, Switzerland, as their meeting place. In 1988 the regulators published their first Basel requirements for determining how much capital a bank needs to set aside as a cushion against possible loan losses. For community and most regional banks, Basel was a nonissue in Era 3.

Era 4: Digitization, Deregulation, Debt, and Dismay (1995–2009)

Two challenges exist in trying to describe Era 4. First, it is fresh history, and fresh history lacks the time and distance needed for cold analysis. Second, attempts to encapsulate the banking industry from 1995 to 2009 inevitably raise questions like "How could you leave such and such out?"

It is not easy to appreciate the wild changes endured by the banking industry from 1980 on. One measure is to examine the list of the top 50 banks in the U.S. in 1980. Twenty-five years later, only seven of those 50 banks still existed. Of the seven, only Citicorp, Northern Trust, and Pittsburgh National Corporation (PNC) survived and retained the name of their bank from 1980. Four others—Bank of America, JPMorgan Chase, U.S. Bancorp, and Wells Fargo—actually were acquired by banks that chose to save the monikers. Wells Fargo is really Norwest Bank of Minnesota; U.S. Bancorp is First Bank System, also of Minnesota; JPMorgan Chase is Chemical Bank in New York; and Bank of America is NationsBank of North Carolina.

So why did so many banks merge? As Era 4 began in 1995, many bank directors faced a critical decision: Do they sell the bank or invest substantial capital to compete in a rapidly changing industry? Two external events and one personnel-related issue raised these two options to the forefront in the mid-1990s.

The first was the relief many bank directors felt knowing their bank could have been one of the 3,000 financial institutions that failed during the banking crisis of the late 1980s and early 1990s. Banks began to recover beginning around 1993. Directors of banks that had experienced near-death as well as a crushing fall in stock price had about as much fun as they could stand. Faced with a chance to sell the bank at a premium to book value, some boards jumped on the opportunity.

Bank boards had a second motivation to sell banks in the mid-1990s. Some of the nation's banks were led by CEOs and chairmen on the cusp of retirement. Many bank directors emerged from the banking crisis concerned about the talent benches in their banks. Uncertain the bank could replace a CEO hired in the 1950s, some boards decided to sell their banks.

Perhaps the most profound but least understood driver of the frothy bank consolidation was the role played by Bill Gates. In 1995, Gates called banks dinosaurs. Gates described a new 10X risk. He predicted digital banking would render modern banking unnecessary. Bankers who failed to evolve and go digital, he argued, would die like dinosaurs. Needless to say, the comment by the world's richest man generated a ton of media attention.

The inflammatory comment backfired on Gates, however. Bankers interpreted the statement as Microsoft's threat to enter the online payments business. His attempt to buy Intuit (Quicken) a year earlier had already spooked a lot of informed bankers. Gates's decision to buy into several payments companies reinforced banker worries.

Eventually Gates realized bankers were actually important customers of his company and he backed off public comments about them.

Most bank boards and bankers were indeed utterly "clueless" (as a 1995 *Fortune* magazine cover story blasted) about how to compete in a digital banking future. Many were like deer caught in the headlights, struggling even to gather sufficient information on the cost of building and competing in such a world. By 1996, a few banks had leaped ahead of the others in building online banking capabilities. Concerned with so much uncertainty, some bank boards, especially banks with an aging CEO, decided it was time to sell.

By the end of the 1990s, bank consolidation left the industry with a handful of megabanks. CEOs of the largest banks joined forces with public policy advocates of free markets to promote the reversal of Depression-era banking legislation. The Gramm-Leach-Bliley Act (GLB) of 1999 meant profound industry change. GLB gave birth to universal banks. This new breed of banks was designed to compete globally, to reduce risk through diversification, and to foster the innovation of new financial products needed in the 21st century.

Like the Garn-St. Germain Act nearly 20 years earlier, GLB led to unintended consequences. Old-line investment banking partnerships quickly took their companies public. With the infusion of new capital, the investment banks helped partners liquefy their holdings and, in the process, think less like partners than get-rich-quick investors. The capital also gave the firms the ability to compete with the aggressive universal banks. GLB unleashed a torrent of new capital just in time for the dot-com boom. Chastened by the dot-com 10X risk bust as well as 9/11, the financial industry slowed temporarily. By the end of 2002, however, a combination of clever financial innovation and Keynesian "animal spirits" unleashed a virtual financial services arms race. New risks emerged, some not well understood. Seven industry-wide risks went largely undetected until the full blast of the financial crisis hit.

First, just as fast as big banks bought smaller banks, cash-rich investors were eager to back entrepreneurial bankers eager to start new banks. In too many states, regulators approved these banks without enough appreciation for the risks associated with approving so many in such a short time. As documented throughout this book, inexperienced or naïve directors and bankers were given too much leeway to grow their banks. Unchecked by prudent regulators or directors, new banks blew through their initial business plans in search of higher and higher profits. Eager to keep up with the Joneses, older banks stepped on the gas and pumped out record profits until the day of reckoning struck.

Second, because of the power of credit scoring models, banks were no longer dependent on a highly trained consumer credit expert to grow consumer loans. Nationwide consumer loan production, especially with credit cards, rose dramatically. Credit scoring introduced new challenges and risks. Perhaps the biggest challenge for most community and even some regional banks was their inability or unwillingness to compete with big banks and credit card companies for consumer loans. As a result, a new risk appeared. No longer able to profitably attract consumer loans, many of these banks concentrated their lending on local businesses, especially those with needs tied to commercial real estate.

Third, by Era 4 the free checking movement included most of the nation's community banks. As interest rates fell steadily throughout the 1990s and the 2000s, banks could no longer count on making as much money from the spread between deposits and loans. Consequently, banks developed new ways to capture fees from the so-called free accounts. By the middle of Era 4, the free checking movement evolved to a strategy to reap fees from customers who wrote bad checks.

As the banks "earned" more money from bad-check fees, they gained a heroin-like addiction to bad-check fees to drive profits. Like the story of how to boil a frog—place it in a pot of room-temperature water and gradually turn up the heat to a boil—banks of all sizes ever so gradually saw reputation risk increase with growing free checking fees. Although free checking was not the only factor, by the end of Era 4 the banks' reputation damage would prove so great that Washington lawmakers formed a new federal agency to protect consumers.

Fourth, Era 4 brought abundant evidence that too many banks lacked effective bank director governance. For banks of all sizes, governance practices in Era 4 looked a lot like those practiced in Era 1 some 40 years earlier. Quite simply, the skills of bank directors failed to evolve from the 1950s. No longer was banking a "paint by number" business. The industry was changing by the day. Suffering from overconfidence and not eager to be challenged, too many bank CEOs seemed perfectly content to have underskilled directors on their boards. Ultimately, the absence of directors with advanced banking skills came back to bite many of these same CEOs. As Era 4 ended, the need for industrial-strength governance cultures was crystal clear.

Fifth, the rapidly changing era also made it quite apparent that the industry suffered from a vast shortage of skilled and wise bank executives. Combined with weak boards, banks with underskilled management succumbed to tantalizing opportunities for rapid-fire growth and potentially cup-runneth-over profits. The years from 2002 to 2006 amounted to banking on steroids. Enabled by cheap and abundant capital, an accommodating Federal Reserve, imprudent consumer lending, and a gluttonous global appetite for mortgage debt, bank profits soared.

In some bigger banks, new CEOs were often investment bankers, accountants, and lawyers. Very few of these new CEOs had commercial bank experience. It is unlikely any of them ever worked as a branch manager or made a small business loan. For that matter, many of these CEOs had little to no actual lending experience. Despite the experience gap, or perhaps because of it, many CEOs performed radical makeovers of their banks' risk profiles.

Sixth, in Era 4 bankers relearned the lesson that overconfidence is their worst enemy. Good bankers are by nature worriers. They don't sleep well. They especially don't sleep well when times seem too good. From 2000 to 2007 the banking industry had little patience with bankers who refused to believe "this time is different." Investors rewarded banks for fast growth. Banks that did not grow like their neighbors were punished with low stock prices, and their boards were pressed to replace management.

As always when times are good, bankers whose institutions did well from 2001 to 2006 grew in confidence. Each year of success reinforced their sense of brilliance. No surprise that compensation, especially for the high-profile, name-brand CEOs, skyrocketed. Worse, in too many cases, CEOs gained imperial power; bank cultures softened so that neither the board nor risk managers felt empowered to challenge them. Royal Bank of Scotland is a case study of this problem, as seen in Chapter 8.

Compounding the cultural issue, many risk management organizations failed in Era 4 to develop skilled people, forward-looking control processes, and real-time systems capable of identifying, mitigating, monitoring, and reporting risks in fast-growth businesses. Unaware that the banking industry is a barometer of the economy, too many bankers' confidence slipped into hubris. Operational risk management skills diminished, undermining critical disciplines and processes necessary to protect against "bet the bank" strategic risk initiatives.

Seventh, bankers and directors were not alone in believing "this time is different." Even the normally steely-eyed brotherhood of bank regulators drank the elixir. Not all, but some across the many regulatory arms of government dropped their guard from 2000 to 2006. Some critics of the bank regulators—most notably the majority view expressed by the Financial Crisis Inquiry Commission—insinuate that the regulators were asleep on the job. Such a view has dire ramifications that will be examined more closely in the next chapter. In reality most regulators were not asleep but preoccupied by other activities.

As late as early 2008, there is significant evidence that regulators were much more concerned with possible CRA injustices and concerns for fair lending than the crippling issue of potential bank failures resulting from systemic banking problems. In addition, post-9/11, the regulators assumed a quasi-police role. In this capacity, they devoted enormous resources to ensuring banks' compliance with a growing burden of new regulations (most notably anti-money laundering, Bank Secrecy Act, Office of Foreign Assets Control) designed to prevent terrorists from tapping U.S. banks as a funding vehicle. In the absence of much bigger budgets, something had to give when regulatory resources were reassigned to social engineering and protective services. The fact is, regulators went where Congress told them to go.

Also during this time, U.S. regulators were occupied with a global effort to develop coordinated bank oversight. Under the leadership of Basel, global regulators largely rewrote the rules of bank supervision. In a 21st-century global economy, such new rules are critical for long-term success. The downside, however, was that such an effort required a lot of management attention. An arguably second downside was the reality that the new rules emerged at a time when economies across the globe were weakening. It is possible that the new regulatory guidance, checklists, and highly complex capital modeling actually contributed to the U.S. regulators missing the forest for the trees.

Once full of promise, Era 4 ended with western civilization awash in debt and dismay. Of course, all the banking problems landed on the front doors of 435 U.S. representatives, 100 senators, and the White House. Determined to "just do something," the lawmakers ushered in Era 5 in 2010 with a series of new banking laws and rules. In addition, the lawmakers formed the Financial Crisis Inquiry Commission (FCIC) to investigate the causes of the financial crisis.

The FCIC's report, released in January 2011, was actually three reports. Unable to agree among themselves, the 10 commission members separated into three groups. The four Republicans on the so-called bipartisan committee did not even agree among themselves. Consequently, the Republican view required two different mini-reports. The actual, official report was signed off by the six Democrats who made up the majority of the commission. Their first two conclusions about the causes of the financial crisis were:

- "We conclude this financial crisis was avoidable."
- "We conclude widespread failures in financial regulation and supervision proved devastating to the stability of the nation's financial markets."

Given the second conclusion, it is especially appropriate to examine the role of bank regulators in the next chapter, as they may be the key to how Era 5 will unfold in the years ahead.

Regulators: The Latest Bubble?

The sentries were not at their posts.

—FINANCIAL CRISIS INQUIRY COMMISSION, JANUARY 2011

Yesterday, December 7, 1941—a date which will live in infamy—the United States of America was suddenly and deliberately attacked by naval and air forces of the Empire of Japan.... Hostilities exist. There is no blinking at the fact that our people, our territory, and our interests are in grave danger.

—PRESIDENT FRANKLIN DELANO ROOSEVELT, DECEMBER 8, 1941

On December 6, 1941, America slept. On December 7, 1941, America awoke to a nightmare. On December 8, 1941, Hell's fury was unleashed.

Imagine life in America the day before the attack on Pearl Harbor. America was detached from what Winston Churchill later called "the gathering storm." The next day devastation struck. In hours a nation was transformed. The pendulum of life in America swung wildly from casual and comfortable to panic-stricken and vigilant. Within days of the attack on Pearl Harbor:

- The FBI intensified its investigations of anti-American activity.
- Citizens on both coasts created shore patrols and ensured homes were "blacked out."
- Voluntary enlistment into the military shot up.

Within a few weeks of the attack:

- The internment of Japanese-Americans began.
- Rationing of all necessities of life began.
- Women entered the workforce in unprecedented numbers.
- The Civil Air Patrol was established and civilian spotters searched the skies for enemy planes and ships 24 hours a day.
- The general and admiral responsible for protecting Pearl Harbor were dismissed.

Calamity provokes sudden and violent change. Often the change is necessary. In the heat of the moment, it seems anything is better than nothing. However, sometimes the swing in the pendulum is so violent and hyperbolic that it leads to counterproductive activities.

To many bankers today, the pendulum of regulatory scrutiny has swung too far. During the past year, I have spent time talking to individual bankers and groups of bankers from community and regional banks. When I ask "What is the greatest current risk facing the industry?" bankers from across the nation identify by a wide margin the intensified regulatory environment. There is clearly a growing sense that the new level of scrutiny is leading to unintended consequences.

It is fair and reasonable to ask: "Who are the bankers to complain? Didn't they bring this all on themselves?" Virtually every banker would say the industry requires more scrutiny. Most understand the need for tighter supervision. I know of no banker who seeks to preserve the status quo of the pre-financial crisis banking system.

It is not at all difficult to understand how and why the pendulum has swung so violently. Put yourself in the regulators' shoes. The Democratic majority who wrote the official Financial Crisis Inquiry Commission report makes it very clear that the regulators were caught unprepared when the crisis hit:

> We conclude widespread failures in financial regulation and supervision proved devastating to the stability of the nation's financial markets. The sentries were not at their posts.... More than 30 years of deregulation ... had stripped away key safeguards which could have helped avoid catastrophe.... The government permitted financial firms to pick their preferred regulators in what became a race to the weakest supervisor.

—FINANCIAL CRISIS INQUIRY COMMISSION, JANUARY 2011

Together with CEOs of big banks, the "sentries" are punching bags for angry lawmakers. Quite understandably, the regulators have reacted. They have a new mantra: "Never again on my watch." And who can blame them? Not only is there strong evidence supporting the FCIC conclusions, there is also a paper trail of documentation left over from the S&L and bank crisis of the late 1980s and early 1990s.

The Good News: The OCC, Federal Reserve, and FDIC Produce Outstanding Analysis

The Federal Reserve, OCC, and FDIC are actually quite good at analyzing and documenting bank failures and, for many years, have produced excellent analyses. Consider three written in 1988 and 1990 by each of these regulators.

The first is an analysis written by the Office of the Comptroller of the Currency in 1988 entitled *Bank Failure: An Evaluation of the Factors Contributing to the Failure of National Banks*. The OCC rightly defined bad credit as the reason the bank failed. Listed below are the internal factors identified as root causes of the failures:

> The major cause of decline for problem banks continues to be poor asset quality that eventually erodes a bank's capital. The OCC's intent, however, was to determine the factors that were commonly responsible for the poor quality.

The second sentence—"determine the factors"—is the key to the analysis. The writers pinpoint internal problems as the root cause of the failures. Below are verbatim quotes from the OCC's 1988 analysis.

Note that the problems identified are operational risk failures: weak management, unskilled directors, and inadequate processes to identify and mitigate risks. Get used to this theme. This will not be the last time you see regulators pin bank failures on bankers and directors who "lacked necessary banking knowledge."

Internal Problems

- *Uninformed or Inattentive Board of Directors or Management*
  - *Nearly 60% of failed banks had directorates that either lacked necessary banking knowledge or were uninformed or passive....*
  - *... the Board should maintain clear lines of authority and accountability and ensure that management understands and carries out the Bank's policies.*
  - *The study showed the following factors, related to poor board or management supervision, to be significant problems for many of the failed banks:*
    - *Nonexistent or poorly followed loan policies.*
    - *Inadequate systems to ensure compliance with internal policies or banking laws.*
    - *Inadequate controls or supervision of key bank officers.*
    - *Inadequate problem loan identification systems.*
    - *Decisions made by one dominant individual.*
- *Overly Aggressive Activity by Board or Management*
  - *Inappropriate lending policies.*
  - *Excessive loan growth.*
  - *Undue reliance on volatile liabilities.*
  - *Inadequate liquid assets as a secondary source of liquidity.*
- *Problems Involving the Chief Executive Officer*
  - *The CEO is probably the most important determinant of the success or failure of a bank.*
- *Other Problems Related to Bank Oversight or Management Deficiencies*
  - *Excessive credit exceptions.*
  - *Over-lending, i.e., high loan amount relative to debt service ability.*
  - *Unwarranted concentrations of credit to one industry.*

External Factors—The Economic Environment

To the OCC's credit, in 1988 it also explored the critical role that external factors played in bank failures. The findings are fascinating as well as worthy of some debate. The OCC contends that banks led by skilled bankers and directors can weather a bad economic environment. Therefore, the economic environment in and of itself is not the cause of failure. I agree!

- *The study did show that an adverse economy was a significant factor in 35% of the failures.*
- *The evidence from healthy and rehabilitated banks also supports our hypothesis that economic conditions are rarely the primary factor in determining a bank's condition.*

The OCC's bank failure paper is remarkable in many regards. First, it is pithy and gets right to the nub of the factors that cause banks to fail: internal problems and external factors. Second, as the writer of Ecclesiastes states, "There is nothing new under the sun." The factors behind bank failure in 1988 are exactly the same factors identified in the bank failure autopsies conducted by the FDIC 20 years later. And third, we are reminded that success in banking requires bankers to display flawless attention to detail and directors to exercise determined governance and oversight.

Two years after the OCC wrote its paper on bank failure, the Federal Reserve Bank of Cleveland issued an *Economic Commentary* on the "Underlying Causes of Commercial Bank Failures in the 1980s." The Federal Reserve Bank of Cleveland noted in its commentary that "banks failed at record rates during the past decade, and no relief appears in sight." The analysis identified "two *probable* causes" of the record-breaking rate of bank failures. But interestingly, it concludes that banks failed because of bad bank management:

- *First, the U.S. Banking System is a regional system. Economic slumps in specific areas of the country, which do not necessarily coincide with national downturns,* may be *partly responsible for the upsurge.*
- *Second, the rise in the failure rate* may be *traced to the behavior of bank management in increasingly deregulated and competitive financial markets.*
- *We conclude that while regional economic problems contributed to the demise of many of the banks during this period, a bank's ability to survive is ultimately determined by managerial factors.*

In essence the Cleveland Fed's findings confirmed the OCC findings two years earlier: The same two root causes and the same determination that local and regional economic problems take a back seat to bank management and governance.

Also, take note of the language used. The choice of words is no accident. Commentary written by the Federal Reserve is almost always couched in qualifying language like "probable" and "maybe." Think about the current Federal Reserve chairman, Mr. Bernanke. Rarely does he make categorical statements. In contrast to the OCC, which places great emphasis on bank field experience, the Federal Reserve remains a Ph.D.-influenced organization. The more academic orientation of the Federal Reserve shows up in most of its research.

At risk of some oversimplification, it is fair to say the OCC view of the world is formed experientially while the Federal Reserve view is formed empirically. The fact that the more experiential OCC and the more empirical Federal Reserve arrived at the same two 10X risk root causes of bank failure is extraordinarily important. It has—*or should have*—a profound influence on how and what bank supervisors do to preserve the safety and soundness of the banking system.

Returning to the Cleveland Fed's *Economic Commentary* of 1990, it is of value to explore the factors it identified in support of the "two probable causes."

Regional System

- *The regional preference for geographically limited banking in this country has resulted in a fragmented regional banking structure at the national level which ties bank performance more closely to the regional rather than the national economy.*
- *This occurs because branching restrictions at the national and sometimes the state level limit where banks can locate their offices.*
- *This, in turn, limits the geographic diversification of a bank's portfolio, as the majority of loans are made in areas where it has a physical presence....*
- *Local economic performance was uneven during the decade, as regions heavily dependent on energy and agriculture experienced severe problems.*
- *Banks in these regions were particularly hard hit.*

Managerial Determinants

- *The ultimate determinant of whether or not a bank fails is the ability of its management to operate the institution efficiently and to evaluate and manage the risk.*
- *As banking markets have become less regulated and more competitive, lending margins have shrunk and the task of managing banks' risk exposure has become more complex and difficult.*

By identifying the regional system as the first factor, the Federal Reserve Bank of Cleveland threw another log on the interstate branching fire that some of the big banks were stoking in 1990. In this commentary, the Cleveland Fed is essentially urging Congress to allow banks to expand outside their state boundaries. The Fed proposes that interstate banking would enable banks to diversify credit exposure and thereby improve risk profiles.

There is no question that community bank loan concentrations present in the banking crisis of the 1980s remained a problem 20 years later. What did the data show in Chapter 1? The fact is that bank failure is a contagion. As no bank is an island, the better the loan portfolio diversification, the better the probability that local bank failures will not trigger other bank dominoes to fall.

For this reason, a bigger bank with broader loan diversification like SunTrust, although headquartered in Georgia, is in better shape than many smaller Georgia-only competitors. However, just to be clear, SunTrust's geographic and loan diversification did not insulate it from the ravaging damage of free-for-all Georgia banking. Yes, the bank survived the financial crisis, but not without pain. SunTrust shareholders felt the brunt of the pain as the bank's stock price declined 79% from January 2002 to January 2012 and 67% for the five years ending January 2012. In essence, the Cleveland Fed back in 1990 was making the business case for banks like SunTrust to expand and diversify the concentration risk associated with geographic borders.

The third and final regulatory document is the FDIC's *The Texas Banking Crisis: Causes and Consequences 1980-1989*, an overview of the unimaginable failure of virtually the entire Texas banking system. The quality of the analysis is remarkable since the work was conducted in 1990 when the banking system in Texas was still in the midst of its own crisis. Too often, real-time analyses suffer from political bias and inadequate data collection; neither was the case in the FDIC Texas report.

Among its main findings, the FDIC identifies two leading factors behind the failure of banks in Texas in the second half of the 1980s. The first is the obvious external factor: oil prices spiked, leading to a real estate bubble that popped when oil prices declined.

- *High failure rates among Texas banks appear to be attributable to a combination of several developments:*
  - *Trend in oil prices ... fell dramatically in 1986.*
    - *The high failure rate among Texas banks ... has its roots in the OPEC oil embargo of 1973.*
  - *Boom and bust in Texas real estate.*
  - *Changes in the composition of the loan portfolios ... concentrations in construction and land development.*

The Cleveland Fed and OCC conclude that bank failures of the 1980s were attributed to two factors: weak management and external event risk associated with the regions in which the failed banks did business. What's interesting, in contrast, is that the FDIC's Texas report is silent about bank management failings. The FDIC report does, however, imply management accountability by highlighting the Texas banks' aggressive loan growth rates as well as the effort by Texas bank holding companies to skirt archaic branching laws by chartering hundreds of new banks across the state.

- *Banking activity in Texas increased greatly during the late 1970s and early 1980s.*
  - *In 1981, Texas banks' asset growth reached a high of 20.5%, compared to 8.6% for all other U.S. banks.*
- *Bank examinations ... the frequency of examinations of Texas commercial banks was among the lowest in the nation for the last decade.*

While identifying the external event of oil price shock as the root cause of the bank failures, the FDIC goes one step further in its analysis to suggest more frequent bank examinations could have mitigated the failure rate. There is no statistical data to support the contention that more exams would have reduced failures. Although the statement may be true, the writer's theory was not supported with evidence.

From a personal perspective, the failure of the Texas banks had a profound impact on my family and career. My family moved to Texas in 1990, shortly after the two largest banks in the state failed. My five-plus years working in Texas banks radically changed my opinion of bankers whose banks fail. While in Florida from 1983 to 1989, I had acquired a rather jaundiced view of the S&Ls and banks that failed. My time in Texas opened my eyes to broader issues related to bank failure.

I spent hundreds of hours talking to Texas bankers about why their banks failed and what lessons could be learned from their experience. From these conversations, I gained tremendous respect for most of the bankers; I could see quite clearly they were well-trained, highly professional, and understood the art and craft of running a bank profitably.

In some cases, I felt great compassion for bankers who had never diversified their own assets beyond their large personal holdings in their bank. It was not unheard of for some bankers to lose their entire net worth. In a few rare cases, faith in the bank was so strong that some bankers kept buying stock as the price fell, sometimes on margin. So when I hear about bankers not having enough "skin in the game," I know that in the case of Texas, there was never any question about the alignment of personal and shareholder interests.

The Texas bank failures also shaped my view of bank risk management. While there, I learned to "major in the majors." Success requires an iron grasp on the few things that matter most. Yes, in banking, everything matters, but some things matter a lot more than others. Texas banks failed, as the FDIC found in its 1990 report, because of a 10X external event risk—the oil embargo—that inflated the Texas economy throughout the period of high-priced oil. When oil prices plummeted, it was as though someone took the air out of a balloon. Pre-bust, the surge in Texas oil money had to find a home. Much of the cash ended up in real estate.

Here is the main point: Identifying, mitigating, monitoring, and reporting external and emerging event risk is an absolutely essential and critical requirement for bank management and boards. The constant fear of unknown but potentially catastrophic external events should always be top of mind for bankers. Bankers must "major" in the identification of emerging risks. Risk appetites must always be curbed during the best of times, especially "when everyone else is doing it."

Now the Bad News: Are Bank Regulators the Newest "Bubble"?

As a reminder, this book is about the kind of banking conducted by 99.7% of U.S. banks.

With that caveat, I want to make it clear: Much of what federal bank supervisors do is good work that contributes enormously to the safety and soundness of the U.S. banking system. To a person, the federal regulators I know are dedicated and motivated to do everything in their power to discharge their duties honorably and effectively. They work hard.

Bankers do not always appreciate the difficult role regulators play. Often bank supervisors are caught between lawmakers who, in some cases, have an incomplete or partial view of the facts and bankers who wish to exercise their roles without someone looking over their shoulders.

The regulatory pendulum has swung so violently of late that, in many ways, it is now the latest banking bubble. Determined to show voters they are on the job, lawmakers are working overtime to create new and more effective laws to control banks. Having been beat up by the lawmakers, regulators are doing everything in their power to show they have gotten the message. All the new public policies and regulations eventually end up on the doorsteps of U.S. banks. Some of those new public policies and regulations are half-baked, some not so useful, and some possibly critical to driving permanent and lasting fixes to a broken U.S. banking system.

Whac-A-Mole

A growing number of community and regional bankers now complain that the flood of new public policies and intensified regulatory scrutiny are bringing unintended consequences. Rather than actually make the system safer, the current bubble of policies and regulatory oversight runs the risk of creating the newest external event risk.

A banker or two now compare regulatory oversight to an arcade game called Whac-A-Mole. The goal of the game is to strike moles popping up from holes on the game table. The more moles the player hits, the better the score.

What if the community and regional bankers are right? What if there are potential unintended and material consequences to the current bubble environment? What might those consequences be? Is it possible that more regulatory scrutiny could be counterproductive? Is it possible to use a tool advocated by regulators, such as scenario analysis, to evaluate the potential for severe unintended consequences? In other words, what might go wrong in the current environment?

Sir Isaac Newton lived a long and productive life. As a physicist and mathematician—modern bankers would call him a quant—Newton described the science behind the world we live in. His three laws of motion coupled with his understanding of gravity shaped scientific reasoning for the next three centuries. It is his third law of motion—for every action there is an opposite and equal reaction—that regulators may wish to examine. Have regulators considered whether hyper-supervisory actions could create equal and opposite reactions that lead to the unintended consequence of more, not less, risk to the banking system?

The regulatory bubble brings five risks that I affectionately call: 1) The Popeye Risk, 2) The Easy Professor Risk, 3) The President Garfield Risk, 4) The Good for the Goose Is Good for the Gander Risk, and 5) The Major in the Minors Risk. The regulators would be well-served to practice what they preach and conduct scenario analyses on each.

The Popeye Risk

Popeye the Sailor Man was a popular cartoon back in the 1960s. Although a mild-mannered guy, on occasion Popeye reached a boiling point when he would blurt out: "That's all I can stands, I can't stands no more."

As this book is being written, a story in *The New York Times* highlights the real-time risk of unintended consequences. Monadnock Community Bank was a New Hampshire bank with less than $100 million in assets and 18 employees. Recently Monadnock's shareholders decided to sell the bank to a credit union. The CEO felt selling the bank was the only option after experiencing the final straw of what he considered unreasonable supervisory demands of his bank examiner, the OCC. The bank's president cited the OCC's recent demand that the bank comb through its mortgage records and document how it handled delinquencies during the financial crisis. Not an unreasonable request, you might say, given the state of mortgage lending across the nation. However, in Monadnock's case, the CEO argued that the request failed the reasonableness test because it would require him to devote nearly 20% of his staff to the effort. Further, he noted, the bank had experienced just two foreclosures over the past four years.

At least two unintended consequences arose from the OCC's request. First, at a time when banks are charter shopping for the "best" regulator, the OCC saw yet another defection. Second, some politicians are cheering on the credit unions while booing the banks. More banks will convert to or sell to credit unions. As they do, the overall risk profiles of credit unions will change. What are the chances the credit unions' regulators are prepared to supervise credit unions that are really banks? My educated guess is that credit union supervisors are probably just as prepared to regulate banks as were the savings and loan regulators back in 1982, when many S&Ls started acting like banks. Apparently some credit unions agree. Must we go down this road again?

KEY QUESTIONS FOR ALL BANK EXAMINERS TO ASK THEMSELVES: 1) Does our request pass the common sense test? 2) Are we asking for something nice to have or "have to have?" 3) How will we use this information to protect the safety and soundness of the banking system?

The Easy Professor Risk

College students today are not dumb. Leveraging social networks and the wisdom of crowds, at almost every college in America today, it is possible to find an online tracking system that scores the college's professors. These websites provide a lot of valuable information. For some students, the chief value of the scoring system is to discover which professors are the easiest graders.

Despite some evidence to the contrary, bankers are not so dumb either. Although there are no official online scoring systems grading bank examiners, there is powerful word of mouth. Some bankers, like some college students, want to find the easiest grader. Countrywide's decision in 2006 to move from the OCC to the Office of Thrift Supervision allegedly was motivated by a desire for less regulatory scrutiny. The new Dodd-Frank legislation killed the OTS and put the OCC in charge of the OTS-supervised financial institutions.

Intended to improve supervision, the unintended consequence of this move is that the nation's 600 S&Ls are now shopping for a new regulator. The regulators of choice today are the National Credit Union Administration (which requires S&Ls to convert to or sell to credit unions) and state bank examiners. As will be discussed in the next chapter, America's system of financial institution oversight is unique in allowing banks to "shop" for a regulator. Not only are certain regulators perceived to be easier, but some actually offer more reasonable supervision at a lower cost. Taking cues from Walmart, "every day lower prices" are a competitive advantage at a time when bank margins are so tight.

Maybe the most egregious example of regulatory shopping gone bad occurred in June 2008, when the $25 billion Colonial Bank swapped out the apparently tough professor OCC for easier professors—the Alabama State Banking Department and the FDIC. Facing an imminent cease and desist order from the OCC, Colonial bought some time by changing regulators. Fourteen months later the bank failed. Colonial cost the Bank Insurance Fund $3.8 billion. Only in a nation where the banking system is broken can a $25 billion bank on the verge of failure simply switch regulators. Thankfully, Dodd-Frank legislation makes charter shopping more difficult.

KEY QUESTIONS FOR ALL BANK EXAMINERS TO ASK THEMSELVES: 1) Are you the examiner of choice because your oversight practices are perceived to be lax? How do you know? Why would the FDIC allow a big complex bank like Colonial to exit the OCC for a state regulator? 2) Are you the examiner of choice because you are too close to those you examine and do you erroneously view the institutions as "clients" or "constituents"? 3) Why are state/FDIC regulators less expensive than national regulators? Are state regulators taking shortcuts? Are the OCC and Federal Reserve Bank regulators weighed down with expensive overhead and superfluous activity? Are cost comparisons even accurate? What really are the factors that drive the disparity?

The President Garfield Risk

James A. Garfield was the country's 20th president. Unlike the 19 before him and the 24 to come after, Garfield is the only man elected president who truly did not seek or want the office. In 2011, a fascinating book was published describing the circumstances of Garfield's death. *Destiny of the Republic: A Tale of Madness, Medicine, and the Murder of the President,* written by Candice Millard, is the tragic story of the failures of Garfield's doctors to use emerging technology to locate an assassin's .44 caliber bullet lodged near the president's liver. Despite tending to the most powerful man in the nation, the doctors refused to adopt industry-leading medical practices that in all likelihood would have saved the president's life.

Banking in 2012 is different from 2002 or 1992, and especially 1952. Tools and technology are available for the modern bank to conduct less invasive yet more effective supervision. And if such tools do not exist, examiners from all the agencies need to work together to develop them. The banking industry is going through its own metamorphosis. Exam practices requiring enormous bank resources are out of touch with the reality of tighter net interest margins and shrinking fee income. The burden of the bank's exam management cannot increase proportional to the decrease in bank revenue. Like everyone else in government and business, regulators need to figure out how to more cost-effectively examine banks, while actually improving the quality and effectiveness of their supervision. This can be done, but it will require new thinking and knowledge of emerging technology.

Also, examiners need to tightly coordinate their requests of banks examined by two or more regulators. One reason Garfield died is because he had nine different physicians thrusting germ-ridden hands into his body. Since every state bank is examined by both the state banking commission and the FDIC (or Federal Reserve Bank), coordination is a must. With the advent of yet another supervisor, the Consumer Financial Protection Bureau, it is critical for examiners to coordinate their operations. Redundant requests are not only expensive for banks, but also lead to potential regulatory overlap that often reveals unclear accountability.

KEY QUESTIONS FOR ALL BANK EXAMINERS TO ASK THEMSELVES: 1) What tools and technology can we use or improve to ensure we do not hold unnecessary meetings with the bankers? 2) Has the regulatory community done everything possible to coordinate requests? 3) If there are two or more regulators examining a bank, is everyone clear about which regulator is accountable for what?

The Good for the Goose Is Good for the Gander Risk

This risk relates to the skills and experience of bank supervisors. In the same way regulators quite justifiably hold bankers and directors accountable for having appropriate skills and experience, it is only fair for the regulatory community to hold itself accountable to the same standards. In fact, the regulators could do the entire industry a favor by taking the lead in publishing the criteria and qualifications for examiner licensing and certification.

How different are the skills of examiners from the various supervisory state and federal agencies? How do the agencies certify or verify that examiners have the skills necessary to discharge their duties? The OCC career path suggests that, at a certain point in an examiner's career, there is strong evidence of subject-matter expertise. The typical OCC examiner spends about two to three years as an assistant examiner learning on the job. If successful, the examiner is promoted to associate examiner, a role he or she remains in for another two or three years. At that point, roughly four to six years after joining the OCC, the examiner qualifies to sit for a week-long exam to become a national bank examiner. The exam assesses the candidate's skills across eight categories of bank supervision. Passing the exam is the equivalent of certifying the examiner's qualifications to supervise banks.

It is not clear if all examiners of community and regional banks go through a similar assessment. Also, it is unclear if the various bank regulatory agencies hold their employees to the same standards and expectations. Once again, the risk of variation in regulatory oversight emerges as a systemic risk to the industry.

What is clear is the need for regulators—including political appointees privileged to lead regulatory agencies—to be documented experts in bank supervision. The fact that political appointees can lead bank supervision while lacking hands-on experience and tested skill makes about as much sense as having banks run by CEOs who have no experience making loans.

A further benefit of examiner licensing and certification is that the practice could and should be extended across the entire regulatory community. As evidenced by regulator "shopping," the current bank supervision system is fraught with inconsistencies and variation. Establishing common criteria for skills and knowledge will enhance safety and soundness by increasing the probability that examiners with common training and certification deliver consistent, reliable, and accurate assessments.

KEY QUESTIONS FOR ALL BANK EXAMINERS TO ASK THEMSELVES: 1) Is there a common understanding of what skills and experience constitute expertise in the various fields of bank supervision? 2) Are all examiners—not just your agency—receiving an adequate investment in skills development? 3) Why is it not reasonable to establish across the U.S. bank regulatory community common criteria for licensing and certification of skills?

The Major in the Minors Risk

By far the greatest risk to the banking system is for the supervisors and bankers and directors to be so focused on the thousands and thousands of compliance and regulatory mandates that everyone—bankers, regulators, lawmakers—fails to "major in the majors" of 10X risks that ultimately lead to bank failure. How many community and regional banks are like Monadnock Community Bank in New Hampshire, which has been asked to divert significant resources for a problem that will not cause the bank to fail? How much bank management and board time is consumed by secondary and tertiary issues that take attention away from the real causes of failure? What is the fine line for the board of directors between whacking a thousand moles and actually governing the issues of institutional life and death?

The reality is that the regulatory community can control only so much of this issue because it is taking direction from public policy and lawmakers. However, it is incumbent on regulators to inventory their demands of the banks they supervise and weigh those demands based on some type of scale. Everything is not equal. As noted earlier, bankers and especially directors have only so much capacity. Are they all focused on the right things?

Consider some disturbing banking facts from the years 2000 to 2007 in Georgia. As was established in Chapter 1, Georgia is the nation's leader in bank failures. Note that regulators missed early warning indicators that could have limited the damage of bad banking. Georgia banks increased their total loans by 75% in seven years, while increasing the percentage of the total loans tied to real estate from 49% to 69%. Also, from 2000 to 2007, the state of Georgia chartered 108 new banks. These three numbers—new banks, growth in loans, and percentage of real estate loans—are the numbers regulators and bankers must "major" in to manage systemic risk.

Not only did Georgia charter 108 new banks from 2000 to 2007, but some of these banks bolted out of the starting block with startling speed. The ones noted below grew so fast that it is almost impossible to understand how they received strong CAMELS ratings in the years prior to their failures.

Integrity Bank was chartered November 2000 and failed August 2008. Between year-end 2004 and year-end 2007, the bank's loan book grew 140% ($386 million to $930 million). The CAMELS ratings in May 2006, two years before failure, included a 2 for management, 1 for asset quality, and 2 for liquidity.

Georgian Bank was chartered in November 2001 and failed less than nine years later in September 2009. Loans grew from 2004 to 2007 by 180% ($611 million to $1.7 billion). The FDIC's CAMELS ratings of Georgian Bank in January 2007 was 211222. A year later, the Georgia state regulator's CAMELS ratings showed a modest decline: 232222. Even when the FDIC came back in November 2008, the CAMELS ratings fell only to 343332, ratings not portending failure less than 12 months later.

Despite mounting evidence by 2005 and 2006 that Georgia banks were growing too fast, regulators approved state charters for 29 de novo banks in those two years. Two of these are worth highlighting given how quickly they failed.

Rockbridge Bank, chartered December 2005, failed in December 2009. From year-end 2006 to year-end 2007, total loans rose from $7 million to $156 million. CAMELS ratings in May 2007 were 112312 (Georgia exam), followed six months later with an FDIC exam: 122332. In October 2008, a little more than a year before failure, the Georgia regulators' CAMELS ratings were 233333.

Alpha Bank was chartered May 2006 and failed just 35 months later after growing loans to $238 million by year-end 2007. Despite rapid growth that would test the controls of any bank, the April 2007 CAMELS ratings showed a 2 for management, 1 for asset quality, and 2 for liquidity.

In addition to Georgia approving 108 new banks in the 2000 to 2007 time frame, at least one bank converted its charter from the OCC to the state. The Buckhead

Community Bank converted from the OCC to a state charter in July 2005. Loans grew 263% from year-end 2004 to year-end 2007 ($186 million to $677 million). The FDIC's January 2006 CAMELS were 222222, followed a year later by a Georgia regulatory exam that yielded the same ratings. The FDIC returned in January 2008 with ratings of 343332.

At least one credit risk expert took notice of the dizzying trends in Georgia during this time. In 2004 the chief credit officer of SunTrust pushed for the bank to beef up its loan loss reserves. Prescient as she was, the SEC rewarded her action with an inquiry into SunTrust's accounting practices. As a result, the chief credit officer lost her job. Nearly two years later, the SEC cleared her of any wrongdoing. There are many lessons to take away from this experience. One of those is for regulators to respect the judgment of on-the-ground risk officers who are courageous contrarians willing to raise early warnings about credit standards and trends.

Banking in Georgia from 2000 to 2007 was like driving in the Indianapolis 500. These banks in Georgia (and Arizona, Nevada, Washington, Florida, etc.) were not just moving fast, they were flying. In retrospect, of course we now know they were flying at unsafe speeds. It is one thing if one bank decides to go so fast it breaks the speed of sound. It's another when the entire banking system looks like the Indianapolis Motor Speedway.

Driving a race car isn't for everyone. Drivers don't wake up one day and say "I want to race in Indianapolis." Race car drivers start as young kids riding go-carts in the yard. If they are good, they graduate to the dirt track where they race their go-cart against other kids in the area. If they are really good, they move up and up in faster and faster vehicles on increasingly challenging courses against increasingly tough competition. Most of the de novo banks were led by the same types of individuals who ran Winesburg's second and third banks described in Chapter 3.

In the words of Ralph Nader, they were like the Chevrolet Corvair back in 1965: *Unsafe at Any Speed.*

Regulators are—or should be—like the highway patrol that uses a radar gun to clock a bank's speed. Better yet, regulators have remote radar; they can watch banks race on their computers. Not only are they receiving information from the bank itself, but gathering information from across the region and the industry. The regulators' bank information dashboards should be packed with all the facts and figures they must monitor.

A good supervisor is watching privacy protection, CRA loan activity in low- and moderate-income census tracts, anti-money-laundering reports, key bank personnel turnover statistics, customer complaints sent to Congress, online banking hacking issues, bank supplier problems, and on and on and on. As the latest problem du jour pops up on the screen, the senior regulator directs people and resources to make sure the problem does not become a big deal.

Then one day something becomes obvious to everyone. The regulators and the bankers and directors have been so busy being busy that they all fail to see the single issue that could actually kill the bank—bad loans. Frankly, how does one miss a 75% increase in total loans in Georgia from 2000 to 2006? How does one miss seeing the rapid growth in real-estate-secured loans as a percentage of all loans in the state? Who is majoring in the majors?

With 20-20 rearview-mirror vision, it is clear that everyone—Georgia investors, bankers, directors, public policy makers, and regulators—was lulled into believing "this time is different." But it was not different. Just as not everyone is cut out to drive race cars, not everyone should "drive" a bank. Just as the Highway Patrol uses a single radar gun to monitor traffic, true regulators can be better served monitoring bank traffic with one or a few tools that "major in the majors."

KEY QUESTIONS FOR ALL BANK EXAMINERS TO ASK THEMSELVES: 1) Are you "majoring in the majors"? In other words, do you know the banks' 10X risks? 2) If not, why not? 3) Since much of your work is directed by Congress, are your leaders talking candidly with Congress about regulatory challenges to majoring in the minors? This last question is an especially important one to ask. Just as regulators expect bankers to be honest and forthcoming about risks, are the regulators walking the talk?

Questions for Regulators and Lawmakers

Questions for Regulators

How do you ensure 10X risks are not missed?

The Financial Crisis Inquiry Commission (FCIC) noted that the "sentries were not at their posts." It is a quotable statement and certainly true in some regards, but it is not altogether fair. The intended consequence of the FCIC comment was to get the regulators' attention. The unintended consequence is a national "bubble" of intense regulatory scrutiny where everything seems to matters equally.

For the moment, we can assume the FCIC is right and the sentries were indeed not at their posts before the financial crisis. The question to ask is, why? Although not an acceptable answer, it is fair to say that the regulators were so busy conducting other tasks that they actually lost view of the big picture. Is it possible that U.S. lawmakers and policy makers need to dial back their expectations for OCC, Federal Reserve, and FDIC oversight of certain duties to ensure adequate coverage of the issues that actually protect the banking system?

In reality, as will be covered in the next chapter, bank regulators need the lawmakers to step in and determine whether some secondary and tertiary "nice to have" priorities can come off the regulators' to-do lists. A prime example of a secondary issue is the Community Reinvestment Act dating back to the 1970s. When does it come off the table? Is it nice to have? Perhaps it is. Is it absolutely necessary? Maybe it was, but it is no longer. Every one of the duties and tasks of the regulatory community needs to be evaluated and considered for elimination unless it is truly vital to the safety and soundness of the banking system. In the same manner that regulators would expect a bank's risk management function to challenge the CEO, the bank examiners need to do the same and challenge Congress about its priorities. Even if Congress chooses not to back off, regulators need to make sure their focus is on the most critical assignment—protecting the banking system.

Does the 21st century require a more sophisticated, forward-looking measure of a bank's risks than the CAMELS ratings system currently provides?

Events of the past five years reveal a significant problem with the CAMELS ratings system. The system acts more like yesterday's thermostat than an early warning system. It is too judgmental and relies too much on old-fashioned on-site exams that are not only expensive to conduct but have not proven to work well during the two past crises. Before the financial crisis became obvious, too many banks continued to receive 222222 scores until failure was imminent. The CAMELS scores are a rearview mirror look at a bank. What is the forward or prospective view? Is it the total number of matters requiring attention (MRAs)? If so, is there a way to translate the more forward-looking MRAs back into the CAMELS score?

The Federal Reserve, OCC, and FDIC need to come together and charge an elite team of examiners and forward-thinking bankers with the responsibility for developing a next-generation CAMELS ratings system. The team should be comprised not only of "old school" subject-matter experts who embrace the value of on-site exams, but also quantitative-oriented examiners who are able to conduct sophisticated statistical analyses. Most critically, as demonstrated with the data provided in Chapter 5, fact-based, statistical analyses need to be conducted to identify root causes of the bank failures of 1985-1992 and 2008-2012.

Can regulators work together to create and maintain systemic early warning systems for large cities, regions, and states?

Early warning systems are common to many professions. Perhaps the best example is meteorology. One of the nation's most important websites is operated by the National Weather Service. They do a remarkable job predicting hurricanes, tornadoes, snow, and ice storms. Although an early warning system cannot be expected to prevent tragedy, it provides a cushion of time for citizens to take cover.

More than just key risk indicators (KRIs), an early warning system should consist of a dashboard of 10 to 15 metrics that allow federal regulators to track and routinely report systemic risks inherent to large metropolitan areas, states, and regions. Just to be clear, "systemic" refers to risks that cut across the industry and impact more than one bank. As seen during the financial crisis, unmitigated systemic risk can lead to a domino effect of bank failures.

Which 10X risk metrics should be part of the early warning systems for large metro areas, states, and regions? A comprehensive study of that question needs to be conducted, but what is known today is the "velocity" of banking across America. An example of a "velocity" metric is loan growth. As this book highlights, the FDIC is already producing valuable bank data. The Federal Reserve does a laudable job of meticulously gathering and analyzing macroeconomic information. Examples of the kind of data that could find their way to the early warning systems for metros, states, and regions are:

- Rate of new bank charter growth.
- Rate and trend of using "hot money" liabilities to fund banks in the market.
- Rate of growth in loan volume (highlighting key components like real estate).
- Employment trends and forecasts.
- Unique external event watch items (oil for the Southwest, weather and farming for the Midwest, etc.).
- Financial health trends for big cities, states, and the country. (The deteriorating government balance sheets and widening income-expense budget deficits could be the single greatest risk to banks over the next 15 years.)
- A "banker watch" report that asks bankers in the metros, states, and regions to assess risk trends across the markets they do business in.

Consider the advantages of having this kind of information available to bankers. First, banks will have a ready list of meaningful external event risks identified. Furthermore, bank management and boards can focus on ensuring their banks build appropriate monitoring, mitigation, and reporting to control for these risks. Of course, this list will not negate the need for banks to identify other issues. Second, by eliminating the guesswork from identifying critical systemic external event risks, bankers and regulators can quickly evaluate residual risk; residual risk is the risk left after banks take action to mitigate the inherent risk. Third, by driving transparency of the systemic external event risk in the market, bankers will be more assured competitors' directors are aware of risks; hopefully, a better-informed board will curb the risk appetites of dumb competitors before they can inflict tremendous damage across the market.

To be clear, the early warning system should "major in the majors." The system must not be bogged down in "nice to know" information not vital to the safety and soundness of the banking system. The great risk to the current bubble of regulatory scrutiny is that boards and management become so busy fixing current directives that they may not attend to the 10X risk issues covered by an early warning system.

Can the various regulatory agencies work together to create more sophisticated early warning systems to better assess the risk profiles of community and regional banks?

In American football, defensive teams can be penalized for piling on, an unsportsmanlike behavior that occurs when a defender jumps on an opposing player who is already down. If the financial crisis were a football game, a lot of flags would have been thrown for piling-on penalties. At the risk of being accused of piling on, one could find considerable value in analyzing the very sad and short life of Alpha Bank and Trust of Alpharetta, Georgia.

Alpha opened May 8, 2006, and attracted more initial investor dollars than any bank in Georgia's history. Despite or maybe because of the strong initial capital, the bank failed less than 900 days after it opened. What lessons can be learned from Alpha that could help regulators, directors, and bankers in the future? The FDIC wrote its material loss review of Alpha Bank in May 2009. About two-and-a-half years later, the FDIC filed a complaint against 11 former directors and officers of the banks.

The FDIC found that "Alpha's board of directors did not ensure that bank management identified, measured, monitored, and controlled" the bank's risks. The lawsuit accuses the defendants of failing to "exercise even slight care in the performance of their duties." Among board oversight failures, several stood out:

- Growth rates well beyond the original business plan submitted to the FDIC when the bank was formed.
- Lack of asset diversification.
- Over-reliance on hot brokered deposits.
- Lack of controls for risk management.
- Payout of bonuses contrary to the bank's bylaws.

As in many other bank failures, Alpha's strong early CAMELS ratings belied its rapidly increasing risk profile. The material loss review (MLR) notes that "after 11 months in operation, asset growth was nearly double the planned projections." Yet, the CAMELS ratings for April 2007 showed a 2 for composite score, a 2 for management, a 2 for liquidity, and a 1 for asset quality. At that time, 75% of the loans were concentrated in construction and development. It is interesting to note that the first draft of the April exam actually contained a score of 1 (superior) for the management rating, according to the MLR. The case manager for the April exam apparently dropped the rating to 2 after it became clear Alpha was growing much faster than planned.

Could the pain of the Alpha failure have been avoided or substantially reduced if the FDIC and the Georgia Department of Banking and Finance used timely, data-driven processes to closely monitor Alpha's increasing risk profile during its first few months in business? Clearly there is a place for judgmental supervision; however, in banking as in investing, history proves over and over again that certain laws of nature are not violated without consequences. Not only do trees not grow to the sky, they do not grow 100 feet high in six months. Quite simply, banks that grow fast are risky. New banks that grow fast are very risky.

It is possible for regulators and experienced bankers to develop a 10X risk heat map of five to 12 performance metrics that can act as an early warning system for regional and community banks of any age. Much like the racing car analogy, industry experts can identify unsafe bank speeds that indicate when the banks' risk profile has "redlined."

In addition to the rate of loan growth, examples include the number of bank acquisitions in a certain time frame; personnel turnover rates on the board, executive management, key lines of business, or overall employee base; growth rates in certain businesses (like mortgage lending) that are historically proven to be highly cyclical; loan concentration rates; brokered CD percentages; acquisitions that have the potential to "bet the bank"; and percentage of directors with no actual bank experience.

Bank directors must know the criteria regulators use for the early warning system. The system should be a common risk management tool for every bank's first (line of business executives), second (the risk management function), and third (audit) lines of defense to monitor and report. Finally, an effective early warning system must not depend on regulatory on-site exams.

Some bankers will complain they do not need to invest in such a system because they are already prudently managing the bank. In such cases, and there are many, the reality is that those bank managers and directors are already using such a system, but without the formality. If at some point they plan to sell the bank or buy another bank, a documented history of a "green" early warning system should give potential partners confidence in the bank's risk management processes and controls.

Can a better process or field test be created to evaluate bank management skills? Can regulators better define the skills and experience required of bank directors?

Perhaps there is no more critical need than a means by which all constituencies can be assured of the effectiveness of bank managers and directors. Judging by the findings from the MLRs, the regulatory process used to assess CAMELS management ratings in the 2000 to 2007 time period did not work as designed. Obviously, the assessment practice needs to be fixed. The simple fact that a CAMELS rating is not a forward-looking score is an obvious problem. Moreover, new and existing boards need to be evaluated and risk-rated for bank-specific experience and skill. Clearly there is more than enough hard data available to create quantitative risk scores based on management and board experience and bank successes and failures. The criteria must be transparent, easily understood, and not subject to high variability depending on the regulator.

Can the states and FDIC assure the banking community that new bank charters are evaluated consistently across the U.S.?

If only one thing is clear from this book, it should be that new banks are dangerous to the health of the industry. In an industry suffering from a shortage of skills and experience, new banks are prone to place inexperienced and unskilled people in positions of management and oversight. The barriers of entry into banking must become higher if the industry is to avoid the problems experienced in the 1980s and from 2000 to 2007. Just to be clear, the industry needs new banks; it just cannot afford many of them entering into business in a concentrated time.

The federal regulators need to take three other steps. First, it is difficult to imagine the FDIC is not now devoting some of its best supervisors to monitor new banks. Recent experience revealed that the FDIC had taken its eye off the task or thought the state banking commissioners were doing the work. The decision to expand the special oversight from three to five years makes sense provided it actually happens. And given the systemic risk implications, federal regulators need to assign highly experienced examiners to these new banks during their first five years in business. New banks are not the place for new examiners to cut their teeth.

Second, monitoring of new banks must evolve from the apparently once-a-year look back to a much more rigorous ongoing scrutiny. Once again, examiners need to avail themselves of 21st-century technology that provides ongoing and remote monitoring.

Third, in what should be a pattern for federal bank regulation going forward, reporting of new bank charter activity risk needs to be public and transparent. What does this mean? New banks pose a systemic external event risk to banks doing business in the new bank's market. Examiners need to be sure directors and managers of the existing banks fully comprehend the risk posed by new banks. In particular, existing banks in the market should be alert to dangerous and dumb actions by the new bank. Examples of such activities can include weak loan underwriting, poor pricing practices, and reckless compensation models. The reality is that incumbent banks will almost always see bad practices before regulators do. And when they do, they should be prepared to notify examiners.

How much variability exists in the skills and qualifications among bank examiners from the various state and federal agencies?

The banking industry needs to raise professional standards. The regulators can accelerate industry adoption by committing to a process for licensing examiners. Skills need to be certified through classroom or computer-based training and experience equivalent to apprenticeship through field experience.

Is it possible for the FDIC and OCC to make their websites easier to use?

The FDIC and OCC feature valuable information on their websites. The OCC's handbooks are great tools for bankers and directors. The problem is that the websites are clunky. It is not easy to quickly navigate the sites to find useful information. Both websites need to be reengineered with an eye on who uses them and for what purposes. For example, if I am a director of a $500 million bank, wouldn't it be great if I could go to the first page of the OCC website and click on a user button that immediately takes me to a page for users like me? In other words, why not set up the website with the users in mind? Such a page can highlight the most critical tools directors, CEOs, and CROs of banks of certain sizes need. And here is a really wild idea: The various regulators should combine their resources into a single site with easy access to all the information bankers and directors need to run a bank. Ideally, the websites should be an "open book" describing not only how banks are most effectively run, but how to pass regulatory exams. It is in everyone's interests to have banks pass exams; the websites should be a prime vehicle for helping banks to do so.

The next chapter raises questions for the regulators' bosses, the U.S. Congress and the president's Cabinet. The role of lawmakers in banking is sometimes underappreciated by bankers. Banking laws establish the ground rules for the industry. Usually bank laws make sense. Sometimes they do not, especially when Congress creates new rules and agencies while allowing old rules and agencies to hang on.

Questions for Lawmakers

First things first: Is Congress worried about the potential impact the U.S. debt and deficit could have on banks over the next eight years? Could the debt prove to be a 100X risk by 2020-2025?

The single greatest systemic risk threatening U.S. banks is the federal budget imbroglio. Open any newspaper and read about Spain's and Greece's banks. The good news is the U.S. is not Spain and Greece. The health of banks requires government to exercise strong fiscal management. The closer a nation gets to a fiscal cliff, the greater the systemic risk to its banks.

Scenario (or war games) analysis should begin now to prepare the banks for the increasing risk of weakened federal, state, and municipal balance sheets and income statements. Models need to be run for all banks that assume higher U.S. debt, lower U.S. debt ratings, a weaker U.S. dollar, higher inflation, higher gold prices, higher interest rates, and creditor-forced austerity. Banks that are already required to conduct stress tests can load assumptions like these into their models. Banks that are not required by regulators to do stress tests would be wise to run at least a back-of-the-envelope stress test that contemplates these potentially disruptive factors.

Is it time to start over and build a new house for bank oversight?

Four follow-up questions are:

- Is bank supervisory accountability always clear?
- Where does the buck stop in a dual system of state bank regulators and the FDIC/Federal Reserve Banks?
- How does Congress know for certain there is adequate regulatory expertise across such a fragmented supervisory system?
- Is it possible for other congressional priorities to get in the way of the highest priority of protecting the safety and soundness of the U.S. banking system?

The current system is an amalgamation of U.S. political history. The system is fragmented, and regulatory accountability is often unclear. U.S. banks are overburdened with multiple regulatory agencies. The problem is made worse today with the advent of yet another new regulator, the Consumer Financial Protection Bureau (CFPB). The dual system of federal and state oversight of the majority of U.S. banks is littered with thousands of bank

121

failures over the past 25 years. The variability in bank failure rates by state is so high that one can only conclude the supervisory processes overseeing state banks are highly inconsistent and, consequently, not reliable; as the protectors of the Bank Insurance Fund, the FDIC's risk managers know the score and they have to know its current supervisory processes are broken.

Congress and state legislators need to consider several questions:

- Is the current regulatory system well designed? Effective? Efficient?
- Is regulatory accountability crystal clear?
- What is the role of state bank regulators? How is the supervisory role of the state regulators different from the FDIC's supervisory role of the same banks?
- Other than political reasons, does the dual system of state and federal regulatory supervision make sense in the 21st century? Does the dual system contribute to role clarity and accountability issues?
- Should Congress design a comprehensive 21st-century framework for bank supervision?

The Financial Stability Oversight Council (FSOC) has the potential to be either the very best output from Dodd-Frank or the worst; it will be closely monitored in its first two years by Congress. In the best case, it gets off quickly to a good start and demonstrates the ability to create a coordinated, forward-looking, preemptive-strike organization that monitors and controls for 10X industry-wide risks. In the worst case, its 10 members are rivals, decisions are political, and accountability is simply further diffused. If the worst case proves true, we could see the unintended consequence of not only an ineffective FSOC, but less effective member agencies.

To ensure clear accountability and to avoid inconsistency and charter shopping, should there be one regulator in the U.S. responsible for supervising community and regional banks? Could that regulator also cover their cousins, the S&Ls and credit unions?

Would not accountability be crystal clear if one federal agency supervised the safety and soundness of all U.S. regional and community banks, savings banks, S&Ls, and credit unions? Would not accountability for approving all new bank, savings bank, S&L, and credit union charters be made indisputably clear? Could this agency also be responsible for supervising vital suppliers of services to regional and community banks, savings banks, S&Ls, and credit unions?

Should the FDIC directly supervise banks and also act as the insurer of banks? Is the FDIC conflicted in having to perform both roles? If the FDIC were strictly an insurance function, would it be more effective in acting as a check and balance to the federal and state agencies directly accountable for supervision?

In the current construct, where the FDIC acts as both a direct supervisor as well as reviewer of the regulator charged to oversee state banks, how is it possible the FDIC is not conflicted? If the U.S. dedicated one regulator to supervise community and regional banks, assuming it was not the FDIC, could the FDIC act as an independent check and balance against the supervisor when acting in its critical capacity of overseer for the

Deposit Insurance Fund? Given the risks charter shopping creates, should the National Credit Union Share Insurance Fund (NCUSIF) be under the FDIC?

What should be the goals of a new bank supervision framework? First, it should eliminate dual coverage for bank supervision; consequently, roles and accountability are clear. Second, it could eliminate the ability of financial institutions to charter shop. Third, although it could possibly eliminate the FDIC's direct supervision of banks, it could also eliminate the FDIC's conflict of interest when it (or more precisely, the FDIC Office of Inspector General) reviews failed banks, many of which are banks the FDIC had been accountable for supervising. Fourth, it could eliminate the high variability of supervision that is unavoidable when the nation has 50 disparate state bank regulators in addition to the federal supervisors.

Is it time to call into question whether a 19th-century invention of state bank supervision is the best way to oversee community banks in the 21st century? To be clear, there are hundreds of excellent bank regulators across the states. No better evidence exists than the 2012 appointment of the former head of the Massachusetts Division of Banks to the top leadership job in the OCC. In addition, the former North Carolina Banking Commissioner is now administering the nationwide mortgage settlement. Both Massachusetts and North Carolina have strong records of bank supervision. The problem, however, is that state performance is so variable and unpredictable that it begs for the need to drive consistent nationwide standards. Could qualified state regulators be folded into federal bank oversight roles and given accountability for driving out a consistent supervision of banks in the U.S.?

By the way, European nations appear to be moving to a single bank regulator structure. It is unimaginable that the United States of Europe will have a more coherent bank regulatory structure than does the United States of America. But it's about to happen.

What can be learned from Texas and Canada? Should the U.S. impose tighter credit underwriting standards on first mortgages, second mortgages, and home equity lines of credit?

Does not common sense suggest that good home-lending guidelines should be written into national law to avoid putting families in the positions millions have been in for the past five-plus years? As a credit trainee, I was taught in 1980 and 1981 the Robert Morris Associates' (now The Risk Management Association) five Cs of good credit underwriting. Time has proven over and over again that sound principles of lending—such as loan to value (LTV) and debt payments to income ratios—are foundational to maintaining sound banking. First and second mortgages as well as HELOCs require greater industry-wide commitment to prudent underwriting. The best way to do this is to do as Texas and Canada have done and set industry standards. However, in return for this greater regulation, lawmakers need to think through which existing regulations and regulatory costs can come off the table in light of these changes.

Did the Financial Crisis Inquiry Commission really address the issues of community and regional banks? Could the U.S. form a banking version of the Bowles-Simpson Commission that could focus on the banking activities (include regulations) conducted by community and regional banks?

Capitol Hill devotes enormous energy to banking. However, as documented in the 500-plus pages of the Financial Crisis Inquiry Commission report, almost all that energy is focused on the megabanks and GSEs and their esoteric activities. In the meantime, the basic blocking and tackling of good old-fashioned banking is receiving inadequate attention. There is not enough appreciation for the significant unintended consequences associated with rules and regulations that are bleeding into mainstream commercial banking. Nor is there enough appreciation in Washington for the challenges community banks face in achieving adequate profitability without over-relying on various forms of commercial real estate lending. Also, it is time to conduct a thorough analysis of the cost and benefit of regulations like CRA. Regarding CRA specifically, it would be helpful if the Federal Reserve chairman updated the comments he gave on March 30, 2007, regarding the "evolution and new challenges" of CRA. CRA must be called into question and it would be helpful to learn the Federal Reserve's current perspective on it. My current view: CRA was needed in the last century; it is no longer needed in the 21st century. Give the bankers some regulatory relief; accept that CRA worked as intended and can now go away.

> Is it not time to engage bankers from community and regional banks in constructing a better banking system for these banks?

Surely not all bankers are evil. Not all bankers put personal greed above the needs of their nation. There are bankers like Old Man Mueller. Can anything good come from a political process that ostracizes bankers? History today does not remember Elbridge G. Spaulding. Back in 1861 and 1862, President Lincoln and Treasury Secretary Chase were desperate to finance the war effort. If not for Congressman Spaulding—a banker from Buffalo—it is possible the National Banking Act of 1863 would not have become a reality. How many bankers are there in Congress today? Who are the real experts on banking in Congress? Is it a political appointee who never made a loan or supervised a bank? If congressional aides are the experts, what are their backgrounds? Were they bankers? Is it a big-time management consultant who actually never underwrote or collected a loan? Is it an academic who never managed a bank P&L? Banking is an easy business if you are not a banker. Yes, there is certainly a place for academics, consultants, and political appointees. But there ought to be a few practitioners at the table too.

One final thought: If Congress chooses to engage bankers, it should avoid the temptation to rely solely on the nation's highly paid and highly profiled CEOs as the single source of expertise for the industry. Yes, they bring a critical eye on the future, but they are not alone in having good ideas for moving the nation's banks forward. Main Street bankers will bring perspectives that the nation needs too.

> What role does and should Congress exercise over bank director selection? Can Congress require that bank directors be truly qualified to serve on a bank board?

Congress does not need to intervene in director selection. Shareholders of banks with unskilled and underskilled directors need to step up and demand better board representation.

But if banks continue to fail because of weak bank directors, when should Congress intervene? Bank governance cannot continue to operate like it did in the 1950s when the community-minded local landscaper found himself on the bank board. Directors require specific banking knowledge and skills. The OCC needs to update its description of director qualifications. If the FDIC and state banking commissions continue to approve under-qualified directors, should the FDIC be permitted to pursue those individuals and banks through the court system? Are there any lessons learned from ERISA laws that defined fiduciary responsibilities and required certification by actuaries? If investors must contractually acknowledge their net worth, skill, and experience to engage in certain kind of investments, does it not make sense that bank directors acknowledge and document their skill and experience to be on a bank board? Should bank directors sign disclosures written by the FDIC acknowledging the risks associated with failures of bank governance?

Do you remember Husband Kimmel and Walter Short?

Husband E. Kimmel was the four-star admiral in charge of the U.S. Pacific Fleet on December 7, 1941. Major General Walter Short of the U.S. Army was responsible for defending Pearl Harbor on December 7, 1941. Within 10 days of the attack, Short and Kimmel were demoted and disgraced. Some people might have argued in 1941 that if Short and Kimmel were not punished severely, other admirals and generals would think they too could get away with egregious errors in judgment. The reality is Kimmel and Short did not stand alone in failing to prepare for a massive, unprovoked, and totally unexpected attack. The system broke down. The nation was not vigilant. Early warning indicators were disregarded or lightly regarded. The leaders—all the way to the office of President Roosevelt—failed to ensure that the Navy and Army were properly led in the days leading to war.

Contrast the treatment of Kimmel and Short with the people being sued by the FDIC for neglecting their duties as board members of small banks. It seems puzzling how the FDIC can take these people to court when in many cases the FDIC itself not only approved their appointments but also repeatedly provided them with CAMELS reports stating their banks were in good shape. Is there evidence the states' banking commissions and the FDIC took reasonable measures to ensure inexperienced directors gained sufficient skills to exercise their roles effectively? Truly, what possible good can come from suing negligent landscapers who had no clue what they had signed up for when they became bank directors?

When Pearl Harbor was attacked on the day that lives in infamy, Kimmel was there. As he looked out his office window as the attack began early that Sunday morning, he ripped off his shoulder board of four stars, acknowledging culpability. When a .50 caliber machine gun bullet crashed through the window within feet of where Kimmel stood, he reportedly said: "It would have been more merciful had it killed me." No, it was not necessary to sue him. Unless directors committed fraud or embezzled money, it's time to stop suing landscapers who had no business being on a bank board in the first place.

P A R T

5

Moving
Forward

2020: Potential "Long Tail" 10X Risk Scenarios

Never make predictions, especially about the future.

—CASEY STENGEL, LATE YANKEES AND METS MANAGER

Probably the best-known professional predictor is Nostradamus, whose reputation rests on his supposed ability to anticipate future events. What makes a good predictor?

The answer has less to do with the quality of the predictions than with the quality of the public relations effort behind the predictor. "Nostradamus" was born in France in 1503; his real name was Michel de Nostredame. When he switched jobs from medical doctor to "seer," he rebranded himself as Nostradamus. He made his living writing almanacs packed with predictions. Not bad work if you can get it. He marketed well, even gaining the attention and support of King Henry II's court. His first almanac sold so well that he decided to write more. In the end he produced 6,338 predictions. A few proved true.

Bankers, despite Casey Stengel's admonition, must make predictions, but the good news for bankers is that we do not need to call them predictions. We call them "scenarios." And like Monsieur de Nostredame, bankers need to identify hundreds, if not thousands, of potential scenarios that may possibly prove true.

To understand why bankers need to evaluate scenarios, it is useful to reconsider reversion to the mean, a risk management tool used to understand probabilities of future events. The mean is a central value around which most potential future events cluster. All tools have limitations. In the case of reversion to the mean, the limitation is the risk manager's tendency to over-rely on the normal distribution of potential events. The risk manager who is prepared for 99% of all events is exposed to a rare one in 100 events.

A bell-shaped curve is a traditional way for statisticians to depict the normal distribution of probabilities. Probabilities that are rare and unexpected fall outside the "fat" bell; they fall along the "long tail" of the bell. Human minds are not well conditioned to imagine and prepare for unexpected "long tail" events. Scenario analysis is a deliberate attempt to force bankers to think outside the box of conventional thinking. The purpose of this chapter is to offer potential scenarios for the banking world in 2020.

Looking Backward was the third most-sold book in America in 1887. Written by Edward Bellamy, the book is the story of a Rip Van Winkle-like character who wakes up in Boston in the year 2000. Bellamy's description of 2000 missed the mark in a lot of ways. Perhaps the greatest value of Bellamy's book was in providing fodder for the people of 1887 to discuss the kind of world they wanted for their great-great-grandchildren.

Consider my thoughts as fodder for debate about the kind of banking world the U.S. needs in the year 2020. The scenarios listed below are not all going to occur. Maybe none of them will prove true. The real value in this exercise is to provide directors, CEOs, risk managers, and bank investors with a set of potential scenarios that could shape how they manage risk over the next eight years.

Each idea listed below is a potential scenario analysis topic. At the risk of being as wrong about 2020 as Bellamy was about 2000, below are listed my concluding observations and "long tail" predictions.

The scenarios that follow are organized into five parts: Big Picture, Bankers, Directors, Regulators, and Lawmakers. Each has five scenarios, except the last, which has four.

2020: The Big Picture

In 2020 the greatest threat to the health of the banking industry will be government (federal, states, local) deficits and debt. Years of kicking the can down the road will mean the banking industry in 2020 faces challenges across several fronts. At some point even the Federal Reserve runs out of quantitative easing magic. Medicare and Social Security in 2020 are real problems, not future ones. Scores of municipalities and possibly even some states could find themselves cut off from capital markets. Heated debates currently flashing across Europe—recession-inducing austerity vs. expanded government deficit spending—will reach our shores in the near future. Even the most ardent Keynesians will throw in the towel if years of government spending prove insufficient to jump-start the economy to reverse deficits and cut debt. As long as one political party objects to raising taxes and another one objects to cutting spending, the only hope is that the economy will grow its way out of its looming crisis. So what are the chances that might happen? How great must the growth rate in GDP be to actually achieve the growth solution to government debt and deficits? Smart banks will consider these questions in 2013, not 2020.

Expect to see significant bank consolidation in "big banking" states with strong banks led by savvy CEOs and boards that understand risk-adjusted profitability. The most likely states with the greatest consolidation will be the 10 states with more than 3,500 combined banks: Iowa, Kansas, Minnesota, Ohio, Missouri, Illinois, Texas, Oklahoma, Pennsylvania, and Wisconsin. In strong banking states like Iowa and Oklahoma, consolidation will be driven by several forces. The first is the aging population of broadly trained and experienced bank CEOs. Boards will realize that replacing this population of Era 2 and early Era 3 CEOs will prove difficult. A second force is the higher costs incurred from greater regulatory burdens tied to the Public Utility Era. Especially during the next couple of years of expected low interest rates (driven by the Federal Reserve), spread income will be difficult to achieve. Not only will big banks cut costs, so will smaller banks. The problem for smaller banks is there is only so much fat to cut before the only real alternative is to merge with other banks facing the same problem. The third factor driving consolidation will be what I call herd instincts. Once a few banks in states like Iowa and Nebraska sell out, more banks will follow. If a few highly respected bank CEOs in these states sell out, expect to see other bankers follow. Do not expect to see acquiring banks pay rich premiums. Sellers will outnumber buyers. Profits will be driven mainly by disciplined purchase prices and tight management of expenses.

Expect to see far fewer banks in the states that experienced the most new bank formation between 2000 and 2007: Georgia, Colorado, Washington, Nevada, Florida, North Carolina, South Carolina, Alabama, and Virginia. Data in this book suggest that overall bank profits are higher in states that monitor and control new bank formation. The corollary is that consolidation will improve profitability provided new bank formation rates are tepid. As one former community bank CEO indicated to me recently, "Community banks are sold, not bought." Plenty of bank boards in states where there has been the most pain are eager to sell. The personal risk-reward trade-off for many bank directors is not compelling. Given a worst-case possibility of bank failure (and getting personally sued by the FDIC) and making maybe $5,000 to $40,000 a year as a bank director, in the Public Utility Era more directors will choose to sell the bank. North Carolina had the fourth highest new bank formation rate from 2000 to 2007. The state is already seeing a spike in bank sales. Based on banks sold recently, it appears sellers no longer define success by how much premium is earned over book value, but by how little haircut is taken from book value.

Expect to see the emergence nationwide of 50 to 100 highly acquisitive community bank holding companies and banks. If there is to be industry consolidation, there must be buyers for all the boards eager to sell. Thankfully, there appear to be buyers. For example, in North Carolina, former bankers from Bank of America, Wachovia, and RBC have formed at least five organizations intent on growing through acquisition. Expect to see one or two become quite successful at building a lean, profitable franchise through mergers. Piedmont Community Bank Holdings, CertusHoldings, and Capital Bank are backed with private equity money. Although their strategies differ modestly, each is determined to grow through acquisition. In addition to the three privately held holding companies, two publicly held North Carolina banks have expressed similar acquisition goals: FNB United of Asheboro and Park Sterling Bank of Charlotte.

It is instructive to examine these two banks because they give several clues as to the acquirers' strategies. FNB United (symbol FNBN, market cap of $260 million in mid-October 2012) has two significant owners, each holding nearly 25% of the stock: Carlyle and Oak Hill. Its executive management and board are nearly all Wachovia and Bank of America alumni. The other bank is Park Sterling (symbol PSTB, market cap of $168 million). The bank's management team is comprised almost entirely of former Wachovia senior managers. This should come as no surprise since three of the seven board members have a Wachovia pedigree, including the chairman, who was actually the former CEO and chairman of Wachovia Bank prior to its sale to First Union. The other four board members include a former CEO of the Virginia Bankers Association, the CEO of an investment advisory firm, a former Federal Reserve SVP, and a lawyer whose specialty is mergers and acquisitions. Review of Park Sterling's shareholder presentations reveals a bank with clear plans to acquire banks in growth markets in Virginia and North and South Carolina. Go to www.parksterling.com and find investor presentations that lay out a crystal-clear path of how the bank plans to grow. These banks will be interesting to watch over the next couple of years, as their fortunes are likely to define community and regional banking for the next quarter of a century. Also worth watching is the role of private equity investors in banks; most will be stern taskmasters.

Expect to see publicly held banks with tired and/or lower-skilled boards of directors sell first. In contrast to the five North Carolina-based acquiring banks with experienced bankers, private equity investors, former regulators, and bank lawyers on their boards, there are still thousands of banks in the U.S. lacking such talent. The acquirers will be banks with confident, skilled, and experienced directors who have a P&L road map for the future. The sellers will be made up of two groups. One is just plain tired. The other includes the banks lacking breadth and depth of needed skills and experience on their boards. The financial crisis is a rude wake-up call to all bank boards, not just those in markets like North Carolina, where the average publicly held community bank experienced a 78% drop in stock price from January 31, 2007, to January 31, 2012. The sellers of banks in North Carolina and elsewhere in the Southeast during 2012 have been banks comprised of Era One-type bank directors. Even though these directors are smart people and no doubt experts in their fields (real-life examples include transportation, property management, biopharmaceuticals, hospital administration, plastics, general accounting, educational software, and cardiology), they have come to realize banking is different. Smart Era 1 directors will cut their losses and sell or work hard to acquire more talent on their boards. Most likely, directors of publicly held banks will move faster to sell than those whose shares are not public. The reason: The scoreboard (i.e., the stock price) is public to everyone. Unlike nonpublic banks, directors of publicly held banks have no choice but to face reality. Consequently, they will put their banks up for sale before the privately held banks do.

Bankers in 2020

Visionary community and regional bank CEOs will lead the industry charge to establish standards and require certifications. A few strong and influential bankers from community and regional banks will pull together and establish CPA-like requirements for certain risk-taking jobs and risk-protecting jobs. Like in the years after the Great Depression, the financial crisis will produce a generation of bankers with a deep respect for cautious and prudent risk management. Rather than wait for regulators to tell them what to do, bankers will set new standards for self-policing the industry. One or more of the industry associations—The Risk Management Association, American Bankers Association, or Consumer Bankers Association—will play a key role in this effort and grow in influence between now and 2020. Regional banking schools will experience a surge in training activity from 2014 to 2018.

Respected CEOs will speak to stakeholders about risk-adjusted profitability. Respect for clearly established risk appetites will translate into more sophisticated analysis of risk-adjusted profitability. A few leading CEOs will establish goals for ROE and ROA based on clearly communicated measures of risk tolerance and appetite. Investors will welcome the change as it will allow for better investment management. CEOs of these leading community and regional banks will speak about return and risk tolerance in the same sentence of their letters to shareholders. CEO presentations to shareholders about target bank profitability will include discussions about historical and projected volatility of earnings tied to various financial scenarios. Banks that lead the move to risk-adjusted profitability metrics will be rewarded with higher price/earnings ratios. Some investors will appreciate a 10% ROE with low volatility over periodically higher ROEs coupled with periodically devastatingly low ROEs.

By 2020, some community banks will reduce risk by cutting back credit concentration through cooperative arrangements with peer banks. Arguably the biggest advantage a large regional bank has over community banks is its broader diversification of risk. Much of the risk mitigation enjoyed by large regionals comes from credit portfolios that are better diversified not just geographically but also by loan type. Community banks often struggle not only with geographic concentrations, but also with insufficient scale to gear up for consumer lending activity. In the future, community banks will discover efficient and risk-effective ways to pool resources in order to benefit from geographic diversification and build the scale needed to promote consumer credit loan programs.

Banks of all sizes will experience a shift from fixed to variable labor. By 2020 banks will use temporary and part-time labor as a much higher percentage of their total labor expenses. Four forces will work together over the next eight years to create a long-term shift in how banks (and other industries) employ workers and get work done. First, the supply of highly skilled bankers and directors will remain tight for the foreseeable future; one way banks will combat this challenge is by entering into short-term engagements with consulting firms and individual contractors with specific skills. Second, cost pressures will lead bank boards and management to evaluate and use new ways to control fixed labor costs, which represented 50% of most banks' total expenses in 2012. Third, although traditional consulting firms will continue to do quite well in the years ahead, expect to see staffing companies develop cost-effective means for smaller banks to gain access to deep subject-matter experts in areas like strategy, risk management, scenario analyses, compliance, policies, marketing, relationship-building, reporting, and regulations. Fourth, after years of cutbacks in full-time employment, a higher percentage of the U.S. workforce will be accustomed to life as "permanent" temporary workers. The trend in America to higher percentages of variable labor will not peak until closer to 2050.

Operational and strategic risk management will improve significantly across the banking industry. Directors will shape risk cultures by ensuring careful attention to both the operational and strategic risk management disciplines. Operational risk management will be viewed as a foundational requirement for all banks. However, unlike the megabanks that are subject to AMA (advanced measurement approaches) for determining capital allocations, non-AMA banks have the huge advantage of not having to devote time to expensive and sometimes unproductive exercises of AMA capital legerdemain.

Instead, community and regional banks will use operational risk management to develop the foundational blocking and tackling discipline of prudent management of material risks associated with people, processes, systems, and external events.

Directors in 2020

Expect to see serious director attrition problems compounded by the severe challenge of persuading new directors to join bank boards. As a backlash to bank problems and especially FDIC lawsuits against directors, many community banks in the nation's worst performing banking states will experience major problems staffing their boards of directors. Smart business people lacking backgrounds in banking increasingly recognize that the risk-reward trade-off is often unappealing. No longer do directors enjoy the intangible benefit of stature traditionally associated with being on a bank board. The inability to retain and attract qualified directors will drive some boards to post for-sale signs on their banks. However, not all banks that want to sell will find willing buyers at virtually any price. Consequently, some banks will be seriously challenged to meet regulatory expectations for director oversight. It is possible some banks will close simply for lack of having directors in place. To remediate the problem, wise directors will expect their banks to provide access to formal bank director training. If the problem of retention gets too bad, do not be surprised to see bank regulators in some cases issue commitments to not sue directors who agree to certain fair and reasonable stipulations in the exercise of their director duties.

Prepare to see a new breed of professional bank director enter the industry who works for three to five banks. To respond to a shortage of qualified bank directors, truly independent, professional bank directors will emerge from the financial crisis. These individuals will be qualified to direct banks in Era 5 based on long and varied careers across bank management, bank law, bank accounting, and bank supervisory oversight. Some will lead the drive for director certification. They will invest considerable time in ongoing training provided by bank schools, associations, and new for-profit businesses formed for this purpose. By the year 2020, there will probably be 1,000 to 1,500 directors who work in three to five banks. None of the banks in which these directors work will compete against each other. However, because of their banking acumen, these individuals will influence the institutions they direct to think differently about risk and return. Not only will they bring a stricter, by-the-book risk management mind-set to their banks, but some will also bring novel business models for diversifying and expanding earning assets in community banks. Banks with headquarters in certain locations like resort and college communities will enjoy a competitive advantage in attracting this new breed of bank director. Consequently, these banks will gain access to strong board talent at below-market cost. Smart banks will move quickly to attract the new breed of professional bank director, and since the supply is finite not all banks will have access to them.

New compensation models will evolve for bank directors. The current Era 1 Potemkin Village director model is broken and will change significantly over the next few years. In today's community banks, there are two kinds of director pay models. One is for the directors who have very significant ($1 million plus) personal investment in the bank; in their cases, their payoff is from expected price appreciation in the value of their stock. (Many have learned that this model does not always work as planned.) In almost all community banks, no more than two or three directors fit this equity appreciation model. The much more common model is a variation of the hourly pay model. Individuals who are compensated this way are community leaders who have been persuaded to join the board by the bank's CEO and big shareholders. They make anywhere from $5,000 to as much as $45,000 a year serving as directors of community banks. In most cases, the combined annual pay of all directors—cash and, in rare cases, equity—amounts to about the total annual pay of the bank CEO. This model is a quintessential Era 1 practice, effectively treating board work like paid volunteer work. It is remarkable it has lasted this long. This quasi-volunteer model is ineffective in attracting the talent required to meet bank director duties.

Expect to see director compensation evolve to three tiers. The highest paid will be highly qualified bank chairmen who have the ability to shop their skills to any bank across the country. These people will be deep subject-matter experts in banking, regulation, and risk management, and well connected with industry leaders. Even though they may not be full time, in some cases they will earn total compensation approaching 50% of that earned by the bank CEO. Higher compensation will be more common in cases where the bank clearly has a less-seasoned CEO who will benefit from greater mentoring. The second tier of director compensation will be for professional directors who have significant banking experience and skills. To coax highly qualified individuals to take on director roles, banks will find it necessary to pay them higher rates. In return, the bank will have highly skilled directors who invest considerable time and energy going to director training and meeting in industry groups to review banking issues. Depending on the bank, compensation for these individuals could be $25,000 to $80,000 per year. Expect banks to pay top dollar for such talent. The third tier of the compensation model will be for traditional directors who are experts in their local communities, but lack the experience and skills of the new breed of directors. These individuals will be paid at roughly the same rates their banks currently pay directors. Although a few will resent the pay scale differences, most will appreciate the risk mitigation associated with having highly skilled fellow directors. Finally, to offset the higher director costs, do not be surprised if board size in many community banks shrinks to between five and seven directors.

The public utility era for banking will produce highly engaged shareholders who will "take over" some banks. Among the greatest challenges facing directors of public banks will be shareholder activism. Some bank boards will resist the activism. Some will pay lip service to it. The best will develop new models for shareholders to influence the banks they own. New and emerging shareholder rights will create a special challenge for underperforming publicly held banks. Do not be surprised to see Congress create laws that provide shareholders with greater rights. Also, for the 50 to 100 privately held acquiring banks, expect no-nonsense private equity shareholders to wield considerable direct influence over management.

Some regional bank boards will struggle to determine what kind of bank they want to be over the next eight years. The best regional bank boards will ask themselves if they are adequately skilled to exercise their role of independent challenge. The good news: These boards will find very significant opportunities to acquire banks. Like the nation's exist-ing SIFIs, they will face greater regulatory and public scrutiny as they grow in size and influence. Prudent regional bank boards will ask themselves if they want to be a SIFI. Some will deliberately tap on the brakes of expansion. Some CEOs of regional banks will find it difficult to resist the temptation to become SIFIs; enticed by bigger pay and more prominent national profiles, some of these CEOs could find themselves at odds with a growing number of their directors. Expect to see the composition of a few regional bank boards change significantly as some existing directors determine the need to replace themselves with real banking experts. However, as long as directors of regional banks continue to be paid $140,000 to $280,000 per year, they will be tempted to persuade themselves that "our bank is different" and "we do not need directors who are actual bank experts." Until their bank is under the kind of pressure seen at RBS, Citibank, or Wachovia, do not expect to see regional bank boards vote themselves out of such well-paying part-time jobs.

Regulators in 2020

By 2020 bank regulation will be less fragmented and not as messy as it is today. Perhaps wishful thinking, some will say. The driving force is not what you might expect. Just as it took the Civil War to build a national banking system in 1863, in the next eight years the war on debt and deficit will force politicians to deal with the reality that the current bank supervision structure is not only antiquated but grossly inefficient and uneconomical. A tidal wave of re-alpolitik will hit America late in this decade. The force will be akin to the socio-political forces behind Salmon P. Chase's and Abraham Lincoln's creation of the Office of the Comptroller of the Currency. As a result, a future high-powered Bowles-Simpson Deficit Commission will investigate wasteful government spending. For the first time in the history of the United States, bank supervision will be examined comprehensively and not piecemeal. Politics as usual will give way to a new reality (imposed by the Chinese?) that the U.S. must change its ways. The scrutiny of bank supervision costs will result in a dramatic reduction in wasteful overlaps and role-clarity problems. By 2020 a new, simpler model for bank supervi-sion will be in place. Community and regional banks will have a single domestic regulator fo-cused exclusively on their activities. The U.S. will design this new regulator by studying the Office of the Superintendent of Financial Institutions (OSFI) in Canada. SIFIs will have their own regulator integrally connected with Basel and other nations' regulators who oversee global banks. SIFIs will be defined not only by size but also complexity. Banks with broker-dealer operations will all be defined as complex and supervised as a SIFI. A third regulator will cross both the SIFIs and the community/regional banks to oversee the banks' compli-ance with quasi-police activities such as AML. The good news about the advent of this new regulator is that it comes with the shuttering of many other regulators. In addition, it will allow the two bank supervisors to attend to 10X risk and not be distracted by compliance is-sues that, although important to society, do not cause banks to fail.

Federal bank regulators will face a shortage of seasoned bank examiners. Speaking of government deficits and government debt, bank supervisors can and do retire in their mid-50s after 30 to 35 years of service. Their pension plans assure them of 75-80% of their final years' pay plus full access to the federal government's best-in-class medical insurance program. Exacerbating the retention issue is the opportunity regulators have to consult the very banks they once supervised. Go to www.calculatedriskblog.com and read some of the regulator enforcement actions. You will see regulators currently require some banks with enforcement actions to hire an approved consultant to independently assure the regulators that the bank is addressing problems identified in the actions. Who better to act as bank-to-regulator go-between than a consulting firm comprised of former bank regulators? Who blames a retirement-eligible bank examiner for retiring and going to work as a consultant? The numbers are compelling: Why would anyone work for $25,000 to $40,000 a year (the difference between current regulator pay and retirement pay) when they can make an incremental $50,000 to $250,000 a year working part-time or full-time as a consultant? Ironically, because demand for bank consultants with regulatory experience is so great, the challenge of retention is exacerbated. Further irony, unless the state bank examiners are folded into a single national bank regulator, federal regulators will solve their problem by hiring former skilled commercial and investment bankers to work as bank examiners. Unlike their government counterparts who have lucrative pensions, after the financial crisis many bankers have seen their retirement assets wiped out (and politicians want to talk about pay at risk?). The "good news" is that these bankers will need work. There is precedent for bank regulators hiring former bankers. Back in the early 1990s, the Resolution Trust Corporation hired an army of former bankers to clean up the post-crisis mess.

U.S. bank regulators will be especially challenged in the supervision of technology. Technology is evolving so fast that regulators will be challenged to attract and retain the personnel capable of monitoring the rapidly changing nature of this risk. Through 2012 no banks have failed from a system's 10X risk. However, since many community banks outsource virtually all technology to key suppliers, systems risk has become a systemic risk. The failure or near-failure of systems suppliers could create systemic risk for community banks. Because the systems risks are so complex and the potential for failure is still not well understood, expect to see regulators require banks to make extensive use of scenario analyses to evaluate the full spectrum of potential risks associated with technology. In the absence of a deep bench of in-house experts, regulators may find it necessary to engage independent consultants to play this role. Likely this work will not come cheap given the shortage of talent available to do it.

U.S. bank regulators will develop an entire division to monitor suppliers to banks. As U.S. banks rely more on suppliers and temporary workers to address systems and technology requirements, between 2013 and 2020 regulators will develop an organization or possibly a new interagency effort with clear and direct accountability for managing systems suppliers. Expect the new organization to embed examiners in the offices of the key suppliers. The precipitating event may be a systems or process failure by a key supplier to multiple banks.

CRA does not celebrate a 40th anniversary. For those who do not recall their Community Reinvestment Act history, it goes back to 1977. A new president will be elected in 2016 who pledges to cut costs. The following year CRA will be dramatically pared down. Using data from the Federal Reserve, the president will proclaim CRA "did the job and is no longer needed." Congress will sign off.

Lawmakers in 2020

Two issues will dominate social, political, and economic life in 2020. The first is the politics of debt and deficits. Related to the first issue, the second issue may be containment of inflation and associated high interest rates. For bankers with strong core deposits, initially the higher interest rates will be welcomed. Profits will improve as a benefit of the long-awaited improvement in net interest margin tied to a normal yield curve. On the other hand, as in the late 1970s and early 1980s interest rates will reach a point so high that normal commerce like buying and selling a home is impeded. For federal, state, and local governments, the higher interest rates will bring higher debt service; higher-cost debt will create even greater budgetary challenges.

The perceived failure of Republicans and Democrats to fix the deficit and debt will produce a legitimate third party in America. By 2020 the nation will engage in a war on debt and deficits with an acrimonious spirit not seen in America since Vietnam. A third political party will emerge and assume leadership for the movement. Over the next eight years, there will be a growing perception that the countries' two political parties protect the status quo and are unable to solve the war on debt and deficits. Both parties, but especially the Republicans, will see massive defections of party loyalty. Independent voters who represent a third to 40% of voters today will represent more than half the nation's voters by 2020. Voters in the 22-39 age bracket will gain enormous political influence as the younger generation grows exasperated with problems they believe were created but not solved by their elders.

The U.S. will have two classes of older Americans, and this will develop into a contentious socioeconomic issue for the country for the next 30 years. The aging baby boomers will be divided into the haves and have-nots. The have-nots will represent roughly half the baby boomers by 2030 and will be dependent on the government. The have-nots and younger Americans will challenge whether generous pensions being paid to retired municipal, state, and federal workers are moral and just at a time when public education and other services must be cut back to balance budgets.

Many states and municipalities struggle mightily in 2020 with debt burden. As difficult as federal debt and deficit spending will be over the next eight years, even more challenging will be the financial problems that some state and municipal governments will experience.

Common Sense: Four Ideas to Fix Basic Banking in America

A merican history does not give Thomas Paine his due. If you can read only one biography of a founding father this year, Craig Nelson's brilliant 2006 story of the life and times of Paine—*Thomas Paine: Enlightenment, Revolution, and the Birth of Modern Nations*—would make an excellent choice.

Paine's 40-page pamphlet, *Common Sense*, was published in January 1776. Influenced by Enlightenment philosophers, Paine wrote that "Society in every state is a blessing, but government even in its best state, is but a necessary evil." Paine flamed the passions of revolution. In a fledgling nation of 3 million people, one in 10 purchased a copy of *Common Sense*. General George Washington's troops reportedly read the pamphlet on the eve of great battles. It is not hyperbole to suggest that without Paine there might not have been an American Revolution. Too bad Paine is not around today to help sort out our nation's broken banking system. We need a revolution in common sense.

This final chapter offers four common sense ideas for fixing banking in America. Now is the time to major in the majors and not get lost in details and numbers.

Many Americans forget that not all colonists supported revolution and separation from Mother England. The Tories, loyal to the Crown, had no interest in challenging the status quo. In the eyes of the Tories—estimated to be 20% of the colonists—revolutionaries like Paine were dangerous.

America's banking system has its share of Tories. Protectors of the status quo, the Tories of banking fight off new ideas like a body cell warding off an invading virus. The Tories of banking acknowledge our system's flaws—they are always, by the way, someone else's fault—but refuse to accept any blueprint for fixing the broken banking system that threatens their coveted role in the status quo.

What follows are four common sense ideas. Tories beware.

Bankers Need Formal Training and Licensing

No bank is an island. Good banks and bad ones drink from the same community well. Let a bad banker poison the well, and good banks suffer too. Bankers and directors have to protect the water supply. Too often, failed and problem banks lack experienced, skilled directors and management. Our reality is that there are a finite number of experienced professionals capable of running and overseeing America's 7,246 banks.

The average community and regional bank CEO today is 57.8 years old; 40% are 60 years of age or older. By 2020, many of these CEOs will have retired. Unfortunately, the pipeline of successors to today's CEOs is beginning to run dry. The industry is now paying the price for not training bankers in the 1990s, when bank consolidation caused CEOs to focus more on cost cutting than next-generation talent development.

Is there any question why the industry is in bad shape? Common sense should prevail. Industry leaders must take action immediately to put banking on the right course for America in the 21st century.

A chief challenge the banking profession faces is its unwillingness to establish standards for what it means to be a banker. Professional bankers should push for the industry to have the highest ethical and professional standards. By doing so, they will help consumers and businesses in need of prudent advice and trained, professional counsel. In addition, bankers and directors can protect themselves from the pain this industry seems to endure every 20 to 25 years.

Leading bank CEOs should engage the industry in an unprecedented effort to define and subscribe to standards for testing and certifying bankers in risk-taking and risk-protecting roles. Similar expectations need to be established for bank directors in their critical execution of bank governance. Beyond establishing standards, the banking community must put in place annual continuing education requirements for bankers.

The banking industry lags other professionals in understanding the importance of licensing. Bankers would benefit from studying the American Academy of Actuaries, which sets and controls the standards for the actuarial profession. Importantly, the Academy has the power to expel, suspend, and publicly reprimand members. Bankers need self-policing powers and the ability to block corrupt, untrained, and imprudent want-to-be bankers from the profession. For bankers to exit the penalty box of public opinion, they must evidence uncompromising integrity and the ability to understand and balance competing interests. Industry-wide standards, formal training, and licensing for bankers and directors will move banking into the 21st century.

Standards must address four fundamental requirements. First, bankers and directors must understand the history of banking in the U.S. Our best teacher is failure, and U.S. banking history is rich in teaching material. We must understand why banks fail and how good banks avoid failure and prosper. Such training should include the "natural laws" of banking. History proves over and over again that banks that grow too fast or make too much short-term profit or cut costs too fast can and do fail. Natural laws govern banking and those laws can be taught just as physics is taught. Banking history shows that it is unnatural for a bank to grow too fast. The FDIC once had the "rapid growth rule" that barred new banks and troubled financial institutions from growing faster than 10% per year. Even though U.S. regulators withdrew this rule in the 1990s, bankers would be wise to self-police and monitor banks that notch double-digit growth rates. Fast-growing banks must be monitored closely, as they represent a threat to the water supply.

Second, bankers must understand the duty and moral imperatives that come with being a banker. As new physicians must acknowledge the Hippocratic Oath, bankers must be sufficiently skilled to acknowledge an oath to serve their clients, especially borrowers. Such a duty requires bankers, like medical doctors, to "never do harm to anyone." But duty goes beyond oaths. Duty requires bankers to balance competing interests and to recognize the special burden bankers have to society. Duty means bankers have an obligation to all their constituents to build banks that last, not banks driven by quarterly earnings.

Third, bankers and directors must be trained to understand good bank governance. Like the U.S. government, banks must have systems of checks and balances. Although it is human nature for highly successful bankers to believe in their own supreme good judgment, bankers must be taught to worry when they become confident. Case studies in weak governance should be required reading for all bankers and directors. The cyclical nature of boom and bust in banking can only be broken by people with long memories and systems that regulate and moderate exuberance.

Fourth, good banking is hard work and requires years of experience and training to understand the nuts and bolts of the business. People who run banks must know all aspects of risk management, especially credit, strategic, and operational risk. Lenders must take classes in underwriting loans. Skills must be tested. The five Cs of credit must be reintroduced. No one should be appointed to lead a bank P&L who is not trained in all aspects of consumer, small business, and commercial credit. It is simply stunning how many bank executives move into big jobs without a solid understanding of how banks make money or what successful credit risk management looks like. However, training must not be limited to credit. Industry leaders should develop a comprehensive program for training and licensing risk-takers and risk-protectors.

Bank Directors Must Be Real Banking Experts

More than 50% of the directors of U.S. community and regional banks have professional experiences outside banking, accounting, investing, or law. Less than 10% of today's independent directors have hands-on banking or bank regulatory oversight experience. Like bankers, the directors of our banks have underinvested in training and skill development. Consequently, too many bank directors lack not only the real-world experience needed to govern, but lack even the means to acquire the skills required to govern.

Former directors of the nearly 3,500 U.S. financial institutions that have failed since the mid-1980s must appreciate Groucho Marx's letter of resignation from the Friars Club in 1949: "I don't want to belong to any club that would accept me as one of its members."

The proverbial Bank Directors Club of America is not as exclusive as you might think. In a nation of 7,246 financial institutions, the club has roughly 75,000 members. How many are qualified to be a bank director? The answer may surprise you. They all are.

How do I know? Take a look at the job requirements according to the Office of the Comptroller of the Currency. The OCC Director's Book (http://occ.gov/publications/publications-by-type/other-publications-reports/director.pdf) lists six qualifications to be a national bank director. The list includes these five requirements: "basic knowledge of the banking industry," "a willingness to put the interests of the bank ahead of personal interests," "a willingness to avoid conflicts of interest," "knowledge of the communities," and "a willingness to … commit the time." There is a sixth qualification: "background, knowledge and experience in business or another discipline to oversee the bank."

In other words, if someone has the time and is honest, he or she is qualified to be a director of a U.S. bank. Standards and testing for basic knowledge do not exist. Individual banks' board-nominating committees presumably establish their own definition and test.

Let's ask the question about directors another way: How many of the 75,000 are *truly* qualified to be directors? To answer this question, it is useful to examine lessons learned from failed banks. The 457 U.S. banks that have failed since 2008 provide keen insights into director qualifications.

According to the FDIC, 665 director and officer professional liability lawsuits tied to 80 banks have been authorized since 2009. Of that total, 40% were authorized in 2011 and 44% in 2012 through October 12. The FDIC notes that "professionals may be sued for either gross or simple negligence." That statement raises several questions. Does America have "professional" bank directors? What is a "professional" director? Is the term even defined?

A close examination of the FDIC's 98 material loss reviews (MLRs) provides clues as to what is expected of professional directors. In 97 of the 98 MLRs, ineffective bank directors are identified as a primary cause of bank failure. (The one exception, inexplicably, is 1st Centennial Bank in California.) One MLR is especially helpful in describing the responsibilities of a bank director. In the Imperial Bank MLR, the FDIC writes: "An institution's Board is responsible for establishing appropriate risk limits, monitoring exposure, and evaluating the effectiveness of the institution's efforts to manage and control risk."

Is it reasonable to expect someone with "basic knowledge" of banking and "experience in business or another discipline" to set bank risk limits, monitor exposure, and judge management's risk controls? Having spent 31 years in banking, my professional opinion is that it is unreasonable and unfair to expect someone with basic knowledge of banking to meet the FDIC's standard for director qualifications. I have reviewed board data for 430 U.S. banks of all sizes. My conclusion: The director selection model for too many U.S. banks does not reflect the industry's risk profile realities of 2013.

Despite our nation's history of high bank failure rates, we see little evidence that director selection has evolved from the 1950s era of paint-by-number banking. Back then, interest rates were regulated, net interest margins were guaranteed, and lending policies were overseen by bankers who survived the Great Depression. None of that is true today.

Citigroup's board has been transformed since 2007, when it was a who's who of Fortune 50 CEOs. Today, only one director predates 2007. Seven of the 11 outside directors have substantial experience in banking, bank supervision, and financial oversight.

In contrast, consider the boards of 37 banks with assets between $10 billion and $299 billion. Of the 476 directors, 16% are bank executives. Directors who are not bank executives include 6% with commercial banking backgrounds and 1% with regulatory experience. Another 9% are from private equity/investments, 7% are lawyers, and 9% are CPAs/CFOs. More than half (52%) have business, academic, and nonprofit experience outside of banking or investments.

The U.S. banking system suffers from a severe shortage of directors with the hands-on experience and formal training to govern our banks. Unfortunately too many bank directors are unaware of their shortcomings until something bad happens. Usually the problems occur because the board overestimated the skill of management and the wisdom of its competitors. Bank directors should take three common sense actions to protect themselves, their communities, and their shareholders.

First, set standards for skill and training. Today only the "audit experts" are documented and acknowledged experts. In the future every director must have documented skills tied to specific governance functions such as talent assessment/succession planning, compensation practices, bank and corporate strategy, control design and reporting, and risk management (with sub-specialization in credit, operational, market, and liquidity risks).

Second, directors must understand bank profitability and financial statements. Anyone who joins a bank board and cannot analyze bank financial statements quite simply should step down for their own protection. The language of banking is different from other languages. Too many bank boards are like tourists in France who don't speak French; they rely on one or two members of the traveling party to do all the talking and interpreting.

Third, directors would serve their investors well by clearly documenting their qualifications to form bank strategy, set risk limits, and monitor controls. Too many bank proxy statements either fail to identify their directors' qualifications or gloss over the qualifications with broad-brushed generalizations.

The Bank Directors Club needs to be more exclusive. Unqualified directors would be wise to heed Groucho Marx's counsel.

Bank Regulators Should Do Less to Achieve More

"The sentries were not at their post." Those seven colorful words delivered by the Financial Crisis Inquiry Commission (FCIC) in January 2011 pin the financial crisis on U.S. bank regulators. Implied are three messages. One, the sentry's job is to protect the banking system. Two, there were not enough sentries. Three, the sentries were somewhere other than at their posts. Let's agree for the time being that the FCIC is correct. If so, what are the implications?

It is only natural that bank regulators will spring into action when criticized by their employer. As a result, sentries become more visible, carry more powerful weapons, and establish new "get tough" rules. Sentry management will make it clear: "Never again on my watch!"

But what if the FCIC was wrong? What if the government inquiry into the root causes of the financial crisis led to the wrong conclusions?

The Cold War divided Germany. The U.S. and its World War II allies moved into West Germany. The Soviet Union occupied East Germany. "Deterrence" was the goal. A wall was erected. Troops were amassed. Fortified checkpoints were manned. More troops, more military equipment, and taller walls meant more protection and greater deterrence. More meant more.

The FCIC's analogy of U.S. bank regulators as "sentries" is meaningful. Consider the implications. Like in the Cold War, the regulators are soldiers placed at the "front" to deter the "enemy." The sentry analogy is just plain wrong. It is 17th-century thinking, and it is taking this nation down the wrong path. Banks are not the enemy. Regulators are not soldiers.

What is needed is a thoughtful analysis of the root causes of not only the recent crisis but all the bank crises that have plagued this nation since its founding. What is needed is a 21st-century solution for bank supervision. The FCIC's 17th-century thinking is yet one more setback for bank supervision in America.

Weak as the military analogy is, it is useful in one regard. Congress has bank regulators fighting yesterday's war with yesterday's strategy and tactics. More of everything is not the answer. Paradoxically, just the opposite is true: Less is more.

The Italian economist Vilfredo Pareto gave the world the "80/20 rule." The Pareto principle suggests that focusing on 20% of something will yield 80% of the desired outcome.

Here is what's needed to improve bank oversight in America. First, toss out the notion that banks are the enemy. Nothing is a greater hindrance to moving our banking system forward than this attitude. Banks and federal overseers have a symbiotic relationship. It is in the best interests of well-run banks to have well-designed bank supervision. As in Canada, regulators need to engage bankers in forming 21st-century strategy and tactics for protecting the banking system.

Second, reject the military analogy that suggests bank regulators should fight a 17th-century "conventional war" against U.S. banks. Such antiquated thinking leads to more sentries, more regulation, and more costly financial burdens borne by banks. Ultimately, it is the same thinking that has followed every banking crisis in America. It partially explains why the U.S., unlike Canada, continues to have banking crises every 25 years or so.

Third, less is more. When criticized, it is understandable for regulators to do more of everything. The trap the FDIC fell into in 1990—when it concluded without fact and data that more bank examinations would have prevented so many Texas banks from failing—is exactly the trap regulators are falling into today. We need to identify the 20% of bank supervision and strategy that matter.

My analysis has identified one action that is more critical than any other: Revamp the CAMELS bank ratings system. No one can possibly argue that it works. The evidence of 457 failed banks less than 25 years after nearly 3,000 banks failed simply overwhelms any argument for the benefit and usefulness of CAMELS. And anyone who argues that CAMELS works, but "we just didn't do it right," is someone who does not live in the real world.

Now is the time for common sense. The U.S. needs a new 21st-century model for identifying, monitoring, and reporting bank risk. The new model must be forward-looking, not backward like the CAMELS ratings. It must consider the bank's momentum as well as emerging risks. The new model should be transparent to bankers, depositors, and investors in bank equity and debt. Finally, it should be based on objective measures.

Bankers and regulators should collaborate in designing a process to replace CAMELS. My research and analysis of failed banks reveals five factors to focus on. Two factors relate to "velocity": How fast are the market's (city, region, state) loans growing and how fast are an individual bank's loans growing? In my view, the most important factor is to evaluate the skill and experience of the bank's board to oversee strategy, management selection, risk appetite, and controls. Another factor is to detect loan and asset concentration risk. The last factor relates to strategic risk, particularly if the bank plans to grow through acquisition.

Important as it is to improve CAMELS, it is equally important to identify regulatory activities that do nothing to protect the banking system. Everything should be on the table, including the roles banks play in enforcing social policies and laws.

Less can be more.

Lawmakers Need to Scrap the Current System for Bank Supervision

"We hold these truths to be self-evident." Thomas Jefferson wrote these words in the second paragraph of the Declaration of Independence. But was he right? Were the ideas "that all men are created equal" and "are endowed by their creator with certain inalienable rights" truly self-evident? Jefferson's recognition of equality and inalienable rights was hardly self-evident to English men and women living prior to the 18th century.

What should be self-evident in America in 2013 is that our system for regulating our banks is broken and nothing less than a complete overhaul is needed. But is this really understood? What greater evidence is required than 12,000 bank failures and closures during the past 80 years, including 457 in the past five years? What also should be self-evident is that bank regulatory oversight in this country is dysfunctional and broken. Five brief illustrations will make my point.

First, the variation in banking across America is evidence that the regulatory system is broken. Engineers at Motorola were the first to introduce American business to the rigor of Six Sigma to manage quality. The ideas behind Six Sigma are fairly simple. The main tenet is that "variation is the enemy," meaning variation leads to an undesired outcome. Six Sigma practitioners use cold, hard facts and data to measure the inputs that go into producing a product. The goal is to eliminate defects. The statistical term "sigma" is used to measure the number of defects in a process. "Six Sigma" means the process is 99.99966% free of error.

This book reviewed the wide variation in bank chartering, failures, and profitability that existed across the U.S. over the past dozen years. The variation in bank performance by state is so significant that it suggests but one thing: The current regulatory processes are incapable of producing consistent, satisfactory results. On our current path we can expect another round of bank failures concentrated in five to 10 states in the years 2032 to 2037. To avoid future pain, it is time to fix the broken processes used to supervise banks.

Second, based on the history of bank failure in this nation, we must question whether U.S. federal regulators are paying appropriate attention to the nation's community banks. Unintentionally, the former head of the FDIC, Sheila Bair, provided abundant evidence of her own view of the importance of small banks. In her book, *Bull by the Horns* (2012), Bair devotes only one chapter out of 27 to the subject of small banks. And what was the title of that chapter? "Too Small to Save."

The FDIC is the federal bank regulator with primary oversight of the majority of community banks. Despite having direct federal supervisory accountability for 5,000 banks, under Bair the community banks that failed under her watch were—in her words—just "too small to save." She chalks up hundreds of community bank failures to banks that simply "were poorly managed and took excessive risks." The reader never learns what the FDIC did to correct the courses of poorly managed banks that took excessive risks. Nor are readers provided with her insights as to why the dual system of bank supervision is wise for America after ample evidence of its shortcomings.

Third, Bair's book is also instructive in its insights about the internecine war U.S. bank regulators wage on each other in their pursuit of power. Bair has opened the curtain and shown America what its bankers long thought: The bank regulators do not coordinate with each other and they sometimes do not cooperate. In risk language, when regulators fail to coordinate and cooperate, systemic risk is introduced into the banking system. This is a very serious national policy issue.

Lawmakers should be concerned that vital information is intentionally or unintentionally "stopped up" in the communication pipes of our bank regulators. Lawmakers who believe the FSOC (Financial Stability Oversight Council) will unstop the pipes would do well to examine the failure of the FFIEC (Federal Financial Institutions Examination Council), which Congress created in 1979 for virtually the same purpose.

Fourth, if regulators do not readily cooperate with each other, it should come as no surprise that accountability for bank supervision is often murky. Members of Congress from states with the highest bank failure rates need to ask one simple question: Who was accountable for supervising the banks that failed in my state?

What they will learn is that accountability is diffused. In some cases it was the Federal Reserve. In some others it was the OCC. For the vast majority, the failed banks were supervised under a dual system shared by the FDIC and state bank examiners. When problems occur—such as hundreds of cases where failed banks were given satisfactory CAMELS ratings just a year or two before failure—it is unclear if the FDIC or the state examiners or both fell short in the exercise of their duties.

The issue of unclear accountability goes beyond community banks. When the problem with the "London Whale" became apparent in 2012 and JPMorgan Chase lost billions of dollars, several members of Congress wanted to know which regulator was responsible for overseeing the bank. What a strange question. Why would it even be asked? How could bank supervisory responsibilities for banks be possibly in question after everything that has happened in this country over the past few years? Unfortunately, the answer is simple: JPMorgan Chase is supervised by the Federal Reserve and the OCC. And there are the SEC and the Commodity Futures Trading Commission. Oh, and don't forget, the FDIC is a backup and the CFPB can step in as well.

The fifth and final concern relates to the benefit and cost of a bank regulatory system that provides so many layers of redundancy. John Allison, former chairman and CEO of BB&T, a top 10 U.S. bank that made profits throughout the recent financial crisis, wrote a book in 2012 that underscores the concern with redundancy. About half-way through *The Financial Crisis and the Free Market Cure*, Allison describes what he calls a "redundant system on top of a redundant system." In the case of BB&T, the bank is audited and examined by internal auditors, external auditors, the North Carolina state banking examiners, the FDIC, and the Federal Reserve. As Allison puts it, "These are auditors auditing auditors auditing auditors."

BB&T is far from alone. Ask any bank CEO and he or she can rattle off a litany of examples of unproductive and sometimes even conflicting overlap. Ironically, even though the current redundant system has been around for decades, it did little to actually protect the industry when the banking crisis hit. Perhaps the current system lulled everyone into a false sense of confidence. Perhaps it best serves to diffuse accountability for mistakes. Sadly, Congress has responded with more burdensome regulatory oversight, arguably greater redundancy, and certainly the potential for greater diffusion of accountability. Our current system for supervising banks has two serious unintended flaws: unclear regulatory accountability and a system weighed down by duplicative, unproductive costs.

By now it must be self-evident: Common sense says the system and processes for regulatory supervision are fatally flawed. U.S. lawmakers must build a system where regulatory accountability is crystal clear and finger-pointing is impossible. Lawmakers should assign one regulator 100% accountability for the megabanks that compete globally and have complex business strategies that cut across commercial banking, trading, capital markets, and investment management. In addition, lawmakers should assign 100% accountability to another regulator for all other U.S. banks and thrifts. Rather than reinvent the wheel, it would seem to make sense to appoint the Federal Reserve as overseer for the megabanks and the OCC for the remainder.

The mission of the Federal Reserve and OCC should be to preserve and protect the banking system. Both must major in the majors of focusing their attention on the health of U.S. financial institutions and the interrelationships they have with each other. In addition, the U.S. should evaluate and adopt certain best practices used by Canada's bank regulator, including a heavier emphasis on emerging-risk evaluation, principles-based supervision, and a complete redesign of the failed CAMELS system.

If bank regulators are to be inspectors and enforcers of social policies and laws, Congress would serve its constituents well by conducting a thorough analysis of the costs and benefits of all bank compliance programs. Such an analysis should include an inventory of the programs and a clear accounting of the direct and indirect costs of each. Bankers clearly share the burden for protecting the nation and advancing certain social policies. Do all compliance programs designed to meet social and law enforcement policies still make sense in 2013? Can some be sunset because they no longer make sense or because the costs are clearly greater than the real or perceived benefit? For sure, some of these burdens are disproportionately onerous for community banks.

The FDIC should perform two specific roles. First, it should act like a conventional insurer by evaluating and measuring systemic risk (as State Farm does with potential hurricanes and other natural disasters) and assess and evaluate the effectiveness of the policies and procedures of the primary bank regulators (similar to how a reinsurer evaluates an insurer that has sold off risk to the reinsurer).

The FDIC's second responsibility should be to evaluate and report on the root causes of all bank failures. The current model for evaluating bank failures makes no sense because it lacks independence. Bank regulators should not conduct MLRs on the banks they supervise. The Federal Reserve and the OCC do not need an Office of Inspector General to write MLRs on failed banks. The U.S. should have one independent office under the FDIC to analyze bank failures.

Congress should finish what Lincoln started and shut down state bank regulators. Depression-era politics that permitted states to oversee state banks was bad public policy in 1933 and remains bad public policy in 2013. As long as the federal government provides the insurance backstop, states should cede bank oversight to federal overseers. That is not to say there are not very capable state bank regulators across the country. The best are clearly needed by federal bank regulators, which face serious staffing challenges in the years ahead as the generation of examiners hired in the last banking crisis retires.

By now it should be self-evident: A radical redesign of the current regulatory system will create clear accountability, better communication, and lower cost of supervision.

Postscript

Did you know Thomas Paine was so concerned about accusations of sedition that when he first published *Common Sense*, he did so anonymously? Why would common sense truths about liberty and justice and freedom be so threatening to the Crown?

Although I never seriously considered writing this book anonymously, more than a few people have told me that my common sense prescription for fixing banking in America will not be well received in places of power. To which I respond in the words of Martin Luther: Here I stand, I can do no other.

APPENDICES

Tools for Bankers and Directors

Operational Risk Management: The Banker's Swiss Army Knife of Risk Management

S witzerland has a population of fewer than 8 million, yet it seems to have an outsized influence on the world. Bank regulators from around the world have gathered in Basel for almost 25 years to hammer out bank rules. Every year the World Economic Forum meets in Davos, where the high and mighty and their minions debate global economic issues.

Most people know the Swiss are diplomatically neutral. During World Wars I and II, although surrounded by war on all sides, the Swiss avoided armed conflict. Unknown to most Americans, Swiss law requires every able-bodied Swiss male to serve in the army and to provide his own uniform and equipment. (Women can volunteer for the army, but are not conscripted.) Speaking of equipment, have the Swiss made any greater contribution to the world than the Swiss Army knife? It does it all: scissors, screwdriver, can opener, cutting blade, and most importantly, corkscrew to open wine bottles.

The Swiss Army knife goes back to the early 1890s, when Karl Elsener started manufacturing the knife in a reported effort to stem the tide of skilled laborers leaving town in search of work. Although Elsener was apparently a manufacturing genius, he was arguably a less skilled marketer. On the plus side, he is credited with designing the famous cross and shield logo found on every knife. On the flip side, he had some branding problems, having chosen a rather unwieldy name, *Schweizer Offiziersmesser*, for anyone but a native speaker of German.

By World War II, German soldiers carried the knife. Like the German pistol known as the Luger, during and after the war American soldiers were interested in collecting the knife. Unable to pronounce the German name of the product, American soldiers simply called it the Swiss Army knife.

What does the Swiss Army knife have to do with bank risk management? The answer: Operational risk management is the Swiss Army knife of banking. In this appendix, we will examine several very practical tools found on the operational risk Swiss Army knife.

As a reminder, operational risks cover people, processes, systems, external events, and strategic risks. All great banks have excellent operational risk management programs. They may not call it operational risk management, but great bankers understand that these risk management skills are the bedrock for managing and governing banks. All community and regional banks can improve their programs by committing to and executing a few key actions.

The Emerging Risk Committee

Every bank, large and small, should have an Emerging Risk Committee that includes the bank's leadership team. To be most effective, the committee should meet monthly, and members should do their homework prior to the meeting. Committee members should regularly identify emerging risks that could threaten the bank's earnings or its reputation. The definition of an emerging risk is one that the bank could face three months to five years down the road. Meetings should have a formal agenda, a chair, and follow-up actions.

All risks should be tracked in an Excel database. Open issues should be assigned to committee members who will be responsible for mitigation and monitoring. At all times, committee members should focus on material risks, especially the 10X risks that can cause bank failure. Monthly meeting minutes should be submitted to the board of directors.

Issues that come before the Emerging Risk Committee should focus principally on operational and strategic risks. The committee must consider risks associated with people, process, systems, and external events, risks not often covered in other forums. The Emerging Risk Committee should not discuss credit risks, which should be covered by the bank's Loan Committee. Examples of issues the Emerging Risk Committee could discuss include the following:

- **External Failure and Loss Analysis:** *American Banker*, FDIC reports such as material loss reviews, and the enforcement actions found at www.calculatedriskblog.com are excellent sources for issues the Emerging Risk Committee could discuss. Management can learn by studying bank failures and enforcement actions. In addition to bank failures, the Emerging Risk Committee should monitor other banks' losses due to fraud, employment practices, workplace safety, natural disasters, systems failures, and business practices failures.
- **Internal Loss Analysis:** Most community banks and regional banks have not taken big losses from the seven categories of operational losses. However, there is a significant benefit in tracking and analyzing losses over a certain threshold (a recommended $1,000 for community banks and $10,000 for regionals). Internal losses often reveal control failures that expose the bank to future losses unless they are mitigated and monitored.
- **Reputation Risk Management:** Reputation risk management is the next generation of risk management practices. As a risk discipline, it is where operational risk management was 10 years ago. Key risk indicators, well-documented policies, and processes for managing reputation risk are still in development. Leading banks are already pushing forward on formal management and board reviews of this critical risk.

Periodic Scenario Analysis Sessions

Underused and underappreciated in the U.S., scenario analysis is one of the best formal processes bankers can use to discuss big-picture risks. At least twice a year, the Emerging Risk Committee should run a special meeting three to four hours long. The extended time allows management to quantify and risk-rate the most important emerging risks under evaluation. Examples of issues that might be discussed at a scenario analysis session include:

- Natural disaster in the marketplace (hurricane, earthquake, tornado, drought).
- Failure of the bank's supplier of online banking.
- Highly contagious disease spreads across the bank's workforce.
- Public worker strikes cause public service interruptions.
- The euro fails, leaving every member of the European Union to resurrect its own national currency.
- The local county goes bankrupt.

Some community banks might assume issues of this magnitude are not germane to their business. Maybe they are right. On the other hand, maybe they are wrong. A good banker must sleep with one eye open, fully conscious of the devastating potential for 10X risk to arise from unexpected sources. How many bank CEOs and boards of the 9,000 financial institutions that failed during the Depression could possibly have understood the ramifications of Black Thursday on October 24, 1929? Scenario analysis is not necessarily about nailing the risk before it occurs; it is about the process that improves the bank's risk culture.

For the Emerging Risk Committee and scenario analysis sessions to be most effective, all participants must be highly engaged in the process. There is a problem if one person dominates the sessions. Scenario analysis sessions must always be alert to the potential for bias that derails effective analysis. Similar to blinders on a horse, bias limits discussion and blinds the bank to the full spectrum of risks.

Another caution: It is not uncommon for banks to have a person on staff whose experience and position are respected by all members of the organization. If you recall from Chapter 2, despite being the most respected person in the room, Old Man Mueller made a point of talking last when the bank debated the important issue of loan concentration strategy. Well-run banks recognize the risks associated with a potentially dominant individual. Often this respected yet dominant person's ideas can go unchallenged. Several FDIC material loss reviews identified bank failures where a dominant banker's ideas went unchallenged. In at least one other failed bank, the dominant CEO was the go-to person for everything. Sadly this person died. Because there was no effective bench strength behind the CEO, the bank unraveled and failed. A special risk is created for the bank when the dominant personality is a highly successful CEO.

Some banks find it helpful to bring in an outside resource to facilitate the scenario analysis discussion, to ensure broad engagement, and to steer debates away from debilitating bias. The ideal facilitator not only is knowledgeable about the process, but has a strong working knowledge of national and global social, economic, political, and regulatory issues.

Risk and Control Assessment (RCA)

Every bank should ask its employees to identify operational risks. Every employee can be involved in this work. An Excel spreadsheet should suffice for community banks as the record for the bank's risk and control assessment. Regional banks may benefit from more robust, commercially available RCA software.

Issues should be identified and rated high, medium, or low in inherent risks—risks identified before banks take action to mitigate and control them. The Excel spreadsheet should include columns or rows that describe steps for mitigation, monitoring, and control. Based on the strength of these actions, residual risk is determined—the risk that remains after mitigating action has been taken. Residual risks should be expressed as high, medium, and low.

Ideally, every bank, even very small community banks, should have a person or department that plays a challenge function. The job of this person or department is to evaluate the risks identified by the employees. It is critical to the integrity of the process that the challenger not be engaged in writing the first draft of the RCA. In larger organizations, this function is performed by the bank's risk management organization. It is the role of the challenger to ask questions and push back when and where appropriate. In addition, the challenger can independently add issues to the RCA that other employees missed.

Suppliers require special attention during the RCA process. Bank management must design effective means to evaluate supplier risks. It is becoming common for banks to require suppliers to adhere to the same rigorous risk and control assessments that the bank conducts. Banks should always stipulate this requirement in their supplier contracts. However, it is important to recognize that suppliers are getting similar requests from a growing number of client banks. Over time, banks should expect suppliers to develop a standard risk and control assessment report that works for all banks. Of course, bankers cannot rely solely on the word of suppliers. Banks will need a process to challenge and monitor the suppliers' self-assessment. Over time, bankers are likely to develop consortiums to conduct such challenge work.

Failure mode and effects analysis (FMEA) is one of the best tools bankers can use to rank and evaluate risks as part of the risk and control assessments. FMEAs are used to rank residual risks. Once the residual risk is identified, it is evaluated on three criteria: *severity* (if the risk occurs, how bad can it be for the bank?), *detectability* (is the risk obvious or hard to detect?), and *occurrence* (what is the likely frequency?). Each criterion is assigned a value of 1, 3, and 9, where 1 is low and 9 is high.

As an example, a Tampa bank is concerned about hurricanes. The bank knows hurricanes are devastating and can interrupt service for weeks, if not longer, so severity is a 9. Hurricanes usually come with some warning, so detectability is a 3. Occurrence of a hurricane threat is not infrequent and so merits a 3. The three scores are multiplied (9 x 3 x 3 = 81). In a similar manner, other residual risks are measured. Residual risks with high scores must be elevated to the bank directors for discussion. In some cases, directors will choose to spend money to further mitigate the risk (in this instance, to buy additional insurance or backup electric-power generation).

People risks often do not get appropriate or accurate assessment. The failure of 457 banks since 2008 requires bank directors to step up their scrutiny of bank management and management succession plans. No longer is the board in a position to accept informal and undocumented processes that leave directors vulnerable to FDIC lawsuits. Consequently, all banks, regardless of size, must have formal, fair, and accurate processes to evaluate the bank's management and succession plans.

Processes do not have to be administratively burdensome; however, some administrative burden is fine if it means the board gets a clear picture of management strengths, weaknesses, and development needs. Succession planning requires more than a one-page list of names. The succession plan should clearly identify:

- *Who* are potential successors for key jobs?
- *What* are their development and experience needs?
- *How* will those needs be met (for example, by attending training outside the bank or being assigned a special project)?
- *When* will successor candidates be ready to succeed the person currently in the role? Successor readiness will always vary. One of the most critical factors is whether the successor candidates are internal (working at the bank) or external (needing to be hired away from another employer).

Rigorous and Disciplined Strategic Risk Management

Strategic risk management must be a shared responsibility between the board of directors and the bank's CEO. Strategic risk management requires each bank to clearly state its appetite for risk. The CEO and board must have a strategic risk framework that lays out a three- to five-year vision and plan for the bank. It should include:

- Profit and revenue growth targets.
- Target client or customer markets.
- Ten to 15 key risk indicators (KRIs) with red/yellow/green heat maps. Each KRI will include a range of metrics that describe green (on target or plan), yellow (marginally or slightly off target or plan), or red (substantially off target or plan). The KRIs should be tracked easily on one page and act as early warning indicators.
- Identification of key processes to control the bank's risks (for example, use of the Emerging Risk Committee, tools like scenario analysis, and external sources for benchmarking and external event risk identification).
- Talent planning, including confidential employee succession, as well as detailed plans to train and upgrade the skills of key bank personnel.
- Competitor risk analysis, including an assessment of the talent and risk profile of key competitors.
- A candid assessment of SWOT: strengths, weaknesses, opportunities, and threats.

Banks of all sizes should expect bank directors to become more active and determined to understand, develop, and ultimately own the strategic risk framework. CEOs and bank executives will also need to demonstrate comprehensive skills for identifying external event risks. The Emerging Risk Committee and scenario analysis sessions should be excellent sources of insight for the board of directors. In addition, bank management will want to develop, if it does not exist already, a short list of key external event risk indicators for board discussions. These risk indicators should be big picture and forward-looking. Bankers should take advantage of excellent economic analysis conducted by the Federal Reserve. In addition, banks will want to develop an understanding of how to use the statistical concept of reversion to the mean as a strategic risk management tool.

Reversion to the Mean as a Strategic Risk Management Tool

Unless you are from the North Carolina mountain town of Rutherfordton, likely you have never heard of Harold "Gomer" Hodge. Hodge was a professional baseball player, but not just any player; he was on my beloved Cleveland Indians for part of the 1971 season. Cleveland Indians baseball in the 1960s through 1980s was pitiful. Every spring training started with promise, and every season the hapless Indians broke our hearts.

In the days of my youth, my heart knew only hope. In 1971, the Indians' spring training camp was in Tucson, Arizona. As a kid who had never been west of Chicago or south of Wheeling, West Virginia, Tucson seemed as far away to me as the moon. Every morning, I would wake up early and devour the sports pages of the *Cleveland Plain Dealer*, eager to learn the latest news out of spring training. News reports from Tucson during the spring of 1971 were especially upbeat. Apparently the Tribe had discovered a great baseball talent out of the remote mountains of North Carolina. His name: Harold Hodge. Because Harold looked and sounded like the TV character Gomer Pyle, the newspaper changed his name to Gomer Hodge.

Gomer made the 1971 team as a backup player and pinch hitter. In the first game of the season, Gomer pinch hit in the eighth inning. He lined a single, driving home a run. In game two, once again he came in to pinch hit in the eighth inning. Again Gomer delivered, drilling a double and scoring the Tribe's first run of the game. Staying in the game, Gomer stood at the plate in the bottom of the ninth inning with two runners on base and the Tribe down 2-1. Again, Gomer delivered—stroking a single and driving home both runs for a victory. In his next game, Gomer was called upon once again to pinch hit and knocked a double. While relishing his success after the game, he proudly told the reporters gathered around him "Golly, fellas, I'm hitting 4.000."

What's the point? The law of averages caught up with Gomer during the season. He did not hit 4.000 or even .400. Gomer hit .205, batting only 79 more times that season before being sent down to the minor leagues, never to return to the majors. As for the Indians in 1971, they broke our hearts again. Despite starting the season 3-1, they managed to lose 102 games.

Statisticians prefer the term *reversion to the mean* over the law of averages, but they both mean the same thing. Reversion to the mean is an important strategic risk management tool for bankers. Investors understand its power. The truly great "deep value" investors use the concept to take large positions in industries that no one loves and whose stock prices are deeply discounted.

From the early 1990s to 2007, too many bankers forgot the power of reversion to the mean. Sometimes people get so caught up in "this time is different" that it is easy to lose a big-picture perspective. Banking from 1995 to 2006 was like going to the roulette table in Vegas and watching the little white ball fall on red 11 years in a row. Banking back then was like watching Gomer Hodge get four hits in a row and thinking he was the next Babe Ruth.

The truth is, a Babe Ruth comes along once every 100 years. What were the telltale macroeconomic signs bankers should have been watching from 1995 to 2006?

Financial Services Share of S&P 500 Earnings

The S&P 500 is an excellent tool for community and regional bankers to look at every quarter or so. The key is studying the profitability of industry sectors. The S&P has been reporting this metric since 1926. Historically, the financial sector has averaged somewhere around 12-15% of the S&P 500 earnings. From 2000 to 2006, the financial sector soared to 30% or so. Even in 2007, the sector achieved 18% of the S&P 500 earnings. From 2000 to 2006 no other sector contributed more than 15% of total S&P 500 earnings. In a classic case of reversion to the mean, the financial sector got pulverized from 2008 to 2011. When financials produce outsized profits, it is time to dial back the risk (source: *The Wall Street Journal*, Feb. 11, 2009).

GDP Growth Compared to Bank Profit Growth

Going back to 1950, U.S. gross domestic product has grown about 3% a year. Some years it is a little more; some years it is a little less. When the banking industry's earnings grow faster than GDP, it is time to evaluate the bank's risk appetite.

Some bank CEOs will argue that bank earnings should grow much faster than GDP when the economy is recovering from a recession. This is certainly a fair argument. However, this argument assumes that bank earnings fall much faster than GDP declines during a recession. In fact, that is exactly what happened beginning in 2008. The result is earnings volatility. The greater the volatility, as successful investors recognize, the greater the inherent risk. Banks that produce less volatile earnings over time are safer than banks that do not. Banks with lower volatility and steady profits have better risk-adjusted returns.

Banks that grow faster than GDP do so in one of two ways: 1) by increasing productivity/efficiency, or 2) by taking on more risk. In baseball, there will always be players who are better-than-average hitters. Likewise in banking, some banks will always be better-than-average banks. Unlike baseball, however, banking introduces risk in addition to skill to improve performance. Bankers who achieve higher returns are often fooled into thinking their superior performance is based on skill. Like the roulette player who rolls the ball on red four times in a row, the banker's best friend can be luck. Time and reversion to the mean will eventually catch up with the roulette player and the banker who fails to discern whether superior returns have come through skill or luck. If bank profits grow faster than GDP, the banker must be able to explain why. Recall Old Man Mueller's Second Law of Banking: Gravity pulls objects down to earth at 9.8 meters per second squared and bank revenues grow only as fast as GDP allows; try to defy these two laws of nature for long and bad things can happen.

Banker Compensation and Employment

Bankers may be surprised to learn that banker employment and compensation numbers are another excellent risk management tool. On April 28, 2008, *The Wall Street Journal* carried a chart from New York University economist Thomas Philippon. According to

Philippon, financial services workers' share of the all U.S. workers' income grew steadily from 3% in 1940 to 10% in 2007. Employment numbers for the financial services industry are also a good barometer of the health of the industry. As a rule of thumb, when both incomes and employment grow, bankers need to become more cautious. By the time payrolls are cut through layoffs and lower compensation, the damage to the industry has already been done. The big question from a risk management perspective is whether the long-term upward trend in financial services compensation is now reversing in a substantive way. Likely it is. It seems conceivable that the financial services workers' share of national incomes will revert over time to a lower number. As this occurs, all things being equal, bank profits and capitalization will improve.

New Bank Chartering (Formation)

By now it should be quite clear to the reader that new banks pose extraordinary risk to banks that are in the market where the new bank will compete. New banks are not formed in tough times, but tough times do not last. There will be a day in the not-so-distant future when banking will seem easy again. When that day comes, bankers and bank directors need to be assertive and vigilant in their assessment of the risks new banks bring to the market. The early warning indicator will be a jump in applications for charters.

APPENDIX

Scenario Analysis: The Best Tool to Manage 10X Risk

S cenario analysis is the single most critical risk management tool available to bankers seeking to manage 10X risk. Although not all bankers would agree with that view, former CEOs of failed banks might. European bankers are more likely to use scenario analyses than Americans because of the number of very large operational losses recently experienced in Europe.

- Barings: a $1.4 billion loss in 1995 put the bank out of business.
- Societe Generale: a $7.2 billion loss in 2007-2008.
- UBS: a $2.1 billion loss in 2011.

Losses of this magnitude are so extraordinary that standard risk management practices fall short in preparing an institution to identify and control for them. A risk management tool is needed to evaluate the risk of catastrophic problems, and the scenario analysis process was invented for such a purpose. Although designed to identify big losses like those noted above, the tool has much broader application.

Bank boards and managers who demonstrate strong risk management skills will make broad use of the flexible capabilities of scenario analysis. It is particularly helpful as a formal process to evaluate how a potential external event risk may affect strategic decisions like acquisitions or divestitures. Some of the world's best investors make frequent use of scenario analysis (which some call war games or what-if analysis). Typical examples of issues to which scenario analysis can be applied are:

- What if there is a hurricane in the Gulf of Mexico?
- What if a barrel of oil goes to $250?
- What if the Russian ruble is devalued by 33%?
- What if the global production of corn falls 20%?
- What if high-frequency trading causes the stock market to go haywire for a day?

Beyond traditional applications of scenario analysis, the tool can also be used to evaluate issues such as these:

- What if a well-capitalized new competitor enters our market and attempts to quickly build earning assets by lowering credit standards?
- What if local housing prices fall another 10%?

159

- What if a major employer in our market goes out of business?
- What if local unemployment rates drop another 3%?
- What if the Republicans sweep Congress? What if the Democrats sweep Congress and hold the presidency?

When bank managers decide to conduct a number of scenario analyses simultaneously, they are, in effect, creating the key components of a stress test. If the board of directors asks management to couple the scenario analyses with detailed financial forecasts, the end product is a stress test. Not all stress tests need to be highly detailed forecasts. Quite often, it is sufficient to conduct a "poor man's" stress test by developing the most relevant scenario analyses and converting them into high-level financial forecasts for the board to evaluate and debate.

Let's take some examples of issues that may be germane today to a number of community and regional bankers and boards. The bank's directors want to discuss and analyze several very complex questions. As a result, they pose the following scenarios for analysis:

- What if the number of banks in America falls from the current 7,246 to 1,500 in 2020? What is the probability? Why?
- What if Congress abolishes the state bank commissions by 2015 and appoints the OCC to supervise all banks as a way to stop charter shopping and drive more consistent bank supervision? What is the probability? Why?

The first thing the bank's risk executive does is gather the bank's most senior bankers as well as one or two external subject-matter experts to evaluate each of the questions. Given the gravity of the questions posed, management then chooses to use a professional facilitator to ensure the management team approaches its task without bias, which could produce an inaccurate assessment.

The typical amount of time needed to address three or four scenarios is three to four hours if the participants are knowledgeable and have done their homework. When the session begins, the facilitator points out the goal: The participants are to discuss and evaluate the question. Then, each participant independently identifies the probability of the event occurring and the potential worst-case financial outcome. A composite score is developed by simply averaging the collective viewpoints.

Let's assume I am a participant in this exercise. As a seasoned banker, I come to the meeting with experience to address the questions posed. However, I also know I need to do my research because the issues require me to come to the meeting with the most informed and current insights I can gather.

I do my homework. I go through my analysis before the meeting. Here are my notes as I walk into the meeting:

Question 1: What if the number of banks in America falls from the current 7,246 to 1,500 in 2020? What is the probability? Why?

My view: There is a 15% probability. Ten forces are at work that could result in an 80% reduction in the number of banks operating in the United States by 2020.

Loss of political capital in Washington and the Public Utility Era. When the S&Ls failed in the late 1980s, Congress felt burned. They had put their necks out by passing Garn-St. Germain. There was no appetite post-crisis to give the ailing S&Ls a helping hand. Consequently, the Office of Thrift Supervision had a free hand to put weak S&Ls to death. Perhaps not quite so ominous, the Dodd-Frank legislation foreshadows a difficult time ahead for banks. Political support for banks of all sizes has evaporated. It is unlikely lawmakers will take action any time soon to create a more benign environment for banks to make money. As a result, fee income will not grow and margins will remain tight for a while. It is also unlikely Congress will lose interest in banks soon; in the Public Utility Era, regulators will remain aggressive and highly active in their audits and oversight.

Exasperated and worn-out directors. Following the bank crisis of the 1980s and early 1990s, directors of banks that came close to failure could not wait to find a respectable exit. As a result, a merger boom took place in the mid-1990s. Similarly, burned directors of surviving banks will go through their own calculus and conclude they can maximize shareholder value by merging or selling the bank. Also, although not an explicit driver, bank directors minimize personal risk by selling, a benefit that cannot be overstated in a time when the FDIC is eager to punish directors of badly managed banks.

An industry-wide talent shortage. Although the industry-wide talent shortage is broad, two specific bank functions will be the principal drivers behind bank mergers. First, there are simply too few qualified Americans to serve as bank directors. No longer do people qualify based on the criteria from the 1950s. The bar has been raised over the past few years. Adding to the challenge, fewer people today want to be on bank boards. As a result, director pay will go up, as will their time commitment and duties. As boards realize how difficult it is to attract and retain skilled and experienced directors, some will consider merging or selling the bank. Second, directors are carefully assessing their bank management and often concluding that the CEO and bench strength behind him or her are inadequate. Unable to attract the kind of management needed in this era, banks lacking such talent will run to those that have it. Directors who sell banks with marginal management will realize a price haircut as buyers have their pick of potential banks to buy.

Healing balance sheets. The economy is healing and so too have bank balance sheets. Ultra-low interest rates squeeze net interest margins, but a low-rate environment also eases payment schedules for borrowers whose balance sheets need time to heal. As banks are getting back on their feet, some directors have already put their institutions on the block. Until their banks are sold, expect to see those directors dial back their banks' risk profiles and work hard to document evidence of strong risk cultures.

Lackluster earnings forecasts. The problem is revenue and the answer is cost reduction. Bankers do not see light at the end of the tunnel. Strong borrowers—high-net-worth or small business or commercial enterprises—are in the catbird seat as they are courted by all the banks. As a result, the real cost to borrow money is declining. Even banks that succeed in growing loan balances will find they must trade off net interest margin for asset growth. Some banks will become strong niche players (e.g., high net worth, asset lending) and choose to stay independent. As seen in the mid-1990s, a select number of community banks and many of the regional banks will exploit the next five years to buy smaller banks. Such a strategy bets on superior operational skills. If successful, acquiring banks will develop scale advantages that presumably will translate into improved profitability. Such a strategy is always logical, but not always easy to pull off without incurring substantial operational and strategic risk.

Economies of scale to improve productivity and drive down costs. Although scale in banking has long been touted as an advantage of bank mergers, in the past costs have not always fallen as expected. In the near future, this will change as more banks continue to leverage size and volume to pressure key suppliers, especially technology-telecommunications-operations providers, to lower costs. In addition, given the high probability of excess real estate, owners of commercial real estate who lease premises to bankers will be forced to deal with significant supply-and-demand problems. Consequently, the most aggressive commercial real estate owners could choose to cut rents in order to keep banks as tenants of branch buildings and office parks.

Double whammy: Bank demand for real estate falls as interest rates rise. Because of the U.S. government's failure to reverse deficit operating budgets and rising debt, at some point in the next few years interest rates will go up. Not only will bank consolidation have a big impact on commercial real estate demand, but it will also occur in an environment where interest rates rise. Higher interest rates will be triggered by inflation (designed to make U.S. debt easier to pay back in cheaper U.S. dollars) and/or China's and other creditors' determination to be paid an appropriately risk-adjusted return on U.S. debt. The impact of rising rates bodes poorly for owners of commercial real estate, who will have no choice but to translate higher capitalization rates into higher rent. In a proverbial vicious circle, higher rent will chase some tenants out. Bankers who think this will be a big problem are already reducing their appetite for commercial real estate lending to retailers.

Technology complexity and concern about emerging competitors. The pace of technology advancements, especially in telecommunications and social media, creates two challenges for bankers and directors. As when Bill Gates called bankers "dinosaurs" in 1995, bankers now are wary of the role of new technology. First, more bankers worry that the long-expected end of brick and mortar is finally near; the big investment Capital One made in ING suggests the smart money is preparing for such a day. Second, and perhaps an even bigger concern, is the emergence of Facebook and Google as potential sources of disintermediation. The more likely scenario is the emergence of an alliance between a powerful telecommunications company and a Visa or MasterCard. The greater the uncertainty, the higher the probability that bankers and investors in banks will cash in their chips and sell their banks when opportunity comes knocking.

Difficulty for suppliers to manage banks. The burden of the Public Utility Era of banking is not limited to banks. Bank suppliers are just now starting to feel the first round of such pressure. It is highly likely that the regulatory scrutiny of banks will be felt aggressively by suppliers. These pressures only intensify every time a big supplier is hacked, creates a privacy event, or experiences extended service disruptions. As regulators put more pressure on banks to monitor suppliers, these suppliers will experience a significant increase in the cost to serve the banking industry. Those costs will be passed back to the banks eventually, another reason for the industry to consolidate.

Credit unions. Some politicians love credit unions and are pushing legislation in Washington to make credit unions look a lot more like banks. For sure, credit unions have come a long way. When they began, workers in the same company used their credit unions to help each other out. If one person had excess savings and another needed to borrow money, the credit union facilitated the transaction. Those quaint days are gone. A growing number of credit unions today act like for-profit banks. Credit unions not only have the advantage of political support at a time when banks have none, but they have two other advantages. First, their regulator is perceived to be less aggressive in its oversight than other bank regulators. Second, being exempt from income taxes makes it possible for them to pay higher purchase premiums to banks eager to sell.

> Question 2: What if Congress abolishes the state bank commissions by 2015 and appoints the OCC to supervise all banks as a way to stop charter shopping and drive more consistent bank supervision? What is the probability? Why?
>
> My view: the probability is 25% by 2015. The inherent risk is actually higher for five reasons. However, the residual risk/probability is lowered to 25% for one important reason: a lack of political will.

Quality of supervision varies. The financial crisis has highlighted the weaknesses of a system where 50 states oversee banking in 50 different ways. Informed members of Congress are frustrated that regulators vary too much in their effectiveness. Some states appear to do very good work supervising banks, while others have poor records of oversight. Unfortunately, as witnessed over the past 10 years, supervision of state-chartered banks by federal regulators has proven inconsistent as well. The current system does not produce consistent and reliable protection needed to ensure a safe and sound banking system.

False economies. State banking commissions claim they are less expensive regulators than the OCC, but a 2006 study published in *FDIC Banking Review* challenges that view. The authors of "Challenges to the Dual Banking System: The Funding of Bank Supervision" provide evidence that "a substantial portion of the cost of supervising state-chartered banks is thus borne by the FDIC and the Federal Reserve." In other words, although the states market themselves as cheaper than the OCC, according to the authors of this study, if the full costs of the FDIC and the Fed were accounted, the true cost of dual supervision of the state and FDIC is much greater than currently charged out to state banks.

Safety net is national, not state. When the FDIC was introduced in 1933, the states retained their independent banking commissions while benefiting from national bank insurance. Back in the 1930s, many Americans craved states' rights even more than today. Naturally, key legislators fought hard to protect their interests in state banking. The reality is that the states have no skin in the game. If a state's bank supervisors mess up, Uncle Sam swoops in, cleans up the mess, and hands out checks. Unless the states want to assume the contingent liability of deposit insurance, which of course none will do, it's time they give up the bank oversight.

Bank shrinkage. The number of banks is shrinking and new charters have screeched to a halt. At some point, states need to ask if it makes sense to have a banking department overseeing a smaller number of banks. As the number of state banks continues to shrink, state banking commissions will in all likelihood need to cut back their resources. As state banking commissions shrink in relationship to state banks, there will be a serious question of whether the commissions will have the scale to do their jobs.

Budget deficits. The last nail in the coffin of state banking oversight is the cost of redundant public service. In an era of tight state and federal budgets, it would seem all parties would endeavor to cut costs wherever possible. It is possible to argue that state banking commissions actually break even since the commissions pass through their costs to the banks they supervise. However, as already noted, services provided by the FDIC and Federal Reserve are not free.

On the other hand, community banks continue to have some strong advocates in Washington. If enough community banks make sure their local representatives protect the status quo, it is likely the industry can protect the dual supervision system. Before the crisis, community banks clearly had sufficient political capital. It's less clear now; thus the 25% risk.

The Influence of Bank Chartering Rates on Bank Failure Rates in the United States: 2000–2012

Hypothesis

The probability of bank failure increases when too many new banks enter a market (a town, city, or region) within a couple of years of each other.

Implications

If it is true that new-bank formation rates influence bank failure rates, it means bank directors need a strong handle on competitor behavior and activity when forming bank profit targets and risk appetite. Also, if true, it means banks—especially smaller banks that lack geographic diversity and broad loan mix—need to be conducting much more effective competitor analyses than most currently do today.

Purpose

1. To highlight the potential to use bank chartering rates as a leading key risk indicator for systemic risk (where "systemic" can be defined as a town, city, or region, not just the nation).
2. To offer a theory as to why newly chartered banks are inherently risky and why the entry of new banks heightens the risk of bank failures for its local competitors.
3. To identify specific activities bank directors, bank executives, regulators, lawmakers, and D&O insurance providers can take to mitigate the risks associated with new bank chartering.

Background for Hypothesis

During the 1980s, I was a young banker in the Tampa Bay region making loans and providing cash management services to small and mid-size companies. Over the course of a few years, I witnessed the entry into the market of dozens of new competitors. Enabled by the Garn-St. Germain Act in 1982, S&Ls in the mid-1980s aggressively pursued commercial real estate loans. Around the same time, bullish bank investors launched de novo banks. Lending standards deteriorated as lenders stretched to book earning assets. Based on my readings of books about corporate strategy by Michael Porter (*Competitive Advantage*, The Free Press, 1985) and Bruce Henderson (*Henderson on Corporate Strategy*, New American Library, 1979), I sensed in the late 1980s that the banking industry did not understand the influence bank competition had on corporate strategy, bank profitability, and bank failures.

Methodology

This analysis would not be possible without the good work the FDIC has done to make detailed bank data available since the early 1990s. The data for this analysis comes from FDIC databases, except for the number of problem banks, which is reported by a website that compiles the data from FDIC, Federal Reserve, and OCC reports. Combining multiple sources of FDIC data, this analysis studies the aggregate number of banks, new bank formation rates, failures rates, problem rates, and profitability for each of the 50 states. Earlier dates were considered and evaluated. The year 1995 is the starting point because it was in that year that bank failures reached a 10-year low after nearly 3,000 failures and assisted transactions in the prior 10 years. It is important to note that this analysis assigns all banks to the state in which they are headquartered. For example, although JPMorgan Chase operates in 23 states, for the purposes of this analysis, it is defined and tracked as a New York bank. Before drawing too many conclusions about the implications of this limitation, let's review the data as constructed.

Data and Statistics

Bank Failure 2008 to October 12, 2012: Variation by State

The dates above should look familiar because they were shown in Chapter 1. As was true during the banking crisis of 1985-1992, bank failures during the recent financial crisis were concentrated in 20% of the states. Figure A.1 shows the number of commercial

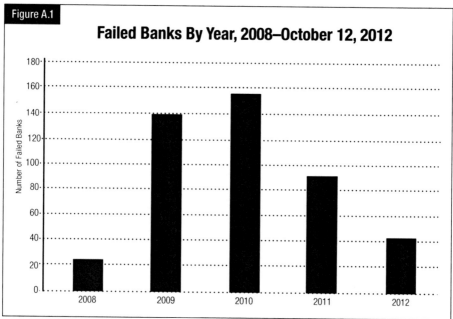

Figure A.1

Failed Banks By Year, 2008–October 12, 2012

Source: FDIC

bank failures in the U.S. from 2008 through October 12, 2012. Figure A.2 shows the distribution of bank failures experienced in the 10 states with the most failures (327 or 72% of U.S. total) during this time period.

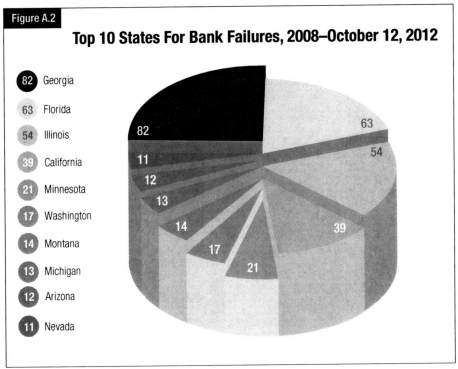

Figure A.2

Top 10 States For Bank Failures, 2008–October 12, 2012

- 82 Georgia
- 63 Florida
- 54 Illinois
- 39 California
- 21 Minnesota
- 17 Washington
- 14 Montana
- 13 Michigan
- 12 Arizona
- 11 Nevada

Source: FDIC

Bank Formation Rates by State, 1996-2010

Table A.1 is a snapshot of Florida bank activity from 1995 to 2010, showing the additions and subtractions of commercial banks headquartered in Florida during that period. Similar data can be found for every state at the FDIC website. Florida is used as an example for all 50 states. Highlights from Table A.1 follow:

- The column showing new charters represents the number of new Florida banks for every year since 1995. For our purpose, we will focus on the new charters issued from 1996 through 2010.[1] For those 15 years, Florida approved 196 new charters.
- The number of new banks (196) formed between 1996 and 2010 as a percentage of total institutions in business at year-end 2010 (220) is 89%.
- The number of institutions from year-end 1995 to year-end 2010 shrank by 34% (from 333 to 220). The net reduction is because new bank formation in Florida was less than the combination of bank mergers and failures in the state for the time period.
- Between 2000 and 2007, 119 new banks were chartered.

Table A.1

Changes in Number of Institutions, Florida (FDIC-insured Commercial Banks, 1995–2010)

Years	Additions		Deletions				Total Institutions at Year-End
	New Charter	Conversions	Unassigned Mergers	Merger	Failures Paid Off	Other	
2010	0	0	11	24	0	-2	220
2009	3	0	9	10	0	2	253
2008	9	2	18	2	0	1	271
2007	24	0	13	0	0	-1	281
2006	21	0	14	0	0	0	269
2005	18	0	12	0	0	0	262
2004	13	2	19	1	0	2	256
2003	10	1	9	0	0	-1	263
2002	6	0	5	2	0	1	260
2001	11	0	14	0	0	0	262
2000	16	0	23	0	0	0	265
1999	37	0	13	1	0	3	272
1998	12	2	30	0	0	-2	252
1997	9	2	33	0	0	2	266
1996	7	2	54	0	0	-2	290
1995	4	2	28	0	0	2	333

Source: FDIC

■ Important: Using the year 2000 as a baseline (265 banks), Florida's total number of newly chartered banks from 2000 to 2007 is equivalent to a 45% increase over the number of banks in the state in 2000.[2]

Similar data was compiled and analyzed for all 50 states.

Table A.2 shows the percentage change in the number of banks headquartered in each state between year-end 1995 and year-end 2010. Note that 90% of the states actually had fewer banks headquartered in the state in 2010 compared to 1995. The midpoint on the list is Massachusetts, which experienced a net 33% decline in the number of banks headquartered in the state from 1995 to 2010. Five states saw the number of banks headquartered in the state decline by more than 50%: Indiana, Colorado, Maine, Vermont, and New Hampshire.

Only four states showed a net increase in the number of banks headquartered in the state from 1995 to 2010. Utah led the nation with a net increase of 20%. The other three states to show net increases were North Carolina (18%), Arizona (15%), and Nevada (8%).

Table A.2

Change in Number of Banks in States, 1995–2010

State	% Change	State	% Change	State	% Change
Utah	20	Oklahoma	−29	Illinois	−39
North Carolina	18	North Dakota	−29	Texas	−39
Arizona	15	Louisiana	−29	Pennsylvania	−40
Nevada	8	Iowa	−30	Ohio	−43
South Carolina	−11	Michigan	−32	Connecticut	−44
Rhode Island	−13	South Dakota	−32	Maryland	−47
Idaho	−16	Montana	−33	Arkansas	−49
Mississippi	−21	Missouri	−33	Delaware	−49
Washington	−23	Massachusetts	−33	West Virginia	−49
New Jersey	−25	Florida	−34	Hawaii	−50
Minnesota	−27	California	−34	Alaska	−50
Alabama	−27	Virginia	−34	Indiana	−52
Tennessee	−27	Georgia	−35	Colorado	−54
New York	−27	Kentucky	−35	Maine	−55
Oregon	−28	Wyoming	−36	Vermont	−55
New Mexico	−29	Nebraska	−36	New Hampshire	−61
Kansas	−29	Wisconsin	−37		

Source: FDIC

Deeper Examination of New Bank Formation Rate by Time Period

Table A.3 examines new charter activity by state. The second column shows new charters formed between January 1, 1996, and December 31, 2010, as a percentage of banks headquartered in the state at year-end 2010. The third column shows new charters from 2000 to 2007 as a percentage of banks headquartered in the state in 2000. The states are ranked based on the new charter activity in column 2. Note the difference in the two rates among states. Column 3 actually gives a better insight into the pace of new chartering in the eight years immediately before 2008, when bank failure rates accelerated significantly.

As a reminder, the higher the number, the greater the new bank charter activity. Arizona and Nevada "led" the nation in new bank charters based on the data shown in both columns.

Note the variation in new bank charter rates by state. As already noted, in Arizona and Nevada new bank charter activity was great in both the 1996-2010 and 2000-2007 time frames. On the other side of the coin, roughly 40% of the states chartered new banks at a slow pace throughout the 1996-2010 time frame. The vast difference in new chartering rates, once again, highlights the wide variation that exists in banking practices across the 50 states.

Table A.3					
New Bank Growth Rates by State					
State	New Banks 1996–2010 as % of All Banks 2010	New Banks 2000–2007 as % of All Banks 2000	State	New Banks 1996–2010 as % of All Banks 2010	New Banks 2000–2007 as % of All Banks 2000
Arizona	167 %	93 %	Alabama	25	17
Nevada	137	75	Massachusetts	24	7
Idaho	137	28	Kentucky	23	8
North Carolina	94	51	West Virginia	22	7
New Jersey	90	37	Mississippi	21	7
Florida	89	45	Wyoming	21	9
New Hampshire	89	13	Louisiana	19	4
Oregon	82	36	Texas	19	9
Connecticut	82	39	Indiana	19	6
Utah	80	46	Illinois	18	7
Washington	77	34	Minnesota	16	8
South Carolina	72	27	Montana	16	10
Rhode Island	71	57	Missouri	16	7
Colorado	69	13	Ohio	15	6
Delaware	67	21	Arkansas	14	3
California	66	43	Wisconsin	12	5
Virginia	60	19	Iowa	11	3
Georgia	42	32	Maine	11	7
Michigan	41	14	South Dakota	10	3
Tennessee	38	22	Kansas	7	4
New York	37	20	Oklahoma	7	2
Pennsylvania	35	15	Nebraska	7	3
Maryland	31	15	North Dakota	6	3
New Mexico	29	11	Alaska	0	0
Hawaii	29	25	Vermont	0	0

Source: FDIC

Several of the states with lower new bank formation rates from 1996 to 2010, including Texas and New Hampshire, were fairly active in new bank charter creation prior to 2000. However, from 2000 to 2007, these states saw new bank charter activity slow considerably.

Why some states like Texas experienced significant new bank formation rates from 1996 to 1999 but not from 2000 to 2007 is a topic for potential further analysis.

Bank Profitability Comparisons by State

Table A.4 shows the median return on assets (ROA) of the banks headquartered in each state for year-end 2009 and the third quarter of 2011.

As Table A.4 shows, banks in three states (Alaska, Oklahoma, and New Mexico) registered ROAs greater than 1.0%. Nine states that had negative ROAs in 3Q 2010 did not need to be reminded there was a crisis afoot. No surprise, then, that these states experienced heavy bank failure rates.

Table A.4

Bank Profitability by State, 2009 and 2011

	ROA 2009 (%)	ROA 3Q/11 (%)	% Change in ROA, 2009–2011		ROA 2009 (%)	ROA 3Q/11 (%)	% Change in ROA, 2009–2011
Alaska	1.17	1.05	−0.12	Maine	0.43	0.61	0.18
Oklahoma	1.07	1.34	0.27	Colorado	0.42	0.7	0.28
New Mexico	1.05	1.12	0.07	Massachusetts	0.38	0.56	0.18
Louisiana	0.98	1.07	0.09	Tennessee	0.37	0.79	0.42
Iowa	0.90	1.31	0.41	Hawaii	0.34	0.82	0.48
Arkansas	0.87	1.1	0.23	Utah	0.32	1.39	1.07
Texas	0.86	1.06	0.2	Connecticut	0.28	0.40	0.12
Nebraska	0.81	1.14	0.33	New Jersey	0.27	0.51	0.24
North Dakota	0.81	1.29	0.48	Michigan	0.23	0.68	0.45
South Dakota	0.75	1.33	0.58	Virginia	0.18	0.67	0.49
West Virginia	0.73	0.71	−0.02	Rhode Island	0.18	0.37	0.19
Montana	0.72	0.95	0.23	Alabama	0.17	0.73	0.56
Wyoming	0.7	0.96	0.26	North Carolina	0.09	0.24	0.15
Mississippi	0.70	0.89	0.19	Maryland	0.08	0.42	0.34
Kentucky	0.68	0.87	0.19	Delaware	0.02	0.51	0.49
Kansas	0.65	1.01	0.36	South Carolina	−0.06	0.31	0.37
Missouri	0.59	0.94	0.35	Oregon	−0.40	0.31	0.71
Vermont	0.59	0.67	0.08	California	−0.61	0.66	1.27
New York	0.58	0.73	0.15	Washington	−0.84	0.43	1.27
Minnesota	0.54	0.93	0.39	Idaho	−0.91	0.12	1.03
Ohio	0.48	0.73	0.25	Georgia	−0.96	0.26	1.22
Wisconsin	0.47	0.84	0.37	Florida	−1.46	0.23	1.69
Pennsylvania	0.47	0.76	0.29	Arizona	−2.36	0.42	2.78
Indiana	0.45	0.75	0.3	Nevada	−2.87	0.74	3.61
New Hampshire	0.45	0.60	0.15	**Average**	**0.24**	**0.76**	**0.52**
Illinois	0.44	0.75	0.31				

Source: FDIC

The 2009 ROA data does not include banks that failed prior to September 30, 2009. If it were somehow possible to include failed banks, obviously the states with heavy failed bank activity would show even worse overall profitability.

Bank Failure and Problem Rates by State

Table A.5 provides bank failure data by state. It also includes problem bank data; a problem bank has not failed but has been identified by its regulator as a weak bank requiring an enforcement letter or some other form of additional attention. Column 2 data (No. of Banks) is from September 30, 2011; column 3 (No. of Problem Banks) is from February 24, 2012; column 5 (No. of Failed Banks) is from March 5, 2012.

The states are grouped into populations of 10 states. Group 5 states are those with the greatest bank failures and problems. Group 1 states are those with the least. Dividing the 50 states into five groups provides interesting insights that will be further explored in later tables.

Table A.5 rankings are based on adding the number of problem banks (column 3) and the number of failed banks (column 5) in each state and dividing the sum into the number of banks doing business in the state (column 2).

For example, at the top of the list is Arizona, where there were 11 problem banks as of February 24, 2012 (according to www.calculatedriskblog.com) and 13 bank failures from January 1, 2008, to March 5, 2012. Those two numbers are added together (24) and compared to the number of existing banks (33) doing business in Arizona as of September 30, 2011. In the case of Arizona, the data indicates that the ratio of failed and problem banks is 73% of the number of banks still in business as of September 30, 2011.

Viewing the Data in Peer Groups

Examining the data from Table A.5 in peer groups reveals interesting insights. As a reminder, peer group 1 is comprised of the 10 states with the lowest incidences of bank failures and problem banks; these 10 states can be considered the healthiest in the nation for banking at the time of this study. Each successive peer group shows higher problem and failed banks. Peer group 5 contains the least healthy banking states in the nation as of March 2012.

A number of observations can be made from the data shown in Table A.5. First, note the wide variability by state in problems and failures. The worst banking state in the country by this measure is Arizona and the best is Vermont, where there have been no failed banks and no current problem banks. After Arizona, the other lowest-performing banking states are Nevada, Florida, Georgia, and Washington. In addition to Vermont, other top-performing states during the recent financial crisis included Maine, New Hampshire, Massachusetts, Mississippi, Louisiana, and Iowa.

In contrast to this recent banking crisis, it is worth noting that New England suffered proportionately heavy bank failure rates in the 1980s and early 1990s. Massachusetts experienced 50 bank failures from 1980 to 1995, while New Hampshire saw 18 banks fail during this time frame.

The presence of Mississippi and Louisiana on the top-performing list of states may surprise some people, given the high unemployment rate in Mississippi (12%+) and the lingering aftermath of the BP oil spill on the region. From 1980 to 1995, Louisiana and Mississippi saw 131 and 25 financial institutions fail in their states, respectively.

Note the mean of 19% at the bottom of the final column. In other words, the total number of failed banks through March 5, 2012, plus the number of problem banks as

Table A.5

States Ranked on Problems and Failed Commercial Banks (displayed in quintiles)*

State	No. of Banks in State	No. of Problem Banks	Problem Banks as % of All Banks	No. of Failed Banks 2008–2012	Failed Banks 2008–2012 as % of All Banks	Failed and Problem Banks as % of All Banks
			Group 5			
Arizona	33	11	33%	13	39%	73%
Nevada	25	7	28%	11	44%	72%
Florida	233	79	34%	61	26%	60%
Georgia	246	63	26%	78	32%	57%
Washington	73	21	29%	17	23%	52%
Oregon	34	10	29%	6	18%	47%
California	261	62	24%	38	15%	38%
Colorado	109	28	26%	9	8%	34%
Hawaii	9	3	33%	0	0%	33%
Idaho	18	5	28%	1	6%	33%
Total Group 5	**1,041**	**289**	**28%**	**234**	**22%**	**50%**
			Group 4			
South Carolina	80	19	24%	7	9%	33%
Utah	57	12	21%	6	11%	32%
Minnesota	395	88	22%	19	5%	27%
Maryland	85	17	20%	6	7%	27%
Michigan	133	19	14%	13	10%	24%
Alabama	142	26	18%	6	4%	23%
North Carolina	98	17	17%	4	4%	21%
Illinois	585	76	13%	49	8%	21%
New Mexico	50	7	14%	3	6%	20%
Virginia	112	17	15%	4	4%	19%
Total Group 4	**1,737**	**298**	**17%**	**117**	**7%**	**24%**

(continued)

State	No. of Banks in State	No. of Problem Banks	Problem Banks as % of All Banks	No. of Failed Banks 2008–2012	Failed Banks 2008–2012 as % of All Banks	Failed and Problem Banks as % of All Banks
Table A.5 (continued)						
			Group 3			
Montana	73	13	18%	0	0%	18%
Alaska	6	1	17%	0	0%	17%
Wisconsin	271	37	14%	6	2%	16%
Arkansas	127	18	14%	2	2%	16%
Tennessee	188	27	14%	2	1%	15%
Delaware	27	4	15%	0	0%	15%
Rhode Island	14	2	14%	0	0%	14%
Connecticut	52	7	13%	0	0%	13%
Kansas	320	33	10%	8	3%	13%
Ohio	237	24	10%	5	2%	12%
Total Group 3	**1,315**	**166**	**13%**	**23**	**2%**	**14%**
			Group 2			
New Jersey	116	10	9%	4	3%	12%
Missouri	333	28	8%	12	4%	12%
New York	187	17	9%	4	2%	11%
Wyoming	36	3	8%	1	3%	11%
Pennsylvania	209	17	8%	6	3%	11%
South Dakota	83	8	10%	1	1%	11%
Indiana	143	12	8%	3	2%	10%
Texas	600	50	8%	9	2%	10%
Kentucky	195	16	8%	1	1%	9%
Oklahoma	242	17	7%	4	2%	9%
Total Group 2	**2,144**	**178**	**8%**	**45**	**2%**	**10%**
			Group 1			
West Virginia	63	3	5%	1	2%	6%
Nebraska	221	10	5%	3	1%	6%
North Dakota	92	5	5%	0	0%	5%
Iowa	348	15	4%	2	1%	5%
Louisiana	150	5	3%	2	1%	5%
Mississippi	89	2	2%	2	2%	4%
Massachusetts	160	6	4%	1	1%	4%
New Hampshire	23	1	4%	0	0%	4%
Maine	29	1	3%	0	0%	3%
Vermont	9	0	0%	0	0%	0%
Total Group 1	**1184**	**48**	**4%**	**11**	**1%**	**5%**
						19%

*Column 2 as of 9/30/11 per www.bankregdata.com (extracted from www.fdic.gov). Column 3 as of February 24, 2012 per www.calculatedriskblog.com. Column 5 as of March 5, 2012 per www.fdic.gov.

of February 24, 2012, equals 19% of the total number of banks in the U.S. as of September 2011.

It is worth noting how much variability exists in the number of banks headquartered in each state. The state with the most bank headquarters is Texas, with 600. Perhaps the high number comes as no surprise given the size of the state in area and population. More of a surprise may be Iowa, with 348 banks, making it the fourth most-banked state in the nation behind Texas, Illinois (585), and Minnesota (395). Five states have fewer than 10 banks domiciled in the state: Vermont, Maine, New Hampshire, Delaware, and Hawaii.

Table A.6 is a summary view of the same problem and failed bank data drawn from Table A.5. In Table A.6, the data is organized by quintiles of states. For example, group 1 from Table A.5 represents the 10 states that performed best (least failed and problem banks). Group 1 experienced a 4% problem bank rate and a 1% fail rate, which add up to the 5% shown in the third row.

Note the stair-step progression in deterioration that occurs among the five groups. For banks in group 5, it is important to highlight that problem and failed banks equal 50% of all banks doing business in the state as of September 30, 2011.

Table A.7 is a deeper look at the five quintiles of states. Table A.7 adds critical new information derived from Table A.1. As a reminder, Table A.1 shows the additions and subtractions of banks in Florida from year-end 1995 to year-end 2010. Similar data has been pulled for all 50 states and embedded in Table A.7.

Notice the almost steady stair climb in numbers that occurs between each group. Each climb is a steady increase from a low number in group 1 to a higher number for each subsequent group. For example, in the row called "No. of new banks/No. 2010," or the total number of new banks chartered between January 1, 1996, and year-end 2010 as a percentage of 2010 number of banks, group 1 shows the lowest percentage at 21%, group 2 at 28%, group 3 at 32%, group 4 at 47%, and group 5 at a dubiously impressive 83%.

There is one exception to this trend. Row 4 is the percentage change in the absolute number of banks by state from January 1, 1995, to 2010. Although all groups saw net decreases, it is worth noting group 1 declined 40%, the highest of the peer groups.

It is important to highlight several key findings. The highest-performing 10 states were also the states with the biggest reduction in the number of banks headquartered there. They were also the states with the lowest new bank formation rates.

Table A.6					
Comparing ROA and Problem/Failed Rates					
	1	2	3	4	5
Problem Rate[3]	4%	8%	13%	17%	28%
Fail Rate[4]	1%	2%	2%	7%	22%
Problem + Fail Rate[5]	5%	10%	14%	24%	50%

Sources: Bank Reg Data, Calculated Risk, FDIC

Table A.7					
New Bank Activity and Key Metrics by Quintiles					
	1	2	3	4	5
No. of new banks 1996–2010	132	395	205	490	781
No. of new banks/No. 2010	21%	28%	32%	47%	83%
Average bank total 1996–2010	1,171	2,197	1,357	1,881	1,272
Change %, no. of banks 2010 to 1995	–40%	–35%	–37%	–21%	–25%
No. of new banks/No. 1995	11%	19%	21%	42%	70%
No. of new banks/average no. 1996–2010	16%	23%	27%	41%	70%
No. of new banks 2000–2007/ No. 2000	5%	12%	17%	21%	42%
3Q 2011 Unemployment	6.6%	7.7%	8.5%	8.7%	9.8%
Past Due Loans 12/2009	2.8%	2.6%	3.6%	4.3%	5.7%

Source: FDIC

On the other hand, the worst-performing 10 states were those with the greatest increase in the number of banks headquartered there. They were also the states with the highest new bank formation rates.

Patterns appear to be emerging. Without stronger statistical evidence, however, it is difficult to state with certainty that our hypothesis—that new bank formation rates influence bank failure and problem rates—is valid.

Correlation Coefficients

Tables A.8, A.9, and A.10 evaluate the statistical relationship among key data. Table A.8 compares data from Table A.4 (ROA) and Table A.5 (problem and failed rates). At the bottom of Table A.8 are correlation coefficients between pairs of germane data.

Several observations can be made from this data. First, as a reminder, the industry ROAs substantially improved by 3Q 2011 when compared to 2009, just nine quarters earlier. The most important observation worth highlighting is the -.88 correlation coefficient for 3Q 2009 ROA and the 3Q 2011 problem and failed ratio. Just to be clear, what this says is that as the problem and failure ratio increases, the ROA two years earlier decreases at a high correlation. The coefficient increases to -.90 by removing the data from the four states that have fewer than 15 banks. This may be intuitive. However, the near perfect correlation explains how even very well managed banks are pulled down when their competitors perform badly.

Second, at -.45, there is no evidence of a correlation between the states' ROAs in 2011 and the problem and failed bank ratio in the states. This is interesting because it suggests that industry profitability has improved significantly even as the metric of problem banks and failed banks continued to increase.

In Table A.9, the -.83 correlation coefficient between ROA in 2009 and the percentage growth in new banks formed between 2000 and 2007 is statistically meaningful and provides

Table A.8	New Bank Growth Rates by State						

New Bank Growth Rates by State

	ROA 3Q/11 (%)	ROA 2009 (%)	Problem + Failed Banks as % of All Banks 09/30/2011		ROA 3Q/11 (%)	ROA 2009 (%)	Problem + Failed Banks as % of All Banks 09/30/2011
Nevada	0.74	−2.87	72	Delaware	0.51	0.02	15
Arizona	0.42	−2.36	73	Rhode Island	0.37	0.18	14
Florida	0.23	−1.46	60	Illinois	0.75	0.44	21
Washington	0.43	−0.84	52	Ohio	0.73	0.48	12
Georgia	0.26	−0.96	57	New Jersey	0.51	0.27	12
Hawaii	0.82	0.34	33	Kansas	1.01	0.65	13
Oregon	0.31	−0.40	47	Missouri	0.94	0.59	12
California	0.66	−0.61	38	New York	0.73	0.58	11
Idaho	0.12	−0.91	33	Pennsylvania	0.76	0.47	11
Colorado	0.70	0.42	34	Wyoming	0.96	0.70	11
South Carolina	0.31	−0.06	33	South Dakota	1.33	0.75	11
Minnesota	0.93	0.54	27	Indiana	0.75	0.45	10
Maryland	0.42	0.08	27	Texas	1.06	0.86	9
Alabama	0.73	0.17	23	Oklahoma	1.34	1.07	9
Michigan	0.68	0.23	24	Kentucky	0.87	0.68	9
Utah	1.39	0.32	32	West Virginia	0.71	0.73	6
North Carolina	0.24	0.09	21	Nebraska	1.14	0.81	6
New Mexico	1.12	1.05	20	North Dakota	1.29	0.81	5
Virginia	0.67	0.18	19	Louisiana	1.07	0.98	5
Montana	0.95	0.72	18	Mississippi	0.89	0.70	4
Alaska	1.05	1.17	17	New Hampshire	0.60	0.45	4
Arkansas	1.10	0.87	16	Iowa	1.31	0.90	5
Wisconsin	0.84	0.47	16	Massachusetts	0.56	0.38	4
Tennessee	0.79	0.37	15	Maine	0.61	0.43	3
Connecticut	0.4	0.28	13	Vermont	0.67	0.59	0

Correlation Failed + Problem Banks % to ROA 12/2009	
−0.8809	R−sq .78

Correlation Failed + Problem Banks % to ROA 3Q 2011	
−0.4501	R−sq .20

Correlation Failed + Problem Banks % to ROA 12/2009 excluding four states with fewer than 15 banks headquartered in the state.	
−0.9009	R−sq .81

Sources: Bank Reg Data, Calculated Risk, FDIC

Table A.9

Comparing ROA and Number of New Banks

	ROA 3Q/11	ROA 2009	New Banks 2000–2007 as % of All Banks 2000		ROA 3Q/11	ROA 2009	New Banks 2000–2007 as % of All Banks 2000
Nevada	0.74	−2.87	75	Delaware	0.51	0.02	21
Arizona	0.42	−2.36	93	Rhode Island	0.37	0.18	57
Florida	0.23	−1.46	45	Illinois	0.75	0.44	7
Washington	0.43	−0.84	34	Ohio	0.73	0.48	6
Georgia	0.26	−0.96	32	New Jersey	0.51	0.27	37
Hawaii	0.82	0.34	25	Kansas	1.01	0.65	4
Oregon	0.31	−0.4	36	Missouri	0.94	0.59	7
California	0.66	−0.61	43	New York	0.73	0.58	20
Idaho	0.12	−0.91	28	Pennsylvania	0.76	0.47	15
Colorado	0.7	0.42	13	Wyoming	0.96	0.7	9
South Carolina	0.31	−0.06	27	South Dakota	1.33	0.75	3
Minnesota	0.93	0.54	8	Indiana	0.75	0.45	6
Maryland	0.42	0.08	15	Texas	1.06	0.86	9
Alabama	0.73	0.17	17	Oklahoma	1.34	1.07	2
Michigan	0.68	0.23	14	Kentucky	0.87	0.68	8
Utah	1.39	0.32	46	West Virginia	0.71	0.73	7
North Carolina	0.24	0.09	51	Nebraska	1.14	0.81	3
New Mexico	1.12	1.05	11	North Dakota	1.29	0.81	3
Virginia	0.67	0.18	19	Louisiana	1.07	0.98	4
Montana	0.95	0.72	10	Mississippi	0.89	0.70	7
Alaska	1.05	1.17	0	New Hampshire	0.60	0.45	13
Arkansas	1.1	0.87	3	Iowa	1.31	0.90	3
Wisconsin	0.84	0.47	5	Massachusetts	0.56	0.38	7
Tennessee	0.79	0.37	22	Maine	0.61	0.43	7
Connecticut	0.4	0.28	39	Vermont	0.67	0.59	0

Correlation New Bank Formation Rate 2000–2007 to ROA 12/2009	
−0.834527046	R–sq .70
Correlation New Bank Formation Rate 2000–2007 to ROA 3Q 2011	
−0.529589273	R–sq .28
Correlation New Bank Formation Rate 2000–2007 to ROA 12/2009 excluding four states with fewer than 15 banks.	
−0.864964	R–sq .75

Source: FDIC

Table A.10		

Comparing Number of New Banks and Problem/Failure Rate

	New Banks 2000–2007 as % of All Banks 2000	Problem + Failure Banks 3Q 2011 as % of All Banks		New Banks 2000–2007 as % of All Banks 2000	Problem + Failure Banks 3Q 2011 as % of All Banks
Nevada	75	72	Delaware	21	15
Arizona	93	73	Rhode Island	57	14
Florida	45	60	Illinois	7	21
Washington	34	52	Ohio	6	12
Georgia	32	57	New Jersey	37	12
Hawaii	25	33	Kansas	4	13
Oregon	36	47	Missouri	7	12
California	43	38	New York	20	11
Idaho	28	33	Pennsylvania	15	11
Colorado	13	34	Wyoming	9	11
South Carolina	27	33	South Dakota	3	11
Minnesota	8	27	Indiana	6	10
Maryland	15	27	Texas	9	9
Alabama	17	23	Oklahoma	2	9
Michigan	14	24	Kentucky	8	9
Utah	46	32	West Virginia	7	6
North Carolina	51	21	Nebraska	3	6
New Mexico	11	20	North Dakota	3	5
Virginia	19	19	Louisiana	4	5
Montana	10	18	Mississippi	7	4
Alaska	0	17	New Hampshire	13	4
Arkansas	3	16	Iowa	3	5
Wisconsin	5	16	Massachusetts	7	4
Tennessee	22	15	Maine	7	3
Connecticut	39	13	Vermont	0	0

Correlation 2000-2007 New Bank Rate to Problems + Failures % of Banks 2011

0.758003682	R-sq .57

Correlation without four states with fewer than 15 banks.

0.80503	R-sq .65

Sources: Bank Reg Data, Calculated Risk, FDIC

evidence that new bank formation rates influence the overall health of the banking industry at the statewide level.

As a footnote, it is interesting to see that the coefficient actually improves to -.86 when the four states with fewer than 15 banks are removed from the data. The entrance of new competitors appears to introduce risk, and, as evidenced in the data, high rates of new bank formation in the seven years immediately preceding the banking crisis are associated with low and negative ROAs.

Correlations were also run examining the new bank formation activity between 1996 and 2010 and the 2009 ROAs. Taking the ratio seen earlier in this report—the number of new banks chartered between 1996 and 2010 as a ratio of the number of banks in business at the end of 2010—the correlation coefficient is -0.80717. Excluding the states with fewer than 10 banks, the coefficient increases to -0.82985. Again, the high coefficients suggest relationship. If substantial data were available to examine this phenomenon at a smaller market level (like a city or region), it would be interesting to see if the high correlation remains.

Table A.10 further explores the relationship between new bank formation rates and bank problems and failures. The correlation coefficient is meaningful at .758; it increases to .805 when the four small bank states are removed from consideration.

There is indeed evidence that the hypothesis is valid: New bank formation rates have a strong influence on bank failures and problems at a statewide level. This is the most critical finding in the statistical analysis. The data suggests there is indeed a relationship between new bank formation by state and subsequent bank failures and problems.

Why New Bank Chartering Rates and Bank Failure/Problems and ROA Are Related

Based on my research and experience in the banking industry from 1980 to 2012, I have made three observations about systemic risk:

First, the industry does not properly evaluate the risk that competitors, particularly de novos, create for community and regional banks. The data for this study would be even more interesting if the FDIC tracked nonbank lenders in addition to the banks and thrifts. For example, what influence do mortgage brokers have on bank failures and industry profitability?

Second, although free marketers will protest, the banking industry does not have sufficient barriers to entry for investors who want to charter a new bank. Related to the first observation, unlike the NFL and Major League Baseball, which carefully control the number of teams in their leagues, bank regulators and investors do not appear to understand the dynamics of a banking system where bank formation is easy. U.S. bank regulators have belatedly intensified their scrutiny of new banks. The more critical question, however, is how have regulators changed their approval process for investors to start new banks?

Third, the U.S. does not have a sufficient number of professional bank directors and experienced bank executives and risk managers to govern more than 7,246 banks. This third observation is drawn from the review of material loss reports written in the aftermath of the failure of 457 banks since 2008. In a country where the qualifications to be a bank director are low, it is easy to fill board seats.

Staying with the NFL analogy, there is a nearly infinite number of people who could be appointed to play in the NFL. It is possible for the U.S. to field tens of thousands of teams. But at what point is the quality of the product so diluted that fans are unwilling to pay to watch a game?

Why is it not reasonable to believe there is a finite number of skilled directors and bankers capable of governing and managing the nation's banks? Logic suggests that markets that have experienced a rapid growth in newly chartered banks in a short time frame of three to seven years are especially challenged to identify and develop skilled bank directors. As more new banks are formed, especially a large number in a short time frame, the new banks must dig deeper and deeper into a weaker and weaker candidate pool of skilled and competent directors and bankers. Exacerbating the challenge is the sometimes unreasonable pressure presidents of newly chartered banks often face to meet the expectations of the new bank's shareholders, who do not view their equity investment as a long-term holding.

Lessons learned from the banking crisis of the late 1980s and early 1990s were not heeded in the buildup to the financial crisis. Clearly, the FDIC, OCC, and Federal Reserve knew as early as 1988 that operational risks—specifically inadequate oversight by uninformed and unskilled bank directors and weak bank executives lacking necessary processes to identify and mitigate risks—were the leading causes of bank failures at that time. Evidence of this can be seen in three papers written between 1988 and 1990.[6]

Effective regulatory supervision and board governance require a better understanding of the leading operational risk indicators. Such risk indicators should be forward-looking and act as an early warning system alerting supervisors and directors to problems well ahead of realizing credit, market, and liquidity risks. Recent history proves new bank formation rates are an external event risk that creates systemic risk to the banking system.

NOTES

1. The time period of 1996 to 2010 was chosen because this 15-year span represents in many ways a new era in banking. The banking crisis of 1985-1992 resulted in the failure of approximately 3,000 banks and S&Ls. By 1996 the economy was on more sure footing, and investors were once again eager to invest in newly chartered banks

2. As will be shown, the new bank formation activity from 2000 to 2007 proved to be the most statistically meaningful time frame for understanding the influence of new bank formation rates on bank failure and problem rates from 2008 to 2012.

3. Problem rate is the number of banks by state on the www.calculatedriskblog.com website as of February 24, 2012, divided by number of banks in the state as of September 30, 2011, as reported at www.bankregdata.com, a source that compiles and parses bank call report data.

4. Fail rate is the number of banks in a state that have failed since from January 1, 2008, to March 5, 2012, as a percentage of commercial banks in the state as of September 30, 2011.

5. Problem + fail rate is calculated by adding problem banks and failed banks to the same denominator as shown in the fail rate.

6. See the 1988 OCC paper *Bank Failure: An Evaluation of the Factors Contributing to the Failure of National Banks*, and from 1990 the Federal Reserve Bank of Cleveland's *Economic Commentary* on the "Underlying Causes of Commercial Bank Failures in the 1980s," as well as the FDIC's *The Texas Banking Crisis: Causes and Consequences 1980-1989*. All three supervisors highlighted the same causes for bank failures.